Re-Reading Thomas Traherne:

A Collection of New Critical Essays

MEDIEVAL AND RENAISSANCE
TEXTS AND STUDIES
VOLUME 325

Acknowledgements

For years, I have envisioned this project coming to fruition, and now, at its completion, I can sincerely say that the work of the contributors contained herein has far exceeded my initial expectations. They have brought to this volume of essays various approaches and insights that help illuminate the complexities and intricacies of Traherne's corpus. For their labors, I cannot thank them enough. I would also like to express my appreciation for everyone at the Arizona Center for Medieval and Renaissance Studies, particularly Roy Rukkila, who has made my first — but hopefully not my last — experience with the ACMRS a delightful one. In addition, I wish to thank the two outside readers of the manuscript for their careful readings and helpful comments and, especially, Dr. Leslie MacCoull who provided me with numerous references, most of which I have included.

Finally, I want to acknowledge the immeasurable debt owed to three individuals whose guidance, instruction, and enthusiasm for the seventeenth century continue to play no small part in my own love for and work in seventeenth-century studies: Thomas Langford, Hugh Wilson, and, most of all, Robert M. Cooper to whom this volume is dedicated.

ers about his work. Finally, a third limitation of Traherne scholarship has been what seems a general inability — or unwillingness — to discuss Traherne in the context of modern critical trends. Certainly DeNeef's book is an exception, and other works, like Balakier's discussion of consciousness, do bring elements of contemporary critical theory to bear. However, because criticism has for so long been primarily concerned with tracing influences and identifying a philosophical structure in Traherne, modern theory has to this point been limited in its applicability for many critics, and unless Traherne is viewed in light of modern critical trends his longevity is probably threatened. The essays in this volume attempt to fill some of these gaps in the previous criticism; and although the essays differ in their specific approach and subject matter, they each contribute something new for the study of Traherne and demonstrate that Traherne is a complex, culturally relevant writer who warrants continued analysis.

While so many scholars have tried to find unity in Traherne, the first three essays of this collection illustrate the presence and relevance in Traherne of certain paradoxes and the cultural contexts that produced them. Susannah B. Mintz, in "Strange Bodies: Thomas Traherne's Disabled Subject," addresses the interplay between the "able" and "disabled" image of the body in Traherne's work. Consistent with the "long established link in religious discourse between illness and sin," Traherne identifies sin as sickness and "the spiritually pure body . . . finds its depraved counterpart in the ravages of disease." However, Mintz points out Traherne's use of physical impairment, such as deafness and muteness, as a "symbol and preparation for the solitary inwardness associated with mystical apprehension of God." Deafness and muteness become a way to achieve "vehement individuality" and a "superior sense of selfhood." Traherne uses such images of disablement metaphorically, and ultimately empowers the functioning body and excludes the legitimacy of a disabled subject; he thus reinforces the "problematic stereotypes by underwriting the hegemony of an idealized, natural, wonder-inspiring physical form that strives for order against the vagaries of embodiment."

In "'Cursd and Devised Proprieties': Traherne and the Laws of Property," Lynne A. Greenberg examines the conflicting notions of property and ownership in Traherne's writing. Historicizing Traherne's use of ownership within the agricultural and legal reforms of the age, Greenberg demonstrates that in Traherne "notions of propriety, possession, and enclosure function as central topoi in Traherne's poetry," and, even more precisely, Traherne's work reflects the opposing views of ownership in seventeenth-century England. While the unenclosed spiritual freedom of Traherne suggests a kind of prelapsarian bliss that values the idea of common usage rights, there is also, Greenberg illustrates, "a paradigm of property" that reflects an emerging discourse promoting absolute ownership. Just as competing attitudes toward ownership existed in England, "Traherne placed competing cultural meanings of ownership side-by-side" in his writing — sometimes expressing a belief that God bestows ownership of the world on the speaker; sometimes expressing the world as unbounded and belonging to all. Concepts of ownership are central to Traherne's philosophy and those concepts are "paradoxical but consistent with the divided concepts of the period."

Kevin P. Laam turns to *Christian Ethicks*. Laam establishes the nature of the seventeenth-century readership and the development of so called "popular" writing. While *Christian Ethicks* apparently had a very small readership, Laam proposes that by examining other works of its kind that were popular in the period and how Traherne appropriated those works — Richard Allestree's *The Whole Duty of Man* and the anonymous *The Art of Catechising* — Traherne's *Christian Ethicks* can be recognized as being "as socially inclusive as it is intellectually rigorous." Establishing the fact that historically the lines between popular and intellectual writing were being blurred during the period, Traherne's appropriation of Allestree shows that *Christian Ethicks* is a work not just about thought but also about action. By referencing Allestree, Traherne "provides us with a provisional acknowledgment of the wider social context in which both works might have been understood."

Beginning with Cynthia Saenz's "Language and the Fall: The Quest for Prelapsarian Speech in the Writings of Thomas Traherne and his Contemporaries," the next four essays deal generally with various aspects of language in Traherne. Saenz not only deals with the *Poems*, *Centuries*, and *Christian Ethicks*, but also relies heavily on the still largely unpublished manuscript, *Commentaries of Heaven*. Saenz asserts that Traherne was conscious of the Restoration debates concerning language and focuses her argument on the issue of reacquiring prelapsarian speech. Saenz first illustrates that Traherne largely agreed with biblical commentators, such as Andrew Willet and George Hughes, concerning prelapsarian speech; specifically, Traherne accepted that Adam's ability to name things in Eden tied language together with the "essence" of those things being named. Traherne's much-discussed emphasis on childhood, Saenz argues, is connected to the Latitudinarian and pre-Nicene traditions, which viewed the pre-linguistic state of infancy as being akin to Adam in paradise. Finally, Saenz finds Traherne's notion of a "linguistic Fall" as a kind of *felix culpa*, as he ultimately praises diversity and "embraces contrarieties as part of the divine scheme of infinite variety and inclusion."

Raymond-Jean Frontain, in "Tuning the World: Traherne, Psalms, and Praise," discusses Traherne's language as a language of "praise" modeled after David, the assumed author of the Psalms. Although critics have frequently pointed out the relevance of the Psalms to the religious lyric, Frontain argues that David is for Traherne not a model of private meditation but rather "individual devotion put to communal use." The *Centuries*, he posits, is a "complex literary and spiritual operation, one intended to create an ever-expanding interpretive community." Traherne aspires to become "David," the Psalm-singer who inspires singing in others, which leads to a "cosmic harmony," in which the poet's voice is a part. Traherne's language of praise modeled after David's shows him to be not a "private" poet at all, but one who assumes a reader who will "sing" his praises to others, recreating the prelapsarian harmony.

In "Motions of Writing in *The Commentaries of Heaven*: The 'Volatilitie' of 'Atoms' and 'Ætyms'," Finn Fordham discusses the manuscript containing *Commentaries of Heaven*. Arguing for a facsimile edition of the *Commentaries*, Fordham analyzes Traherne's process of composition, noting that Traherne's struggle with revisions directly relates to his philosophical positions. Traherne claims that God's creation is perfect; however, his own creation — his writing — is, by the very nature of language, imperfect. Traherne's revisions represent an attempt at perfectly expressing God's perfections through inherently imperfect means. Fordham illustrates this "oscillation between the perfection of God's world and the imperfections in representing that world," and he shows that the genetic recreation of Traherne's text through revision illuminates both Traherne's theological positioning of his own thoughts and his literary principles, which are inevitably based on his attitudes about God and the nature of that which is "created." Comparing revised and unrevised sections of the *Commentaries*, Fordham shows three fundamental types of revision: 1) canceling doubt; 2) canceling confusion; 3) and canceling the "affections" of sensual "pleasure." Fordham's central thesis is that Traherne's process of composition is intrinsic to the meaning, and only through studying Traherne in facsimile can both his literary and philosophical thoughts be fully understood.

The recently discovered Lambeth MS. 1360 is the focus of Carol Ann Johnston's "Masquing / Un-Masquing: Lambeth MS. 1360 and a Reconsideration of Traherne's 'Curious' Visual Language." Johnston specifically deals with Traherne's "visual" language, which she connects to contemporary debates concerning perspectival versus linear vision. Johnston then demonstrates that much of Traherne's visual imagery, particularly his emphasis on the individual's ability to attain a "Heavenly perspective," is derived from the court masque — something, paradoxically, he criticizes. Traherne portrays God as a king on a heavenly throne viewing the world as a perspectival scene; however, God does not lose sight of objects outside of the centrist point. God is able to combine linear and perspectival vision. Johnston stresses the importance of visional structure in Traherne, who ultimately views the combination of all vision as the goal of the Christian experience. Traherne understands the visual field as spiritual recovery in three stages: 1) the anamorphic stage of a child's vision, untrained and uncorrupted by totalizing perspectival vision; 2) an adult's vision given over to the false objective vision of the perspectival system; 3) the Christian vision, a rediscovery of decentered perspective through the visual field of linear perspective, offering the Christian the best of both visual systems.

The final two essays in this volume focus on the nature of consciousness in Traherne's work. Gary Kuchar, in "Traherne's Specters: Self-Consciousness and

its Others," states that it is through self-consciousness that the subject in Traherne "actualizes its desire"; however, for Traherne consciousness is specified —
or actualized — by the representation of its others, those not a part of self-under-
standing. Traherne uses spectral images, such as the "dumb show," as a contrast
to the fully self-conscious subject that praises God. The "specters" are characterized by a "lack of being," but their necessity for defining *true* self-consciousness
secures their reality within that consciousness. Kuchar examines theoretical notions that reflect and help to situate this spectral quality in Traherne's work:

> Traherne's representation of the human soul and of spirit more generally is
> characterized by its simultaneous evocation and repression of a mode of spec-
> trality that has been accounted for in various ways — from Jacob Boehme's
> notion of the *Ungrund* to Lacan's notion of the *real* to Derrida's notion of *dif-
> férance* — each of which will appear here in order to get a firmer sense of the
> place that this most radical form of otherness — this most resistant remain-
> der of spirit — holds in Traherne's view of the self-conscious soul.

Kuchar demonstrates that Traherne's images of "de-animation," which are used
to give meaning to self-consciousness, in fact draws attention to those images'
"inescapability."

The final essay of this volume, James J. Balakier's "Traherne and Husserl:
The Unitary Act of Consciousness," also applies a consciousness-based approach
to Traherne. Using the phenomenological concept of "a unitary act of consciousness" posited by Edmund Husserl and recent psycho-physiological research into
the presence of a "fourth" state of consciousness — characterized by "restful alertness" — Balakier argues that the mystical experiences represented in Traherne's
work reflect a "reawakening of a non-fragmented, pre-lapsarian sensibility" that
parallels the fourth state of consciouness. Balakier believes that a continued inquiry into the nature of consciousness in Traherne has the potential to show that
Traherne was not a "lightweight idealist" nor his work simply an "exaggerated
metaphor"; such an approach can, rather, help understand his mysticism as the
"sublime experience" of a more sophisticated cognitive awareness.

This volume is not the final word on Traherne but rather, it is hoped, the beginning of a new era in Traherne studies. All of the contributors make one thing
clear: Traherne's work is immensely complex and needs to be read and re-read.
Previous scholars have provided much for our understanding of Traherne, and
the present essays help to further that understanding even more, in ways previously unexplored. Still, the riches of Traherne have only begun to be discovered.
As the essays here demonstrate, only through a continued reading of Traherne
will his true value to literary, historical, and cultural studies of the seventeenth
century be appreciated.

Again, there is much left to do.

STRANGE BODIES:
THOMAS TRAHERNE'S DISABLED SUBJECT

SUSANNAH B. MINTZ
Skidmore College

Much recent scholarship on early modern selfhood has focused on the body as both a literal site and a rhetorical figuring of human psychology. Even beyond the obvious (such as eyes and genitalia), all manner of body parts are now understood to have been invested with subjective meaning, from the tongue to nerves to facial hair, each playing its role in the body/self dynamic. Well into the seventeenth century, the entanglement of physical and psychical, and in turn the notion that the embodied self was highly susceptible to the influence of the world, vexed many areas of the body with a fundamental liminality, a tension between sovereign individuality and the fragility associated with losing control to external forces. The stomach, for instance, a kind of subjective command central, was responsible for maintaining the balance of bodily fluids that affected temperament, while its necessary reception of food made it vulnerable both to the self's own greed and to pathogens from beyond its borders. In a similar way, skin, the organ of touch, occupied a threshold space between inner and outer, marking the collision between the self's ability to discern and distinguish and the contagions inherent in making contact with others. Thrumming with activity and agency, with the urgencies of desire and the threat of disease, the body exerted its constitutive presence in the formation of self — a locus of subjectivity even as it became increasingly subjected to the putatively dispassionate gaze of science.

Given this interdependence of corporeality and identity, no expression of physicality in Traherne's work is neutral; nor are his references entirely metaphorical, precisely because Traherne sought, against the more mechanistic theories of human physiology in late seventeenth-century England, to mount what Jonathan Sawday has called "a whole-hearted reinterpretation of the body's significance."[1]

---

[1] Jonathan Sawday, *The Body Emblazoned: Dissection and the Human Body in Renaissance Culture* (New York: Routledge, 1995), 258.

Like many of his contemporaries, legatees of an anatomical age, Traherne is fas-
cinated by the body's interior, and his interest seeks to align the structural and the
mystical. His concern with how the parts fit and work together attends to their
physical specificity while simultaneously locating the origin of their intricacy in
God's handiwork. As he writes in "The Person," for example, "My Tongue, my Eys,
/ My Cheeks, my Lips, mine Ears, my Hands, my Feet" (60–61) are the "Gifts"
(59) and "Glory" (30) of God.[2] In "The Estate," similarly, he claims that "Mens
Bodies," designed for joy, are "the very Throne / Of Blessedness" (31, 34–35). As
Sawday argues, Traherne joins the anatomist in poring over the strange stuff of the
body; the poet's project, however, results not in demystified mastery, but in a cel-
ebration of what cannot be reduced to scientific classification. In the closing lines of
"Salutation," for instance, the speaker venerates, rather than attempting to explain,
these "Strange Things," "Strange Glories," "Strange Treasures," "Strange all, and
New to me" (38–40).

It has become common to speak of Traherne's "physiological blazon[s]," his
praise of "carnality in all its detail as the expression of the Creator's bounty," to
use Barry Spurr's words.[3] In perhaps his most exuberant celebration of this divinely wrought corporeality, "Thanksgivings for the Body," Traherne performs a
careful dissection of the "inward parts" (66): "Arteries," "Veins," "Sinews" (50–
55); "The Organs of my Soul" (72); "The Chambers for Sounds" and "Recep-
tacles for Smells" (94, 96), and so on. The speaker declares that he is "fearfully
and wonderfully made"[4] (20) (reminiscent of Donne's "little world made cun-
ningly"[5]), and concludes that God has "glorified every body, / Especially mine"
(154–155). Importantly, the taxonomy of body parts both internal and archi-
tectural reaches toward something "Unsearchable" (79); for all the exposure of
anatomy, what lies "Beneath my Skin" (75) involves "Hidden Operations" (78).
Without renouncing the scientist's probing gaze, the poet attempts to reassemble
the mysterious whole that, under the knife of dissection, threatens to "fly away"
(91). Thus the body retains, finally, its "secret depth of fathomless Consideration"
(131), its "involved mysteries" and "inaccessible secret" (136, 138). Over 500 lines

---

[2] Thomas Traherne, *Centuries, Poems, and Thanksgivings*, ed. H. M. Margoliouth, 2
vols. (Oxford: Clarendon Press, 1958). All references to Traherne's poems (volume 2) and
to the *Centuries of Meditations* (volume 1) are to this edition. Relevant line or page numbers are parenthetical in the text.

[3] Barry Spurr, "Felicity Incarnate: Rediscovering Thomas Traherne," in *Discovering
and (Re)Covering the Seventeenth Century Religious Lyric*, ed. Eugene R. Cunnar and Jef-
frey Johnson (Pittsburgh: Duquesne University Press, 2000), 273–89, here 287.

[4] Traherne is quoting from Psalm 139:14.

[5] John Donne, Holy Sonnet V, in *The Complete English Poems of John Donne*, ed. C. A.
Patrides (London: Everyman, 1991), 437.

long, "Thanksgivings for the Body" offers less the explanatory finality of an anatomized corpse than the proliferate bursts of hymnic gratitude.

If the body is a divine gift, a wondrous pattern of godly workmanship, then disease inevitably signifies a loss of that connection to God. Sinfulness, an overvaluation of the trivial objects that bind, but also fracture, social relationships (such as jewels, toys, cabinets, thrones, hobbyhorses, and gold), is characterized throughout Traherne's work as sickness. The spiritually pure body — healthy, odiferous, and worthy of self-scrutiny — finds its depraved counterpart in the ravages of disease and in the less seemly instances of corporeal existence. "Wind," for example, inverse of the "welcom Odours and Perfumes" exuded by the body in its uncorrupted state ("Admiration," 9), appears as evidence of the body's digestive process, the entrails that harbor infection. Sickness "advance[d]" on the world with "Sin" ("Silence," 18–19); "yellow Jandice" obscures "Clear" vision (the *Third Century*, 113–114). "The Instruction" offers the purgative advice to "Spue out thy filth" (1), and "An Infant-Eye" similarly construes sin as an infection that must be "purged" (39) in order for the repentant individual to be restored to grace, "made an Infant once again" (40).

In making such analogies — asserting that "Mankind is sick," "infected with [a] sore Disease" ("Mankind is sick," 1, 30) — Traherne invokes a well-established link in religious discourse between illness and sin. The afflicted body has metaphorical status (its ailments denote spiritual travails), but also material consequence (it must be purged, healed, cleansed in order to rebalance the soul bound up with it). As he writes in "Thanksgivings," the individual experiences proximity to (or distance from) God down to its very *"Marrow"* and *"Bowels"* (442), understood to be the innermost sites of God's literal presence within the believer. At the same time, however, bodies are clearly subordinate to the ministrations of rational minds, whose capacity to make the deliberate turn away from sin earns them the role of "kind Physicians" ("Mankind is sick," 10). In this context, Traherne seems to view the body in both holistic and dualistic terms, straddling what Sawday refers to as the competing "eyes" of late seventeenth-century attitudes toward human physiology: the "visiv Ey" of science and reason against "th'Invisible" eye of the poetic imagination, as its stretches to apprehend divine unity in the workings of the body ("Sight," 23–24).[6]

As has frequently been noted, it is vision, more than any other sense, that Traherne charges with the task of elaborating his concept of the faithful Christian. Physical and spiritual sight are most often conflated in the figure of the innocent infant, the one who sees, as Carol Ann Johnston explains, like God: "Faithless human vision, Traherne argues, is subjective and 'broken' . . . Traherne insists that faith in an objective God overcomes the limitations of human

---

[6] Sawday, *Body Emblazoned*, 264–65.

vision."[7] The "Infant-Ey" (in the poem of that name), "doth see / Ev'n like unto
the Deity" (3–4) because it is free from "all Contagion" (1) and "Infect[ion]" (51);
indeed, its vision is "Refined, subtil, piercing, quick and pure" (8). "The Improvment" explicitly equates sensory vision with understanding, linking "the Eye" to
"The Apprehension, or Intelligence" (68–69). In "The Preparative," the speaker
dispenses with the body altogether, presenting subjectivity as a disembodied and
visionary consciousness: "I / Forgot the rest, and was all Sight, or Ey. / Unbodied
and Devoid of Care, / Just as in Heavn the Holy Angels are" (35–38). "Dumnesse" seems to pursue this hierarchy, eliminating the problematic threshold of
the ear in favor of a more dominant eye. "It was with Cleerer Eys," explains the
speaker (39), that he once reigned over and reveled in God's bounty; in infancy,
he could "see, love, Covet, hav, Enjoy, and Prais" in a "Blessed View" (50, 52).

What has not so often been noticed about what James J. Balakier has called
Traherne's "undivided or deiform Self"[8] is its exclusion of impairment or sensory
dysfunction. The prevalence of images of sight (as well as the reiterated health/
illness binary) underscores a simple but important point about Traherne's body-
language: it is resolutely what has in recent times been termed ableist. Whether
the emphasis on vision is read in the context of infancy and innocence, religious
self-appraisal, humanistic subject-formation, or anatomical discovery, Traherne's
repeated use of the eye as the agent of legitimate selfhood assumes the necessity
of physical sightedness. While many of Traherne's poems seem to eschew various
forms of embodiment as distractions or diminishments from a state of grace, they
nevertheless consistently champion the eye's literal ability to see. Only by being
able to look (and not simply to imagine, understand, or intellectualize) does the
speaker-subject of Traherne's poems make his expansive claims of possession
and joyfulness. When he surveys the wonders of nature, when he "Observ[s]"
the world's "Delights" ("The World," 86, 89) — even when he claims that his
"better Sight" derives from the eye "Beneath my Skin," as opposed to the "Two
Luminaries in my Flesh" ("Sight," 28, 10, 7) — he depends on sensory vision as
the guarantor of an identity he can then cast as the receptacle of "tru Felicity"
(60). He thus apprehends the "infinit" (29) just "as certainly / As I can see / That
I have Foot or Hand" (43–45).

Discussing the complex relationship between early modern advances in ocu-
lar theory and the gaze as a marker of subjectivity, Sergei Lobanov-Rostovsky
contends that as science began to accumulate evidence that the eye receives, rather

[7] Carol Ann Johnston, "Heavenly Perspectives, Mirrors of Eternity: Thomas Traherne's Yearning Subject," *Criticism* 43 (2001): 377–405, here 388–89.
[8] James J. Balakier, "Thomas Traherne's Dobell Series and the Baconian Model of
Experience," *English Studies* 70 (1989): 233–47, here 245.

than emanating, light, its status was reduced from an active producer of both form and essence to a womblike entity in which vision "coalesces."[9] The gaze emerges as a kind of compensation for the loss of control once materially associated with the act of looking; while the eyes might inhabit the body as disturbingly passive (indeed, feminized) orbs, subject to the probing view of the anatomist, the slippage from eye to perception to consciousness restores the looker to a position of stable selfhood. If it is true, however, that the sovereign subject who controls the gaze overcomes the vulnerability of the anatomical eyeball, it is also true that the notion of a gazing subject precludes the viability of a blind self. A construct of discourse, the gazer is one who must also physically see; blind anatomist is an ideological oxymoron.

Traherne's many references to sight, therefore, are both metonymic and able-bodied. Though he subordinates "Those Eys of Sense" to the spiritual vision of his "Mind" ("Sight," 13, 40), the force of the latter depends on repeated assertions of the functionality of the former — a conflation of ability and felicity that readers of Traherne uphold, as when Balakier refers to "[a] pure mind, clean heart, and clear sense," or claims that Traherne's "senses are so clean" that he can "perceive the good inherent in all things."[10] And if sightedness guarantees the gaze that conducts Traherne toward mystical spirituality, it is hardly surprising that the poems so often invoke blindness or impaired vision as a sign of sin. In "Mankind is sick," the speaker derides those who have renounced the "sweetness of Felicity" (72) as "Blind Wretches" (74), "Tormented in their Misery / (Like Mad-men that are blind)" (78–79). The speaker of "The Apostasy" describes his immersion in the trivialities of human greed as seeing through "blemisht Eys" (58), while men who fail to use their eyes in honor of the wonder of creation are "more blind" (13) than "Dead Puppets" ("Walking," 10). In the Third of his *Centuries of Meditations*, where he makes a moral distinction between the natural and the cultural, Traherne writes that while "Evry Man naturaly see[s] those Things, to the Enjoyment of which He is Naturaly Born," it is "the outward Bondage of Opinion and Custom" that "Enthrals and Blinds us" (114–115). A disabled body, in this schema, is not "natural."

Given the idealizing effect of Traherne's examination of bodies, what *is* surprising is his use of deafness and muteness as defining characteristics of the intensely individualized self he was invested in obtaining. Blindness, while superstitiously construed as a sign of ignorance and obscured faith, the physical

---

[9] "Coalescence" is Aristotle's term, according to Sergei Lobanov-Rostovsky, "Taming the Basilisk," in *The Body in Parts: Fantasies of Corporeality in Early Modern Europe*, ed. David Hillman and Carla Mazzio (New York: Routledge, 1997), 195–217, here 199.

[10] Balakier, "Thomas Traherne's Dobell Series," 241, 246.

manifestation of spiritual forsakenness, is also frequently narrated in terms of vatic or regenerate "insight."[11] Though Traherne does not figure himself the blind poet-prophet in the manner of Milton, his recourse to a sighted/blind binary to map out the state of humanity's collective soul depends on the same linkage of vision and consciousness whereby blindness is symbolically repaired through heightened perceptual powers. Deafness, however, has not been invested with any such compensatory mythic significance; prior to the eighteenth century, as Lennard J. Davis has shown, the deaf person "was first and foremost a nonperson,"[12] devoid of sense and intellect, and thus an object of pity and contempt, the proving ground for the regulating — that is, aural — powers of education and science. Why, then, does Traherne present himself in terms of what late seventeenth-century culture deemed a pathological dysfunction, one that would have consigned him to the margins of the human community?

According to Jennifer L. Nelson and Bradley S. Berens, it is precisely *because* Traherne was neither deaf nor mute that he can make use of those conditions to craft a fantasy of boldly singular selfhood.[13] Nelson and Berens argue that, secure in the knowledge of his own able-bodiedness, Traherne turns to deafness

---

[11] See Stephen Kuusisto, *Planet of the Blind* (New York: Delta, 1998), esp. 48–50 and 186–89; Georgina Kleege, *Sight Unseen* (New Haven: Yale University Press, 2000), esp. 21 and 28; and Lennard J. Davis, *Enforcing Normalcy: Disability, Deafness, and the Body* (New York: Verso, 1995), 58. Henri-Jacques Stiker argues that Jesus accepted the disabled, but as Kuusisto ponders in his memoir, Jesus "cure[d] the blind in his lifetime, rewarding their faith before the unbelieving multitudes" (188) and making sight the sign of grace (cf. John 9:1–41). See Stiker, *A History of Disability* (Ann Arbor: University of Michigan Press, 1999), 33–34.

[12] Davis, *Enforcing Normalcy*, 175 n.26. See also Margaret A. Winzer, *The History of Special Education: From Isolation to Integration* (Washington, DC: Gallaudet University Press, 1993).

[13] Jennifer L. Nelson and Bradley S. Berens, "Spoken Daggers, Deaf Ears, and Silent Mouths: Fantasies of Deafness in Early Modern England," in *The Disability Studies Reader*, ed. Lennard J. Davis (New York: Routledge, 1997), 52–74. Nelson and Berens argue that despite a growing interest in deaf education in the mid-seventeenth century, recognition of a legitimate "deaf subjectivity" did not inevitably follow. Indeed, they write, "the deaf are still seen as lacking a defining human trait, and are excluded from society and from full recognition as people with a language of their own — sign language" (66). Educating the deaf is synonymous with "curing" their pathological condition. See also Jennifer L. Nelson's article on the rhetorician John Bulwer, whose language theory was clearly influenced by observing deaf people signing: "Bulwer's Speaking Hands: Deafness and Rhetoric," in *Disability Studies: Enabling the Humanities*, ed. Sharon L. Snyder, Brenda Jo Brueggemann, and Rosemarie Garland Thomson (New York: Modern Language Association, 2002), 211–21.

as both a symbol of and a preparation for the solitary inwardness associated with mystical apprehension of God. Disregarding the real social status of the deaf, and paradoxically appropriating the otherness and isolation of disability, Traherne deploys "elective deafness"[14] and a self-willed aphasia to suggest immunity to the "normal" state of human depravity, and seeks access thereby to the divine. As Nelson and Berens put it, "[v]oluntary silence enables a person to be as one with God and blessedness."[15] But while silence may be celebrated as the pathway toward felicitous and godly instruction, the subjectivity articulated in Traherne's "deafness" poems is a hearing, just as it is also a sighted, one. Silence becomes meaningful insofar as it can be entered into deliberately by a reverent speaker, rather than as a permanent state of physical debility from which one cannot leave at will. The fantasy of not hearing or speaking depends, therefore, on an entirely aural frame of reference, and ultimately serves to empower the hearing speaker, rather than to acknowledge or accept actual physical difference.

The deaf and mute subject seems to epitomize for Traherne a vehement individuality, one that is produced not so much by purity from sin but rather by wholesale rupture of any interaction with other people. In Traherne's paradigm, disablement participates in a radical dividing of things into categories that works to assuage a variety of anxieties about mortal and embodied existence. Nelson and Berens write that "the early modern ear is acutely vulnerable," unable to prevent being penetrated by seditious, seductive words and noises that threaten the stolidity of selfhood (as when the speaker of "Thanksgivings for the Body" admits that "idle Speeches profaned [his] Ears" [473–474]).[16] Ears are only receptive: exposed to the noxious materiality of other people's words, breath, and selves, they produce no sound, possess no gaze, make no gestures, and cannot simply close, avert, or quiet themselves. The fantasy of deafness is one of heroic control over the chaos and complexity of human interaction, revealing a horror of penetrability and an urgent desire for a hermetic self. Ensconced within itself, the deaf-mute subject consumes and dominates the surroundings, his bodily difference guaranteeing his identity as unique and autonomous. In defiance of inadequacy or enfeeblement (either the "natural" state of all bodies or the supposed "deficiency" of the deaf), Traherne configures the borders of the disabled self as sealed and guarded, establishing an aggressively superior sense of selfhood whose symbolic viability presumes both the normality and the desirability of hearing.

The centerpiece of this attitude is the poem "Dumnesse," in which physical breakdown is equated with spiritual purity. The poem appears to rest on a straightforward opposition between faith and fallenness: the speaker declares

---

[14] Nelson and Berens, "Fantasies of Deafness," 61.

[15] Nelson and Berens, "Fantasies of Deafness," 64.

[16] Nelson and Berens, "Fantasies of Deafness," 60–61.

that he was once full of "Light" (31), but now finds himself besieged by impurity. Images of bodily dysfunction — deafness and speechlessness — represent a time of isolation, prior to the loss of innocence, when the narrator of the poem enjoyed ecstatic connection with divinity. In a fantasy not simply of infantile but also disabled self-containment, the speaker claims that when "Man" is born (1), his inability to hear or to speak protects him from death and depravity, plagues and corruption, all "the Errors and the Wrongs" of the world (12). "[I]n himself profoundly Busied" (6), this representative deaf-mute accesses an internal space of meditation where, untouched by sin, he "Contemplat[es] the Eternal Springs / Of God" (2–3). Talking and hearing entail engagement with others, embroiling the self in the vexations of human communication; words and breath, language and ideas seem indistinguishable from vice and deceit. The argument presented at the start of the poem thus imagines that being speechless and deaf could defend against the particular dangers of traffic in the human community.

It is intercourse with other people, specifically — and not simply existence as an adult capable of sinful desires — that so disturbs Traherne's sense of spiritual equanimity. To guard himself from wrongdoing, from the hatefulness that follows irremediably on the heels of human relationships, the speaker disables himself. Denying both the dependency and the necessary (even noisy) interconnectedness of infancy, the speaker sets forth disability as a threshold onto contemplative grace. Only through radical physical impairment can he enjoy silence and solitude, delving into a self he figures as untouched by others. Such drastic measures become necessary because other people are held to be literally contagious, pathogenic in both physiological and theological ways. A cluster of images involving illness and bodily interiors — "depravd . . . Tongues" (11), "accursed Breath" (14), "Corrupted Intrails" (15), "hidden Plagues" (16), "Antidots" (8) — suggests that whatever comes from within the body is polluted by proximity to this inmost site of all that is foul and sullied in people. The speaker registers anxiety about what cannot be seen, the invisible infections borne along by the multitude of exhalations from humanity's collective viscera. But more than a literal fear of disease (hardly remarkable in post-plague London) is at work here. The speaker seems excessively afraid of contact generally, as if other people themselves, and not simply their deleterious breath, could infiltrate his interior space. Intensely worried about what occupies the body, as well as what happens at the threshold of bodies when two selves connect, the speaker of "Dumnesse" conducts himself toward the "Glory, Bliss, and Pleasure" (3) of nature by barricading the boundaries of his corporeal self.

The speaker explains the appeal of this "disabled" state, associated with infancy and put forth as invulnerable and uncontaminated, in a nostalgic reverie about the time before his *"Bliss"* and *"Silence"* were broken by speech (20). Describing a "Non-Intelligence of Human Words" (21) that safeguarded him from interchange with others, he says,

Before their Souls were into mine conveyd,
Before that Living Vehicle of Wind
Could breathe into me their infected Mind,
Before my Thoughts were levend with theirs, before
There any Mixture was; the Holy Door,
Or Gate of Souls was closd, and mine being One
With in it self to me alone was Known. (24–30)

"Wind" connotes breath but also flatulence, the sign of bad digestion, collapsing the processes of living and dying; in a perversion of godly inspiration, those others "inspird" (75) the speaker with the roily concoction of their bellies and selves. "[L]evend," too, suggests not only an insidious infusion or mingling of thoughts (and thus minds, identities), but also that the speaker's thoughts are made more gaseous, less dense or solid, through interaction, as if the mere act of speaking with others makes him liable to dissolution, as if their influence could cause him to float away into nothingness. The speaker seems both to acknowledge and to eschew the flesh, worrying that communication renders him at once a locus of disease and dangerously insubstantial. In his retroactive construction of a sphere of blissful, enlightened being, the speaker thus reveals not merely the heavy burden of his worries about sin, but a concomitant fear about the risks to the self of occupying its place in a social realm.

It makes sense, then, that when the speaker elaborates on what made that prior state so "Blessed" (17), he voices an audacious claim of singularity. "Disabled," he enjoys the "Ten thousand Pleasures" (22) of the whole world. Unnamed "Secrets" are "reveald" only to him (33–34), and he is "in the World [him] Self alone" (36). The fantasy of being deaf and mute is primarily one of total and unbounded connection with the divine, producing in turn assertions of unpermeated self-possession, a kind of world domination. The frank desire for a return to isolationism — the somehow poignant statement that it was "*Mixture*" that opened the "Holy Door," the "Gate of Souls," and let contagion in — signals the speaker's potent fear of contact. Intersubjectivity may expose him to the seductions of less virtuous others, but the possibility of sin seems only one part of the despair that propels this fantasy of disability. Perhaps more acutely, deafness and speechlessness maintain the speaker's sense of distinct identity, guarding him against the friction of difference, the inevitable misunderstandings and failures that disturb participation in the human community. The appropriation of disability becomes an antagonistic act, a way of resisting others and ballasting the borders of self.

Paradoxically, then, because disability allows the speaker of "Dumnesse" to deny anything "other," it also allows him to remain unique. Physical dysfunction has special rewards in Traherne's poetic rendering of it: the speaker's soul can be "One / With in it self" (29–30), "alone" (30), "one" (35), "in the World [him] self alone" (36). Such insistence on solitude (especially noticeable in a poem that repeatedly and directly invokes its audience, as when the speaker addresses "my Dear friends" (17) or responds to a query with "D'ye ask me What?" [39]) implies that bodily breakdown transforms the speaker into a daringly autonomous self. David T. Mitchell explains the literary use of physical dysfunction to set the individual apart from others: "Disability lends a distinctive idiosyncrasy to any characters that differentiate themselves from the anonymous background of the norm." "The anonymity of normality," Mitchell writes, "is no story at all."[17] Disability in "Dumnesse" functions in just this way, assuring a level of seclusion that shields the speaker's identity from dilution. Disabled, he is "Distinct and Seperat" (32), a special "one" potentially lost among the many, the disembodied tongues, words, and entrails that threaten to inundate and even consume him. The assertions of confident habitation in God's "World of Light" (31) hide, and therefore inevitably also expose, a fragile self, profoundly fearful of loss and of sharing, afraid of being subsumed by other people, with their competing claims on the stuff of the world, their "Impetuous Torrent of Wrong Desires" (*Third Century*, 114).

In an even more reckless avowal of ownership and desire, the speaker details the "Work" (37) he performed while deaf and speechless. Far from disenfranchisement — a more probable material condition for a congenitally deaf person in seventeenth-century England — this disabled speaker lays claim to everything:

> It was with Cleerer Eys
> To see all Creatures full of Deities;
> Especialy Ones self: And to Admire
> The Satisfaction of all True Desire:
> Twas to be Pleasd with all that God hath done;
> Twas to Enjoy *even All* beneath the Sun;
> Twas with a Steddy and immediat Sence
> To feel and measure all the Excellence
> Of Things: Twas to inherit Endless Treasure,
> And to be fild with Everlasting Pleasure:
> To Reign in Silence, and to Sing alone
> To see, love, Covet, hav, Enjoy and Prais, in one:
> To Prize and to be ravishd: to be true,
> Sincere and Single in a Blessed View
> Of all his Gifts. (39–53)

---

[17] David T. Mitchell, "Narrative Prosthesis and the Materiality of Metaphor," in *Disability Studies: Enabling the Humanities*, ed. Snyder, Brueggemann, and Thomson, 15–30, here 16, 21.

As all those "all"s begin to accumulate, the speaker's wish to rediscover God's presence in himself through meditation on the divine in nature slides into a less sanctioned dream of sovereign singularity. Bodily dysfunction reintroduces the speaker to what he sets forth as the unmediated, reciprocal world of infancy whose treasures suffuse him as he expands to preside over that wealth. Unity prevails: in his state of "Steddy and immediat" apprehension of "Excellence," of "Endless" and "Everlasting" bounty, the speaker eliminates division, denies boundaries, revels in all-ness. His verbs exult in pleasures both erotic and monarchical: "Covet," "Enjoy," "inherit," "ravishd," "reign." One thinks of Donne's holy sonneteer, begging the ravishment of a domineering and elusive God. But Traherne's speaker imagines intermingling not with God himself, but with a more abstracted "pleasure"; the speaker remembers his unfettered appreciation of things both natural and cosmic as a kind of intimate communion with pure satisfaction, undifferentiated and "Sincere." Indeed, Traherne's vision is really not one of interpenetration at all, since his "reign" is silent, his indulgence specifically isolate. Disablement becomes a pathway toward a host of illegitimate desires — greed, a yearning for power, covetousness, the need to feel singular — which are restyled according to the parameters of religious commitment and pre-adult innocence.[18] Figured as spiritual purity, dysfunction masks a desire to possess and contain wholly, to deny the social requirement of intersubjective exchange, or the inescapable adult realities of loss, separation, and fear.

More than ecstatic piety, the "Work" remembered by "Dumnesse" is one of active sequestration in a depopulated world. Battle imagery enters the poem when the speaker recalls the consequences of having "gaind a Tongue" (68). This marks the second time in the poem that the tongue signals the speaker's worry about the dangers involved in speaking and hearing. Carla Mazzio has written that because the tongue is "the one organ that can move in and out of the body," early modern representations of this "little member" reveal a host of cultural anxieties about the threshold "between the space of the self and the space of the

---

[18] In *Protestant Poetics and the Seventeenth-Century Religious Lyric* (Princeton: Prineton University Press, 1979), Barbara Kiefer Lewalski cautions that Traherne is not to be accused of "egomania or blasphemy," as "the singular privileges of Traherne's speaker are gifts of God." Yet as she suggests of the poem "Hosanna," "curiously, the celebration *is* rather of the self than of God: the rejoicing is for the infinite felicity the speaker experiences as he himself is 'enthron'd' with God" (368; my italics). Spurr views Traherne's isolate self as "the nurturing of an apostolic individuality in his spiritual life" ("Felicity Incarnate," 276). My argument here is that "Dumnesse" conceals the "egomaniacal" fantasy of autonomy in its language of disability. For a further discussion of self-love as an instrument of mystical union, see K. W. Salter, *Thomas Traherne, Mystic and Poet* (London: Edward Arnold, 1964), 92–110.

other."[19] The tongue's synecdochal association with both language and identity make it readily available to the imagination as a corporeal version of the complications of intersubjective exchange. Able to cross the boundary of the bodied self, the tongue encapsulates the body's tendency toward excess and loss of control; symbolic slippage between the tongue and other body parts (penis, heart, and brain, for instance) render its uncanny mobility particularly threatening to the safe borders of other selves, for their part acutely aware of their own penetrability. Mazzio writes that if "the tongue is imagined as the site where discursive and moral contagion begins and ends, it seems logical to detach it in the act of punishing transgression."[20] This is precisely the action taken by the speaker of "Dumnesse," who disables his own tongue in a retroactive fantasy of silent purity, then disarms other people's unruly tongues by deafening himself.

Inside himself, the speaker finds "a Pulpit," "A Temple, and a Teacher" (57–58) that "comment" on the "large Text" (59) of the world; he takes instruction from the "Voices" (67) and "Song" (62) of the stuff of earth. But when he begins to speak, his formerly "Impregnable" fortress of self (54) opens wide, his "Ears let other Noises in, not theirs; / A Nois Disturbing all [his] Songs and Prayers" (69–70), and "Whole Legions" (56) troop in to "Cover and despoyl [his] Coasts" (77). The notion of a beleaguered self "pent" (53) within an impenetrable fort that precedes, rather than results from, intercourse in a hearing, speaking world unveils the sense of weakness behind the speaker's claim of sovereign resiliency. In his fear of interaction, his horror at the thought of penetration from without, he disavows not only the helplessness of infancy or the very real social conditions of disability, but the intersubjective reality of human experience in the most general sense. The speaker's metaphor of impregnability reminds us that bodies, and the selves with which they are entangled, are permeable, prone to transgression; it is impossible, except in fantasy, to barricade the borders of the self so thoroughly as he avows here.

At the end of the poem, the speaker seems, unexpectedly, to reverse his bodily condition, announcing that he did hear, even in infancy:

Yet the first Words mine Infancy did hear,
The Things which in my Dumness did appear,
Preventing all the rest, got such a root
Within my Heart, and stick so close unto't
It may be Trampld on, but still will grow;
And Nutriment to *Soyl* it self will owe. (79–84)

---

[19] Carla Mazzio, "Sins of the Tongue," in *The Body in Parts*, ed. Hillman and eadem, 53–79, here 55–56. "Little member" comes from James 3:5 (56).
[20] Mazzio, "Sins of the Tongue," 64.

In fact, this is not physiological hearing at all, but rather a strictly internal listening to what is already inside of the speaker. The metaphor of rootedness suggests a desire to be connected to something "so close" and firmly as to eliminate all space between. He is a hermetically sealed system, entirely self-sufficient and self-regenerating. Penetration is now considered tolerable only because it occurs within the self, because it is governed from within. The heart's porousness — its openness to "Things" that can take root, such as the "first Words" that "penetrat" it (88) — is a sign of receptiveness to God, whereas the vulnerable ear can neither govern itself nor discern between the good and the bad. The distinction made between ears and tongues, on the one hand, eyes and hearts on the other, underscores the poem's preoccupation with whether or not the embodied subject can maintain control, successfully monitoring what enters and exits its boundaries. Because the body cannot entirely prevent itself from being invaded by the breath or disease or ideas of others, Traherne performs a kind of exaggerated surgery on himself, retreating through sensory incapacitation. Not surprisingly, it is the noble heart, fully internal to the body, that takes precedence in the end as "the ultimate locus of interiority."[21]

Ultimately, disability serves the speaker of "Dumnesse" because it signifies removal from interconnection. Those sections of the poem that say something positive about faith, or that seem to return to a state of innocent bliss, bespeak the loudest anxiety about intimate, intersubjective contact. The poem features an array of body parts: depraved tongues and tongues gained; corrupted entrails; hearts that "grow" and are "penetrat[ed]"; eyes that not only "see" (40) but even perform the function of "Hearers" (60); ears that do not hear at all. In the contrast between disease and disability, the speaker effects a hierarchy of sorts: bodily interiors connote loss, failure, betrayal, and deceit; disability signifies transcendence over the mundane or messy stuff of the earthly realm, a state of superior contemplative powers, and a pathway toward grace. The disabled self is unmixed, unintegrated with the truck of humanity, and thus flaunts its ethical superiority, its deliberate detachment from infiltrating others. In this, I would argue, the poem is darker than it may at first appear, and far from unambiguously joyful. Not only does it map out a condition of withdrawal and separation that precludes entrance into the pleasures of real human interaction, but in falsifying deafness — extrapolating and idealizing a single attribute out of the whole context of a person's experience — it also limits the possibility of a genuine recognition of corporeal difference.

A similar claim can be made about the person introduced in "Silence," said to "possess / All that is Great or High in Blessedness" (1–2). This "quiet Silent" individual (1), busied with "Inward Work" (3), stands apart from the general run

---

[21] Mazzio, "Sins of the Tongue," 63.

of humanity occupied with the "outward Busy Acts" (9) that result from original sin. As in "Dumnesse," the "only Work" (21, 26) required of the subject of "Silence" is to "admire, rejoyce / Sing Praises," and "See, Prize, Give Thanks within, and Love" (23–24) — activities performed wholly "in himself" (22). Muting himself in silent inwardness, the speaker claims, made his "Bosom like the Deity" (76). "To see, Approve, take Pleasure, and rejoice, / Within," he declares, "is better than an Empty Voice" (29–30). Deaf to the external world, he is immune to the "pollut[ions]" of the outer world (56). "No other Thoughts did intervene, to Cloy, / Divert, extinguish, or Ecclyps my Joy" (53–54).

Yet "Silence," like "Dumnesse," unmistakably displays its "audist assumptions."[22] The symbolic effectiveness of deafness and muteness as forms of disconnection from others depends on a problematic belief that those conditions do entail the absence of communication; they are then transformed, through rhetorical control, into bulwarks against the very dependency and contamination that disability has, historically, been made to represent. Despite the emphasis throughout Traherne's work on the body as constitutive of identity, the depiction of disability in "Dumnesse" and "Silence" implies the possibility of transcending the body through language, thus alienating their readers from the facts of embodied experience. Perhaps more troublingly, the presentation of an idealized deaf-muteness, valued as ennobling and purifying, amplifies the "otherness" of real bodily difference, which in turn reifies the boundary between ability and disability. As "Silence" makes clear, the subject constituted by Traherne's disabling metaphors is fundamentally an able-bodied one, firmly established on the safe side of the "hearing line":[23] the speaker of that poem experiences the treasures of the world "with a lively Sence" (51).

In his *History of Disability*, Henri-Jacques Stiker demonstrates a paradigm shift between Old Testament prohibitions against bodily afflictions and the New Testament emphasis on social responsibility. Hebrew scripture, Stiker writes, "exposes a very profound violence, as concerns disability and physical and mental ills. The person who is afflicted is made to bear the burden of sin, the burden of wrongdoing." Forced to carry "a radical social responsibility for evil, and thus for misfortune," the disabled are "expelled victims," "distanc[ed] from the presence of God." In the New Testament, however, "Jesus says explicitly that the sick, the disabled, the marginalized, are the first in the Kingdom of God. His affection for them is due to their closeness to God; he cites them as examples of faith and of grace." Stiker argues that early Judaism was stabilized by a system of oppositions that segregated the

---

[22] The phrase is Christopher Krentz's, from "Exploring the 'Hearing Line': Deafness, Laughter, and Mark Twain," in *Disability Studies: Enabling the Humanities*, ed. Snyder, Brueggemann, and Thomson, 234–47, here 240.

[23] Krentz, "Exploring the 'Hearing Line'," 234.

sacred from the profane, the afflicted from the clean; under Christianity, thought and conduct replace "exterior pollution" as the mark of impurity or sinfulness: "It is what a person says or does to his fellow that constitutes uncleanness."[24] The lines of demarcation between able and disabled bodies do not disappear with Christianity's emphasis on ethics and charity, however; to the contrary, Stiker suggests that because "[t]here are no longer any dictates," "nothing pre-established," those boundaries are entirely determined by social relationships, and are thus fraught with the tensions of self-other dynamics. "[O]ur relationship to disability," Stiker writes, "our relationship to abnormality, depends entirely on ourselves."[25]

Stiker's analysis of disability in a religious context has two implications for my discussion of Traherne's representation of deafness and muteness. Nowhere does Traherne cite Jesus's "affection" for the disabled as made special by grace (in itself a highly paternalistic response to impairment). To the contrary, while his use of physical dysfunction may serve the goal of rendering the desire to commune with God, it also reveals a more complicated purpose — to separate him from humanity — that has little to do (or, perhaps, everything to do) with the lived experience of disability. And while Christianity's response to the disabled may have been to recognize "[t]heir dignity, their right to partake fully of religious and social life," it did not eliminate social exclusions or the tendency to interpret bodily affliction as a sign of transgression or spiritual loss. The idea that cultural reactions to disability manifest horror at "the fragility of one's own life"[26] further

---

[24] See Matthew 15:17–20 and Mark 7:18–23.

[25] The quoted passages are from Stiker, *History of Disability*, 30, 34, 36.

[26] Susan Wendell, *The Rejected Body: Feminist Philosophical Reflections on Disability* (New York: Routledge, 1996), 107. For the idea that the disabled body inspires fear because it literalizes the ambiguity and unpredictability of embodiment generally, see the essays collected in *Freakery: Cultural Spectacles of the Extraordinary Body*, ed. Rosemarie Garland Thomson (New York: NYU Press, 1996), esp. Elizabeth Grosz, "Intolerable Ambiguity: Freaks as/at the Limit" (55–66) and Paul Semonin, "Monsters in the Marketplace: The Exhibition of Human Oddities in Early Modern England" (69–81); David T. Mitchell and Sharon L. Snyder, *Narrative Prosthesis: Disability and the Dependencies of Discourse* (Ann Arbor: University of Michigan Press, 2000); Robert F. Murphy, *The Body Silent: The Different World of the Disabled* (New York: Norton, 1990); Leslie Fiedler, *Freaks: Myths and Images of the Secret Self* (Simon and Schuster, 1978); and Erving Goffman, *Stigma: Notes on the Management of Spoiled Identity* (New York: Simon & Schuster, 1963). The preliminary chapters of Mark Thornton Burnett's *Constructing "Monsters" in Shakespearean Drama and Early Modern Culture* (New York: Palgrave Macmillan, 2002) details the fascination for "monstrous" bodies in the Renaissance. For a further discussion of disability in the early modern period, see also S. B. Mintz, "Dalila's Touch: Disability and Recognition in *Samson Agonistes*," chap. 5 in eadem, *Threshold Poetics: Milton and Intersubjectivity* (Newark, DE: University of Delaware Press, 2003), 175–207.

underscores Traherne's highly paradoxical assumption of an aphasic deafness to reject what might otherwise be the intolerable susceptibility to breakdown and the entanglements of interdependence that characterize embodied subjectivity. While many critics have pointed to Traherne's investment in the body as the proof of humanity's dignity no less than of God's design, it is important to notice that he does not celebrate all bodies, and that his deaf-mute subject is symbolically powerful only to the extent that it is read as figurative, not actual.

The desire to overcome the embarrassment, discomforts, and frailty of the body is vividly expressed in the poem "The Odour." Elsewhere, Traherne disparages jewelry as the gaudy baubles of frivolous and superficial people; here, "Hands are Jewels to the Ey" (1): a bodily ornament as pleasing to the eye as "Wine, or Oil, or Hony, to the Taste" (2). To have hands — specifically to *witness* one's own hands — is to be gratified in a multiply sensory way, visually but even orally. Feet, too, along with all the body's "Members" (5), inspire the speaker to a rapturous outburst:

> Ye living gems, how Tru! how Near!
> How Reall, Useful, Pleasant! O how Good!
> How Valuable! yea, how Sweet! how Fair!
>   B'ing once well understood!
> For Use ye permanent remain intire,
> Sweet Scents diffus'd do gratify Desire. (7–12)

What stands out about this paean to the limbs is its mention of a use-value that derives from understanding. Indeed, the notion of "use" recurs throughout the poem: feet are "us'd" (4), the body's "Uses" flow and endure (19, 30), uses are "*Treasures*" and "sacred" (24, 63), the speaker strives to "apprehend" the use of his senses (66). Malcolm M. Day locates this emphasis in the poem's "quest for the ultimate perception of God." Whatever the sensual pleasures of being a body, it is "the spiritual meaning of any sense perception, its *use*, that is finally Traherne's real concern," Day argues; "sense detail" is merely an invitation to the bodied subject to "contemplate its intelligible idea."[27]

This line of reading has been echoed many times in Traherne scholarship. Years ago, K. W. Salter discussed Traherne's representation of the senses in terms of a self-love that, in stimulating self-knowledge, develops the individual's understanding of the divine. "The senses are to be fully exercised," writes Salter, "because God can be known by them." Employing the "faculties" is a "mode of praising God," whose "Holy Will is to be fulfilled by these active instruments, the bodily senses, the great endowments of hand and eye . . . the senses are to be

---

[27] Malcolm M. Day, *Thomas Traherne* (Boston: Twayne Publishers, 1982), 150–51.

purified by their proper employment."[28] Richard Douglas Jordan has argued that Traherne's "real 'message'" is "to improve the human faculties to the point where they become infinite and divine," while more recently Alvin Snider reiterates the Baconian thread in Traherne's work, citing "Bacon's attempt to create an inductive method of scientific analysis rooted in sensory experience."[29] Even Sawday's complaint — that too much criticism of Traherne ignores the poet's affiliation with contemporary science and falsely aligns him with "the irrational, the inward, the insubstantial" — reinforces the idea that the body Traherne prizes and anatomizes is one of Christ-like complexity and thus a source of wonder. The study of such a body would lead to a fitting acknowledgement of God's mystery, and "[s]ensory experience could be transformed into a hymn of praise."[30]

In these various efforts to articulate Traherne's spiritual and philosophical attitude toward sense perception, critics tend to minimize the ideological implications of the poet's assumption that only a body defined as fully "functional" can be deemed glorious; the physically (as opposed to poetically) disabled sense does not conduct the subject toward God.[31] In "The Odour," a specifically meditative self-scrutiny clearly dominates the poem's presentation of glorious corporeality — encapsulated in the instructions to "*Contemplat*" (47) and to "Talk with thy self; thy self enjoy and see: / At once the Mirror and the Object be" (53–54). But the repeated stress on usefulness, permanence, and functionality suggests a very different relationship to embodiment than the critical accounts of Traherne's body-imagery may imply. The speaker claims that his feet "never waste" and that his limbs do "not consume" delight (4, 6); that his "living gems" (7) are "Valuable," "permanent," and "intire" (9, 11); and that despite its dispersal of "Light" and "Influence," his body nonetheless "Abide[s] the same" (18–19). Such statements may bespeak a mystical trust in the continuity of God's presence as revealed in the human body, but they say something else, too — that the body is disturbingly prone to decay, dysfunction, and death. In its praise of a sweet-smelling body whose "Gifts" (28) continually replenish themselves, "The Odour" insists that a "Good" (8) body is one that doesn't waste away: it transcends aging, illness, and the baser needs of corporeal existence; perhaps most significantly, it *works*. No deafened ears, blind eyes, or immobile limbs inspire the exhortation to "esteem" oneself (43).

---

[28] Salter, *Thomas Traherne*, 54–55.

[29] Richard Douglas Jordan, *The Temple of Eternity: Thomas Traherne's Philosophy of Time* (Port Washington, NY: Kennikat Press, 1972), 45; Alvin Snider, "The Self-Mirroring Mind in Milton and Traherne," *University of Toronto Quarterly* 55 (1986): 313–27, here 325.

[30] Sawday, *Body Emblazoned*, 256, 260–61.

[31] Again, in the *Third Century*, Traherne writes that "the Riches of Nature are our Souls and Bodies, with all their Faculties Sences and Endowments" (116).

The able body so highly prized in "The Odour" is also contained within the same self-enclosure that protects the subjects of "Dumnesse" and "Silence" from infiltration by toxins, both physical and psychical, that originate outside the self. The speaker describes a kind of self-perpetuating, wholly sustainable corporeal system: his body emits and consumes its own tastes, scents, and light; it is the stimulus and gratification of its own desire. The oft-cited specular moment of the poem — "Talk with thy self; thy self enjoy and see: / At once the Mirror and the Object be" (53–54) — exemplifies the closed space everywhere apparent in Traherne's work as the matrix of subjectivity. The self is fractured into spectator and object of the gaze, a mind actively observing and the thing being observed; it is thus an entity *experiencing* being seen even as it does the looking. To be one's own mirror is to be caught in a curious *mise-en-abyme* of self-appraisal. Not simply encountering a version of himself in the mirror but actually reflecting himself back to himself, the mirror/object subject of "The Odour" must *already know what he looks like*; is there, then, any true observation at work, any genuine stimulation of recognition or new awareness? Does such a regard allow for anything unfamiliar — such as a body that does not abide by idealized norms — to be authentically "seen"?

Perhaps this is why the terms of comparison in the poem are not especially provocative or inventive; indeed, they are even subtly disparaged. The speaker likens fingers to "Amber," crowns the head with honeysuckle, and compares eyes to "Stars," cheeks to "Roses" (49–51). Later, after the many references to wine, oil, honey, milk, cinnamon, and myrrh — all introduced (as in the Song of Songs 4:11, 12–14) to establish the body's fragrant and nourishing qualities — he asks, "What's Cinnamon, compar'd to thee? / . . . / Those Fruits and Flowers which in Fields I see, / With *thine*, can not compare. / . . . what is Myrrh? What Cinnamon?" (55–61). To be sure, it is not uncommon for poetic analogies to break down in the very act of linking the stuff of the world and a thing considered to be perfect, particularly in devotional poetry where the subject is, by definition, unimaginable and incomparable. But there is something tautological about Traherne's characterization of the body that precludes inclusion of disabled limbs or unworking senses. The body is "good" because it is "Reall" [8], but the criteria for being "real" lies in a hierarchy that defines realness as goodness; goodness depends on a notion of what is normal, because "lack of Sense the Benefit destroys" (42).

Traherne's tribute to embodiment, then — what Barbara Lewalski has endorsed as "the proper valuation of the glories of man's body"[32] — not only privileges "natural" physicality over what is artificial (such as jewels, superficial

---

[32] Lewalski, *Protestant Poetics*, 359.

wealth, or anything "man-made"), but further demarcates the boundaries of the normal body through an implicit, deeply embedded association between disability and idleness, corruption, and degeneration ("All corruptible things waste and consume away," as he writes in *Christian Ethicks*). The dichotomy between functional and dysfunctional sensory perception is apparent throughout the poems. The speaker of "An Infant-Eye," for instance, states that "Wantonness and Avarice" (37) so obscured his capacity to "discern the Lov / of God" (27–28) that his senses became "feeble and disabled" (41), perceiving only the "grosser" things of the world (11, 20, 30); the speaker of "Wonder," conversely, robust in his "Native Health" (17), boasts the "Vigour in [his] Sence" (20) and listens attentively to "evry Thing" that "Did with [him] talk" (7–8).

"Solitude" offers a more intriguing expression of the primacy of working senses. Here, silence is not a self-imposed defense against intrusive and sinful others, but a result of the speaker's own spiritual failure. "I was so blind," he says (31), that the landscape "silent stood" (49), refusing to calm his mind by speaking to him: "Ye sullen Things! / Ye dumb, ye silent Creatures . . . Will ye not speak / What 'tis I want, nor Silence break?" (41–46). Frantic to hear, desperate for the sensory intercourse between self and nature that signifies for Traherne the felicitous state of connection to the divine, this speaker demonstrates Nelson and Berens's contention that deafness is desirable only when it is appropriated as an act of power over the risks associated with other people. In their words, "actual physical deafness and muteness do not come from the inward, glorious soul, but from the weak body."[33]

Both "The Salutation" and "The Person" make clear that whatever meditative advantage can be garnered from silencing the self has no correlation with nonfunctioning body parts. In "The Salutation," the speaker wonders, "Where was? in what Abyss, my Speaking Tongue?" (6), and says that before he was born, he "Did little think such Joys as Ear or Tongue, / To Celebrat or See: / Such Sounds to hear, such Hands to feel, such Feet" (15–17). "The Person" describes the "Harmony" (62) of "My Tongue, my Eys, / My cheeks, my Lips, my Ears, my Hands, my Feet" (60–61) — which, in a fitting pun, the speaker calls "Organs of [God's] Praise" (64). Such moments exemplify Lennard J. Davis's claim that "one of the foundational ableist myths of our culture" is that "the norm for humans is to speak and hear."[34] At every point, Traherne's revered body works "normally," disabled only as a show of control over the perils of both corporeal and intersubjective existence.

---

[33] Nelson and Berens, "Fantasies of Deafness," 65.

[34] Davis, *Enforcing Normalcy*, 15.

Readings of Traherne have typically stressed the poet's desire for an "objective," "nondual," "organic unity" between the self and the things of the world.[35] "It is more Glorious to lov others," as Traherne instructs in the *Fourth Century*; *"No man loves, but he loves another more then Himself"* (197). But the apparent inclusiveness of that vision does not in any overt way extend to the "extraordinary" bodies of the disabled in Restoration England.[36] Traherne employs disability as what Mitchell calls "an opportunistic metaphoric device":[37] his representations of deafness and speechlessness indicate not a serious grappling with difference, but rather an erasure of the social and material circumstances of disability — an erasure, moreover, that criticism has perpetuated in its focus on parsing the philosophical and spiritual beliefs that motivate Traherne's so-called "vision." My aim here has been to shift that focus from the strictly devotional characteristic of Traherne's body-language toward the interplay of "ableism" and disablement that dominates the work.

Rhetorical references to disability, even apparently positive ones, reinforce problematic stereotypes by underwriting the hegemony of an idealized, "natural," wonder-inspiring physical form that strives for order against the vagaries of embodiment. The poet's symbolic appropriation of deafness or muteness obscures the lived experience of those conditions; at the same time, his enthusiastic celebration of the body as an object both marvelous and mechanically intricate requires the denigration of dysfunction to provide symbolic counterpoint. While much scholarship has been devoted to a study of the exact dimensions of the "infinite" on which Traherne's poetics are presumably trained, that enterprise has tended to overshadow the body behind his "luminescent"[38] perception: the unacknowledged body of disability, which is the true "Heart" of all embodied experience.

---

[35] This trend appears in both mid-century and more recent scholarship. In *The Mystical Poetry of Thomas Traherne* (Cambridge, MA: Harvard University Press, 1969), for instance, A. L. Clements argues of the poem "Dumnesse" that the "developing, conceptualizing intellect" of the child "distinguishes as other what in actuality is nondual, indivisible, inextricably interrelated and interdependent" (108). James J. Balakier calls Traherne "broad-sighted" (235) and "objective" (236), "a poet of a new more liberating consciousness" (247), in his 1989 article ("Thomas Traherne's Dobell Series"). In 2001, Carol Ann Johnston writes that the speaker of "The Odour" promotes "an organic unity between self and world as another means of envisioning the self as God objectively sees human beings" ("Heavenly Perspectives," 396).

[36] The term is Rosemarie Garland Thomson's, from *Extraordinary Bodies: Figuring Physical Disability in American Culture and Literature* (New York: Columbia University Press, 1997).

[37] Mitchell, "Narrative Prosthesis," 15.

[38] Sharon Cadman Seelig, *The Shadow of Eternity: Belief and Structure in Herbert, Vaughan and Traherne* (Lexington: University Press of Kentucky, 1981), 104.

"Cursd and Devised Proprieties": Traherne and the Laws of Property

Lynne A. Greenberg

Hunter College

Over thirty years ago, Christopher Hill suggested that the economic thought of Thomas Traherne and radical Digger Gerrard Winstanley shared certain attributes including traces of "communism," albeit "in the imagination only."[1] Qualifying this observation, Hill nonetheless stressed that Traherne's political thought, eschewing the need for social reform, was far from radical but "entirely self-absorbed, self-regarding."[2] Very little critical work has since developed these provocative claims or interpolated Traherne's deeply meditative poetry within seventeenth-century land law, thereby leaving Hill's suggestions largely unchallenged.[3] Yet Traherne repeatedly relied on legal terms of agricultural and proprietary significance in dispute throughout the period; notions of proprietary possession and

---

[1] Christopher Hill, *The World Turned Upside Down: Radical Ideas During the English Revolution* (London: Maurice Temple Smith, 1972), 414. See also idem, *The Collected Essays of Christopher Hill: Writing and Revolution in Seventeenth-Century England* (Amherst: University of Massachusetts Press, 1985), 1:226–46. For further discussions of the similarities of Traherne's and Winstanley's economic and political thought, see John Hoyles, "Beyond the Sex-Economy of Mysticism: Some Observations on the Communism of the Imagination with Reference to Winstanley and Traherne," in *1642: Literature and Power in the Seventeenth Century*, ed. Francis Barker (Colchester: University of Essex, 1981), 238–57; T. Wilson Hayes, *Winstanley the Digger: A Literary Analysis of Radical Ideas in the English Revolution* (Cambridge, MA: Harvard University Press, 1979), 75–76, 127, 130, 186.

[2] Hill, *Collected Essays*, 1:233–35.

[3] For an analysis of Traherne's political economy and its relationship to that of emerging mercantile political economists of the period, see David Hawkes, "Thomas Traherne: A Critique of Political Economy," *Huntington Library Quarterly* 62 (2001): 369–88. For other political discussions of Traherne's work, see Julia J. Smith, "Thomas Traherne and the Restoration," *The Seventeenth Century* 2 (1988): 203–22; N. I. Matar, "The Political Views of Thomas Traherne," *Huntington Library Quarterly* 57 (1994): 241–53.

enclosure function as central topoi in Traherne's poetry, and the "Ground" both literally and figuratively grounds much of his imagery ("The Salutation," 18).[4]

This essay will historicize Traherne's discussions of property, its ownership, usage, and division, within the agricultural and legal reforms of seventeenth-century England in order to clarify Traherne's vexed, at times ambivalent, at times contradictory, configuration of both the communal ideals of Interregnum radicals and the proprietary concerns of an emerging class of landowners. Traherne's topographical depictions of prelapsarian Eden, in their rejections of enclosures and celebration of the natural world, do suggest a privileging of common usage rights and interests in real property; nevertheless, Traherne's paradigm also voiced an alternative discourse, articulated most influentially by common law judges, legal theorists, and property holders, that advocated the absolute ownership of real property. Exploring his "unpossest" interior landscapes ("The Preparative," 62), envisioned conversely as both delimited and boundless, also reveals a less consistently critical attitude towards the processes and principles of enclosure. The second half of the seventeenth century witnessed crucial changes to the proprietary rights and topography of England, and Traherne's poetry arguably recorded these changes. This essay, while not disputing Traherne's radical proprietary ideas, suggests that his work also bears the influence of evolving legal definitions of property and its ownership that would become dominant by the eighteenth century.

Traherne's communal philosophy predominates in his depiction of the prelapsarian condition, one shared only by children in the fallen world, as a state that rejects material acquisition. He describes prelapsarian Adam as contemptuous of "preternatural" things, a category he defined in the *Centuries* as both real and personal property that had a monetary value, including "gold, silver, houses, lands, clothes" (3.9).[5] Important to this discussion, Traherne repeatedly targeted the desire for houses and lands, or real property, as particularly odious: "But to say this house is yours, and these lands are another man's . . . is deadly barbarous and uncouth to a little child" (3.11). Man's interest in obtaining private and exclusive ownership rights in property, that is, to "think no Realms nor Kingdoms theirs / No Lands nor Houses, that have other Heirs" ("Misapprehension," 40–41), Traherne derided as "false proprieties" (1.33). Traherne also attacked

---

[4] Thomas Traherne, *The Poetical Works of Thomas Traherne*, ed. Gladys I. Wade (London: P. J. & A. E. Dobell, 1932). All references to Traherne's poems derive from this edition. Relevant line numbers are parenthetical in the text.

[5] Thomas Traherne, *Centuries* (Wilton, CT: Morehouse-Barlow, 1986). All references to the *Centuries* derive from this edition. The relevant *Century* and entry number are parenthetical in the text.

attempts to keep property within familial blood lines across successive generations through hereditary schemes: "wise men die, likewise the fool and the brut-
ish person perish, and leave their wealth to others. Their inward thought is, that
their houses shall continue forever, and their dwelling places to all generations.
They call their lands after their own names. This their way is their folly" (3.80).[6]
Traherne's contempt for land bequests has autobiographical corroboration in his
own failure to grant, or even mention, his five cottages located in Hereford when
verbally composing his last will and testament on his deathbed.[7]

Traherne contrasted the materialistic ethics of the postlapsarian world with
Eden: "No Gold, nor Trade, nor Silver there, / Nor Cloaths, no Coin, nor Houses were" ("Adam's Fall," 13–14). He urged the renunciation of claims to private
property ownership, privileging instead non-exclusive property rights shared by
all of mankind: "He called his house the house of Paradise: not only because it
was the place wherein he enjoyed the whole world, but because it was every one's
house in the whole world . . . All things in his house being as much the foreign-
ers as they were his own" (4.22). Attempting to replicate the prelapsarian condition, Traherne repeatedly urged that one should "do as Adam did" ("Blisse," 3)
and abjure possessory interests: "till you delight in God for being good to all: you
never enjoy the world. Till you more feel it than your private estate, and are more
present in the hemisphere, considering the glories and the beauties there, than in
your own house" (1.30). Traherne coupled this rejection of material ownership
with an alternative esteeming of God's created universe. He counseled, in place
of the acquisition and valuation of private property, the enjoyment of the natural world. "Glory and Dominion are invisible joys. And so is that great interest a
man hath to all Kingdoms and Ages, which a true possessor of the World is more
sensible of, than of his houses and lands" (2.98).[8]

The foregoing brief summary of Traherne's communal philosophy suggests,
as Hill detailed, an affinity with the economic theories of Winstanley and other
mid-century radicals; yet paradoxically, Traherne's paradigm offers an alternative topography that graphically configures emerging delineations of property.
As an initial matter, Traherne's interiorized meditations insist upon the sanctity of "private and personal delights" (3.92), an ethos potentially at odds with

---

[6] Traherne is quoting from Psalm 49:10, 11, 13.

[7] Gladys Irene Wade, *Thomas Traherne* (Princeton: Princeton University Press, 1944),
104.

[8] And, again, in the *Centuries*, Traherne cautioned that as the world is "more nearly
and immediately our dwelling place, than our cities and kingdoms and houses . . . Why
then we should not be sensible of that as much as of our dwellings, I cannot tell . . . Those
accidental dwellings may be thrown down, or we may be taken from them, but this can
never be removed, it abideth for ever" (5.2).

a purely communal philosophy. Moreover, he described the "desire to have all alone in our private possession" as a "natural" inclination (1.79),[9] even conceding that some material acquisition, specifically in real property, constituted a necessary feature of worldly life and religious belief: "we must some Estate / Possess," otherwise "No Tenant can rais Corn, or pay his Rent, / Nor can even hav a Lord, / That has no Land" ("The Circulation," 51–53).[10] An examination of the precise nature of Traherne's understanding of such "possess[ion]" reveals the extent to which it parallels and perhaps unwittingly assimilates the ideology of England's evolving land laws.

A critical period in England's transition from a feudal to a market economy, the second half of the seventeenth century transformed England's landscape, as parliament and the commons effected sweeping agricultural reforms, including changes to the laws of land ownership. Prior to the Civil War, the common law restricted individuals' interests in real property to limited rights in rather than more inclusive ownership of land, deferring to the feudal understanding of the king as the sole owner of land in England. Much of the property in England was held in royal tenure and subject to stringent obligations, including military service,

---

[9] One area of Traherne's thought beyond the scope of this essay that merits further inquiry is his proto-capitalistic ideology of the pursuit of wealth. "The Fourth Century," in particular, fluctuates between a disdain for and a simultaneous embrace of material possessions: "Riches are not to be hated, nor coveted: but I am to bless God in all estates, Who hath given me the world, my Soul, and Himself: and ever to be great in the true treasures. Riches are good, and therefore is it good sometimes to want them that we might shew our obedience and resignation to God" (4.89). He rationalized that the insatiable desire of riches was not only a natural human instinct but also indicative of the "nobility of man's soul" (1.22). Traherne, accordingly, urged men fortunate enough to have material wealth to accept it as a sign of God's generosity: "because His love is free, so are His treasures. He therefore that will despise them because he hath them is marvellously irrational" (1.23). While these isolated quotations do not negate Traherne's larger vision, they do locate an anxiety over the roles that material holdings and proprietary possession play in human life and how properly to esteem them.

[10] Traherne's other statements on tenancy likewise suggest a critique, not necessarily of private property ownership, but of feudal notions of ownership. For example, Traherne asserted that "Those Acts which Adam in his Innocence / Performed, carry all the Excellence. / . . . Ploughing and Toyling for a forc't Increas, . . .This was a thing / As then unknown" ("Silence," 7–8, 14, 16–17). The "forc't Increas" could refer to the rack-renting of a landlord, but could also refer to the customary power of a feudal lord to demand exorbitant increases in the form of rents, fees, and other tributes. Another such critique of feudal entitlement occurs in the *Centuries*, in a description of childhood: "I knew not that there were any sins, complaints or laws. I dreamed not of poverties, contentions, or vices . . . I knew nothing of death or rents or exaction, either for tribute or bread" (3.2).

fines, fees, and even exclusive control of the land during an heir's minority. This system of land tenure had the ancillary effect of making the succession of property rights a precarious and uncertain practice.[11]

In 1646, the Long Parliament abolished the Court of Wards and military tenures, thereby dismantling the Crown's customary restrictions on, exploitation of, and intrusions into individuals' property rights. Diminishing the power of the Crown, the ordinance also served substantially to empower property holders in marshalling and protecting their exclusive rights and freedom to alienate land. The confirmation of the abolition of wardship and feudal tenures at the Restoration in 1660 ratified the characterization of property as subject only to individual ownership and control. This re-definition had an immediate effect, creating for the first time a vigorous land market, as property "bec[a]me a commodity in an increasingly competitive society. It could be freely bought and sold, mortgaged and bequeathed."[12]

Traherne's characterization of the natural world as his dominion and possession crucially qualifies his communal philosophy and moreover encapsulates the emerging cultural conception of absolute ownership within its purview. The *Centuries*, woven together by the underlying motif of ownership, infuses its seemingly non-materialistic vision with the competing values and desires of proprietorship. As Traherne rhapsodized: "The streets were mine, the temple was mine, the people were mine, their clothes and gold and silver were mine, as much as their sparkling eyes, fair skins and ruddy faces. The skies were mine, and so were the sun and moon and stars, and all the World was mine; and I the only spectator and I enjoyer of it" (3.3). The use of anaphora in "Hosanna" beautifully illustrates Traherne's ubiquitous, nearly obsessive characterization of the world as owned privately and exclusively by him:

> For Me the World created was by Lov;
> For Me the Skies, the Seas, the Sun, do mov;
>   The Earth for Me doth stable stand;
>   For Me each fruitful Land
>   For Me the very Angels God made His
>   And my Companions in Bliss: (61–66)

---

[11] For background on these changes, see Theodore Plucknett, *A Concise History of the Common Law* (London: Butterworth, 1956); Alan Macfarlane, *The Origins of English Individualism: The Family, Property, and Social Transition* (Cambridge and New York: Cambridge University Press, 1979); A. W. B. Simpson, *An Introduction to the History of the Land Law* (London: Oxford University Press, 1961).

[12] Christopher Hill, *Liberty Against the Law: Some Seventeenth Century Controversies* (London and New York: Allen Lane, 1996), 335.

This litany, importantly, includes the "fruitful Land" within Traherne's purview and possession. Demarcated even more precisely in other works, specific tracts of land, including England's "fields" ("The Dialogue," 1), "Mountains, Valleys, Woods" ("Speed," 17), "Groves, the Meads and Pastures" ("Meditations on the Six Days of Creation, Fourth Day," 23), are naturalized as his own.

Acknowledging the centrality of ownership to his spirituality, Traherne admitted: "The consideration . . . that the world is mine, confirmeth my faith" (2.6). The language of proprietary possession operates as a controlling leitmotif again in his description of Christianity, that further reveals Traherne's tacit acknowledgement of the advantages of private ownership: "As if that City stood on my own Ground, / And all the Profit mine which there was found . . . / What learn I more than that *Jerusalem* / Is *mine*, as 'tis *my Maker's*, choicest Gem" ("Christendom," 39–40, 109–110). This understanding of the land as having an intrinsic material value from which its exclusive owner could profit also permitted Traherne in a metaphoric leap to assume the position of its owner. Rather than denigrating the benefits that derived from such a position as "preternatural," Traherne figured himself reaping them. Similarly, in "Speed," he conflated the privileges of landholders with those of absolute sovereigns and once again bestowed upon himself their dominion:

> I was as High and Great,
> As Kings are in their Seat.
> All other Things were mine.
> The World my House, the Creatures were my Goods,
>   Fields, Mountains, Valleys, Woods,
> Men and their Arts to make me Rich combine. (13–18)

Exclusive possession, quite simply, leads to pecuniary benefits. Of course, such expansive ownership rights Traherne understood in metaphoric, rather than literal, terms; but, nevertheless, it is this engrafting of the language of property ownership onto spiritual conceptions of one's relationship to God and the world that is so striking in Traherne's work.

Yet Traherne's characterization of the world and all its treasures as conversely both individually and communally owned complicates this analysis. In the *Centuries*, Traherne hoped to awaken an appreciation of the possessory rights in the material world that inhered not only in himself but also in others: "It is my design therefore in such a plain manner to unfold it that my friendship may appear in making *you* possessor of the whole world" (1.3) (emphasis added). Fashioning himself in the role of a property owner, he depicted himself transferring property to his reader(s) by gift: "True Love as it intendeth the greatest gifts intendeth also the greatest benefits. It contenteth not itself in showing great things unless it can made them greatly useful . . . Unless therefore I could advance you higher by the uses of what I give, my Love could not be satisfied in giving you the whole world" (1.6). Hence the world, so insistently characterized by Traherne as his alone, in seemingly conflicting passages becomes yours: "All things were made to be yours, and you were made to prize them according to their value: which is your office and duty, the end for which you were created; and the means whereby you enjoy" (1.12).

Through the slippage of personal pronouns, the earth changes hands in a quick succession of owners, by turns "thine" and conversely "all mine own" in a single poem ("The Vision," 38, 52) and at times even "ours" (1.3). In "The Third Century," rights fluctuate from Traherne to every man, from Adam to God, from communal to private in a mere paragraph: "[I]n the beginning, was it made manifest to be mine, because Adam alone was made to enjoy it. By making one, and not a multitude, God evidently shewed one alone to be the end of the World and every one its enjoyer. For every one may enjoy it as much as He" (1.14). Apparently unconcerned with the inconsistencies embedded here, Traherne placed competing cultural meanings of ownership side by side.

The emergence of "capitalist" landowning according to some historians did not progress in a straightforward linear fashion. Rather, it represented an evolving encounter, an "articulated combination," of feudal meanings of "juridical-conditional ownership" and "capitalist" meanings of absolute property.[13] Despite legal and parliamentary reforms, free market land practices had not altogether replaced feudal ones during Traherne's lifetime; many customary and traditional constraints on land use and alienation that discouraged emerging capitalist tendencies flourished well into the eighteenth century.

Traherne's work too arguably represents its own "articulated combination" of divergent possessory espousals, the one exclusive and private, the other non-exclusive and communal. At times, Traherne managed to reconcile them, by insisting that that "all by each, and each by all possess, / Are intermutual Joys, beneath

---

[13] John E. Martin, *Feudalism to Capitalism: Peasant and Landlord in English Agrarian Development* (Atlantic Highlands, NJ: Humanities Press, 1983), 103. For further studies of the rise of capitalism in England, see R. J. Holton, *The Transition from Feudalism to Capitalism* (New York: St. Martin's Press, 1975); R. H. Tawney, *The Agrarian Problem in the Sixteenth Century* (London and New York: Longmans, Green & Co., 1912); David Lieberman, "Property, Commerce, and the Common Law: Attitudes to Legal Change in the Eighteenth Century," in *Early Modern Conceptions of Property*, ed. John Brewer and Susan Staves (London: Routledge, 1995), 144–58, here 153; Eugene Kamenka and R. S. Neale, eds., *Feudalism, Capitalism and Beyond* (Canberra: Australian National University Press, 1975); Macfarlane, *The Origins of English Individualism*; Joyce Oldham Appleby, *Economic Thought and Ideology in Seventeenth-Century England* (Princeton: Princeton University Press, 1978).

the Skie" ("Ease," 27–28). Choosing not to choose between two contradictory proprietary systems, Traherne in "The Choice" explained: *"Eternity* doth giv the Richest Things / To evry Man, and makes *all* Kings: / The Best and Choicest Things it doth convey / To *All*, and evry *One*" (46–49). Traherne thus elegantly managed to have his cake and share it too, as he insisted that each man is the owner not just of a piece but of the whole: "every one [are] sole heirs as well as you" (1.29). This passage, in its borrowing of a legalistic term for grantees, "heirs," also alludes to the practice of private inheritance, endorsing, even legitimating, a practice apparently not rejected wholesale by Traherne.

The other significant reform to the laws of property in the period turned precisely on such inheritance practices. The equity courts in the second half of the seventeenth century[14] recognized and upheld equitable trust arrangements such as the strict settlement which permitted individuals better to protect and control the dynastic inheritance of land through their family lines. The increasing primacy of common law rules of law over customary and manorial rights, the reliance on jointures over dower rights, and statutory limitations on widows' recovery of dower and freebench in the second half of the seventeenth century further served to secure exclusive ownership rights in property. Unhampered by the life tenures and other ancillary interests of widows, heirs could more freely alienate property.[15]

Traherne gestured subtly to such hereditary reforms in his work, if not in his own life. As the rhetoric of property transference dominated his writing, so, too, the underlying principles of inheritance, that is, the contractual bequest of property, centered his faith. He figured God as an all-benevolent, ever-generous "Benefactor" who bequeathed the world by "gift" to man as "His Heir" (1.16) and so merited praise: "The Heavens and the Earth minister unto me, as if no man were created, but I alone. I willingly acknowledge it to be thy Gift! Thy bounty unto me!" (1.64). In "The Evidence," Traherne, again employing explicitly legalistic rhetoric, described God's grant of the world as the transference of "Title"

---

[14] See W. Hamilton Bryson, *Cases Concerning English Equity and the Courts of Equity 1550–1660* (London: Selden Society, 2001); and idem, *Equity Cases in the Court of Exchequer 1660–1714* (Tempe: MRTS, forthcoming).

[15] For background on these developments, see Susan Staves, *Married Women's Separate Property in England, 1660–1833* (Cambridge, MA: Harvard University Press, 1990); Amy Louise Erickson, *Women and Property in Early Modern England* (London: Routledge, 1993); Eileen Spring, *Law, Land and Family: Aristocratic Inheritance in England, 1300–1800* (Chapel Hill: University of North Carolina Press, 1993); Lloyd Bonfield, *Marriage Settlements, 1601–1740: The Adoption of the Strict Settlement* (Cambridge: Cambridge University Press, 1983). For a discussion of the equitable and common-law developments of the period, often philosophically at odds, see Robert W. Gordon, "Paradoxical Property," in *Early Modern Conceptions of Property*, ed. Brewer and Staves, 95–110.

to his "Estate" (12) and depicted this divine bequest as a formal legal proceeding, appropriately formalized by a "Seal," "Witnesses," and "written Records" (5, 7, 8). The authority that accrued from this "estate," also repeatedly referred to as his "inheritance" (1.15, 2.95), led Traherne to argue that "there is not a man in the whole world that knows God, or himself, but he must honor you . . . an heir of the world, and as much greater than the Universe, as he that possesseth the house is greater than the house" (2.93). Again, through the substitutive powers of figuration, Traherne in this passage took on, if not merely sanctioned, the entitlements granted a property holder.

These entitlements were themselves the subject of redefinition in the period. Legal commentators, in response to the parliamentary overthrow of feudal tenure, slowly began to revise the meaning and consequential privileges and interests of ownership in real property. As previously discussed, before 1646, the common law understood ownership to refer to a mere "fee" (or *feudum*), or limited possessory rights, held by an individual against the crown or king, who alone had "full lordship — both of ownership and of use."[16] By the early eighteenth century, legal theorists began to define ownership in real property as full "dominion" (or *allodium*), comprised of a bundle of absolute and exclusive rights and ideally subject only to explicit restrictions created by the will or deed of the individual owner. This bundle of standard and essential rights of absolute ownership in real property included the unqualified and exclusive "right to possess, the right to use, the right to manage, the right to the income of the thing, the right to the capital, the right to security, the rights or incidents of transmissibility and absence of term, the prohibition of harmful use, liability to execution, and the incident of residuarity."[17]

Emphasizing man's exclusive "dominion" (1.64) over the material world, Traherne's understanding of the ownership rights that inhere in individuals parallels this legal redefinition. Indeed, so essential are these rights to Traherne that they serve in "The Evidence" as the very evidence for his ownership of the material parts of the world:

> The Services they do,
>   Aloud proclaim them Mine;
>   In that they are adapted to
> Supply my Wants; wherin they all combine
>   To pleas and serv me. (21–25)

---

[16] G. E. Aylmer, "The Meaning and Definition of 'Property' in Seventeenth-Century England," *Past and Present* 86 (1980): 87–97, here 88. See also Andrew Reeve, "Debate: The Meaning and Definition of 'Property' in Seventeenth-Century England," *Past and Present* 89 (1983): 139–42.

[17] A. M. Honoré, "Ownership," in *Oxford Essays in Jurisprudence*, ed. A. G. Guest (Oxford: Oxford University Press, 1961), 107–47, here 113.

Traherne further insisted that mere ownership of the world did not alone provide an adequate response to God's generosity and urged that one must use it to give appropriate thanks to God:

> As Bride grooms Know full well that Build
> A Palace for their Bride. It will not yeeld
>   Any Delight to him at all
>   If She for whom He made the Hall
>   Refuse to dwell in it.
> Or plainly Scorn the Benefit. ("The Recovery," 33–38)

Once again adopting a proprietary metaphor, Traherne likened man's appreciation for the gift of the world to that of a bride for her husband's gift of a home, suggesting that the value of the dwelling inhered not in its material worth alone but rather in its usage and potential for future profit. Likewise, in "Amendment," Traherne stressed the use one could make of property rather than ownership alone:

> That all things should be mine;
> This makes his Bounty most Divine.
> But that they all more Rich should be,
>   And far more Brightly shine,
>   As usd by Me: (1–5)

Traherne's analysis of how best to make use of God's treasures further resonates with the legal definition of the essential incidents of ownership, as he exhorted man to lay claim to the earth in substantially similar terms: "Do not your inclinations tell you that the World is yours? Do you not covet all? Do you not long to have it; to enjoy it; to overcome it? To what end do men gather riches, but to multiply more?" (1.22) "Dumnesse" provides an extensive inventory of the many uses that man should make of the earth: "Twas to Enjoy *even All* beneath the Sun: . . . / Twas to inherit Endless Treasure . . . / To see, love, Covet, hav, Enjoy and Prais, in one," and further, "To Prize" this treasure (45, 48, 51–52). To "prize" property necessarily encompasses an awareness of its value ("What would Heaven and Earth be worth, were there . . . no enjoyer?" [2.90]), and not surprisingly, Traherne also urged man to "profit" from (2.100) his property.[18] He further disavowed the "waste" of one's "Endowments" ("The Estate," 8): "if you be resolved to prize nothing great and excellent, nothing sublime and eternal, you lay waste your possessions, and make vain your enjoyment of all permanent

---

[18] Again, "*Things prized are enjoyed*. All things are ours; all things serve us and minister to us, could we find the way: nay they are ours, and serve us so perfectly, that they are best enjoyed in their proper places" (4.16).

and glorious things" (4.17). Toppling the king's prior privileges in land and bestowing them on the individual as effectively as parliament and the common law, Traherne advised how to take advantage of one's newly acquired properties: "the way to possess them is to esteem them. And the true way of reigning over them, is to break the world all into parts, to examine them asunder: . . . We being then Kings over the whole world, when we restore the pieces to their proper places" (1.23). Traherne's philosophy of use in short corresponds closely with the key conceptual terms and essential components of property ownership.

This philosophy of use, in its emphasis on the private rights of the landowner, had further ramifications; in particular, it participated in and at times eased the processes of enclosure. Taking place throughout the early modern period and well into the eighteenth century, the enclosure of the wastelands and common fields of England transformed the topography of and distribution of ownership rights in the countryside.[19] The rural landscape, in large areas a hodge-podge of open fields, common pastures, meadows, and waste areas without precisely defined boundaries or ownership, was subjected to rigorous demarcation. Usually hedges and at times ditches, banks, walls, or fences clearly delineated where one discrete and privately owned plot of land ended and another began. The ownership of lands, previously held in common by villagers, now fell under the exclusive control of independent landowners. By the end of the seventeenth century, "[i]ndividual property rights based on written title replaced ancient custom . . . A conception of land as a commodity to be exploited for profit, protected by absolute rights of ownership, had triumphed over an older one under which ancient custom had guaranteed rights of access and use by the community."[20] Characterized as an important step in the

---

[19] Other seventeenth-century agrarian reforms and legislation of equal import but beyond the scope of this inquiry contributed to the transformation of England's topography and laws of land ownership, including the drainage of fens, disafforestation, consolidations, engrossings, compositions, and confiscations. For further background on the agrarian legislation of the Civil War period, see Christopher Hill, *Puritanism and Revolution: Studies in Interpretation of the English Revolution of the Seventeenth Century* (London: Mercury Books, 1958), 153–96.

[20] David Underdown, *Revel, Riot and Rebellion: Popular Politics and Culture in England, 1603–1660* (Oxford: Oxford University Press, 1987), 284. For background on the enclosure movement, see Gilbert Slater, *The English Peasantry and the Enclosure of Common Fields* (London: Archibald Constable, 1907); Mark Overton, *Agricultural Revolution in England: The Transformation of the Agrarian Economy, 1500–1850* (Cambridge and New York: Cambridge University Press, 1996); J. A. Yelling, *Common Field and Enclosure in England, 1450–1850* (Hamden, CT: Archon Books, 1977); Robert C. Allen, *Enclosure and the Yeoman* (Oxford: Clarendon Press, 1992); Eric Kerridge, *The Agricultural Revolution* (London: Allen & Unwin, 1978); Michael Edward Turner, *English Parliamentary Enclosure: Its Historical Geography and Economic History* (Hamden, CT: Archon Books, 1980).

development of a market economy, the enclosure movement further weakened the already-declining foundation of England's feudal economy previously structured on self-sustaining and independent manorial estates. The enclosure movement crystallized the larger struggles of the English legal and economic system, as local and feudal customs, equitable practices, and manorial rights gave way by the eighteenth century to national rules and the primacy of the common law.

Traherne's own position on the process of enclosure seems initially straightforward. Characterizing "Hedges, Ditches, Limits, Bounds" as "Cursd and Devisd Proprieties," he described how in his childhood he "dreamd not ought of those, / But wanderd over all mens Grounds, / And found Repose" ("Wonder," 53, 49, 54–55). In a similar statement on his childhood, he reminisced: "I knew no churlish proprieties, nor bounds, nor divisions: but all proprieties and divisions were mine: all treasures and the possessors of them" (3.3). Making more than just coincidental use of the actual signposts of land delineation, he not only condemned the topography of the newly privatized plots of England but also hearkened back nostalgically to a pre-enclosed countryside in which one could dally on common areas without restraint.

Yet a study of Traherne's own experience of enclosure bears inquiry, as the agricultural history of Herefordshire, the county of Traherne's residence for nearly all of his lifetime, is somewhat unusual. The enclosure of the common fields and pastures of Herefordshire took place early by national standards. While in the Tudor period areas of Herefordshire were open-field arable, at the beginning of the sixteenth century piecemeal enclosure by private agreement had begun to encroach upon the previously arable fields and open common fields of the county. By the seventeenth century, so much of the common-field land had already been enclosed[21] that one early modern tract described Herefordshire as "an enclosed county. Some few remnants of common fields are seen in what is called the upper part of the county; but in general it appears to have been inclosed from the forest state."[22]

Enclosures occurred by consensual agreements between individuals in the early modern period and by parliamentary mandate in the eighteenth century, but did not take place smoothly or in concert; the subject of rigorous debates, enclosures at times led to violent protestations by villagers who had lost their customary rights, particularly in the farming regions of the East, Midlands, and central South of England.[23] Residents of Herefordshire, however, appear to have met the

---

[21] See also Joan Thirsk, *The Agrarian History of England and Wales,1500–1640,* vol. 4 (London: Cambridge University Press, 1967), 203, that dates this process even earlier to the Middle Ages.

[22] Quoted in Slater, *English Peasantry,* 252.

[23] For background on enclosure riots, see Underdown, *Revel, Riot and Rebellion,* 106–45; Buchanan Sharpe, *In Contempt of All Authority: Rural Artisans and Riot in the West of England, 1580–1660* (Berkeley: University of California Press, 1980), 170–82, 202–12.

changes brought about by enclosure "without commotion."[24] A parliamentary act in 1608, recognized as the earliest act of its kind, sanctioned the voluntary enclosure of approximately one-third of the lands in Marden previously held in common.[25] Greeted without hostility, this act, as one historian observed, "recognizes and legalizes what was apparently a usual procedure in this region."[26]

Traherne thus spent the bulk of his life in a region untroubled by the more fractious responses and dire consequences that greeted the enclosure of other areas of England. He would also have grown up amidst the geometric plots of enclosed land without observing at close hand the extremity of this change to the topography. By Traherne's lifetime, a negligible amount of common land remained to enclose in Herefordshire.[27] Certainly, this background cannot serve as definitive, nor can Herefordshire's general placidity with respect to the processes of enclosure be taken as indicative of Traherne's own position. Nevertheless, in one meditation on a country amble, Traherne appears to have accepted the enclosed topography as benign: "To fly abroad like activ Bees, / Among the Hedges and the Trees . . . / While in those pleasant Paths we talk" ("Walking," 31–32, 49).

Traherne's understanding and valuation of the experience and consequences of enclosure, more tellingly, has a metaphoric component, as boundedness functions as an important leitmotif in his work. Initially his aversion to enclosure seems straightforward, as Traherne praised the world for its likeness to an "illimited field" (1.18), again impugning indirectly the boundaries of enclosure: "It hath neither walls nor precipices, nor bounds, nor borders" (2.21). So, too, Traherne routinely privileged the boundless over the bounded, the infinite over the finite, and the endless over the limited, in discussions of man's understanding, thoughts, love, soul, and pleasure, and God's divinity: "What Bound may we Assign / O God to any Work of thine! / Their Endlessness discovers Thee / In all to be Divine" ("Amendment," 22–25).[28]

---

[24] Thirsk, *Agrarian History*, 5:203.

[25] Howard Levi Gray, *English Field Systems* (Cambridge, MA: Harvard University Press, 1915), 93–97, 138–53.

[26] Gray, *English Field Systems*, 150.

[27] One historian calculated that eighteenth-century acts of Parliament enclosed only 3.6 percent of the open fields of Herefordshire, while another historian calculated this figure at 2.5 percent. See, respectively, C. G. A. Clay, *Economic Expansion and Social Change: England, 1500–1700* (Cambridge and New York: Cambridge University Press, 1984), 1:9 n. 73; Gray, *English Field Systems*, 141.

[28] Likewise, Traherne disavowed the pursuit of private property due to its restricted nature: "to have a few riches in some narrow bounds . . . would be to have our delights limited" (2.77). Again, in "Nature," he queried: "Why Treasures and Delights should bounded be, / Since there is such a Wide Infinitie" (47–48).

Nevertheless, in other passages, Traherne adumbrated a subtle defense of enclosed spaces. He described his spirit as "An Univers enclosd in Skin" ("Fullnesse," 8), a "Secret self . . . enclosd within," whose "Bounds [we] can scarcely find. / It did encompass and possess rare Things" ("Nature," 19, 28–29). He envisioned God as "the Ring enclosing all" ("The News," 49) that "Encompass'd" and "Encircled" man ("Adam's Fall," 31, 36), and eternity as "enclos[ing] us" ("Thoughts IV," 41). The heavens "did my richer Wealth inclose" ("The City," 42); and, in another subtle allusion to enclosure, the heavens "Compassed . . . / Great Tracts of Land / Enricht with Fields and fertile Ground" ("Shadows in the Water," 50–52). Similarly, he characterized the earth's boundedness as preferable ("An Earth made Infinite could ne're be view'd. / But all being bounded for each others sake, / He bounding all did all most useful make");[29] and God's "Power" as "bounded, greater is in might, / Then if let loose" (*Centuries* 3.21), as "Infinite worth shut up in the limits of a material being, is the only way to a real infinity" (*Centuries* 3.20).

Further, as Stanley Stewart has most richly elucidated, one of Traherne's central tropes is that of the "Sphere" ("My Spirit," 16; "Misapprehension," 19), that he paradoxically conceived as both "well-bounded" (*Christian Ethicks*,181) and "Endless" ("Thoughts. IV," 29–30).[30] Through this and similar paradoxes, Stewart posited, Traherne "disintegrates the landscape, the settings of place and time." Emphasizing the "tentative quality of various boundaries" in Traherne's poems, Stewart argued that the "distinctions between line and sphere and center and circumference disappear."[31] I would agree that Traherne's poetry both builds and deconstructs boundaries, and further suggest that this paradox reveals a nascent appreciation for the principles of enclosure. "Consummation," in particular, revolves around and devolves out of this contradiction: "a Sphere / Of endless Reach," containing "boundless Distances" (2–3, 14). Similarly, in "An Hymne upon St. Bartholomews Day," he circumscribed the topography and concurrently

---

[29] Thomas Traherne, *Christian Ethicks*, ed. Carol L. Marks and George Robert Guffey (Ithaca: Cornell University Press, 1968), 181.

[30] Stanley Stewart, *The Expanded Voice: The Art of Thomas Traherne* (San Marino, CA: Huntington Library, 1970). Similar examples are legion, including his descriptions of his spirit as a "Sphere" with "No Brims nor Borders" ("My Spirit," 7, 16), his thoughts as "unconfind," "Illimited," "Endless, yet a Sphere" ("Thoughts. III," 33, 34, 69), his soul as "an infinite sphere in a centre" (2.80), and God's omnipresence as "an Endless Sphere" ("Thoughts. IV," 29). For further discussions of this trope, see A. L. Clements, *The Mystical Poetry of Thomas Traherne* (Cambridge, MA: Harvard University Press, 1969), 45–46; Barbara K. Lewalski, "Thomas Traherne: Naked Truth, Transparent Words, and the Renunciation of Metaphor," in *John Donne and the Seventeenth-Century Metaphysical Poets*, ed. Harold Bloom (New York: Chelsea House Press, 1986), 225–41.

[31] Stewart, *The Expanded Voice*, 210, 165.

expanded it: "An Inward Omnipresence here, / *Mysteriously* like His with in me stands; / Whose Knowledge is a Sacred Sphere, / That in it self at once Includes all Lands" (10–13). As these examples attest, the generalized use of the politicized terms of land delineation, including "enclosure," "boundary," and "limit" and their cognates, occur with regular frequency in Traherne's writing. Surveying, so to speak, Traherne's landscape of the mind reveals a less than consistently critical attitude towards enclosed and bounded space. His tendency to fluctuate between opposing systems, as previously observed in proprietary terms, is similarly perceived here in spatial terms.

Traherne's meditations are also mediations of the conflicting meanings of property and its ownership in the period. Traherne's work, a parallax of contradictory proprietary ideologies, documents the changing nature of cultural and legal meanings of property, its usage, ownership, and relationship to the self in the seventeenth century. To align Traherne too rigidly with any one meaning serves to flatten unnecessarily the influences at work both in his writing and in the culture during the period. His multivalent writing and philosophy is neither delimited by older, established conceptions of ownership nor "illimited" by communal or emerging capitalist conceptions. So, too, Traherne's repeated reliance on spatial, topographical, and legalistic tropes levels borders as quickly as he constructed them and is as "groundbreaking" in his poetics as Digger Gerrard Winstanley in his politics. His work finally affirms that as "property and its protection stood at the moral center of England's particular fabric of the law,"[32] the paradigm of property ownership stood at the center of Traherne's spirituality.

---

[32] Lieberman, "Property, Commerce, and the Common Law," 144.

Thomas Traherne, Richard Allestree, and the Ethics of Appropriation

Kevin Laam
University of Southern California

Thomas Traherne's *Christian Ethicks* (1675) is determinedly *not* a part of the popular culture of religion in seventeenth-century England. Scholastic in method, Platonic in spirit, Traherne's systematic treatment of reason and virtue in the Christian humanist tradition reveals itself to be of more advanced thought than the Restoration lay reader would have been apt to appreciate.[1] The author himself makes a point of distinguishing his treatise from the "easie" and "ordinary" treatment proffered by *The Whole Duty of Man* (1658), the most widely read manual of Christian ethics to emerge from the period. *Whole Duty*, generally credited to the Oxford divine Richard Allestree, presents a wholly accessible model of Christian living, written in unadorned prose and partitioned into seventeen sections (with an appendix of supplementary prayers) to ensure maximum readability.[2] Traherne, ill at ease with the work's attempts at classifying the "*Duties* enjoyned by the Law of GOD," professes that his objective is "to carry and enhance *Vertue* to its utmost height, to open the Beauty of all the Prospect, and to make the *Glory* of *GOD* appear, in the Blessedness of Man, by setting forth its infinite Excellency. . . ."[3] It is the boundless potential that lies within man, not the everyday business of holy living — virtue, not virtues — that is of primary interest to Traherne. Vice, in comparison, he trusts will "appear like *dirt* before a *Jewel*" (*CE*, 4); there is no need to speak on its behalf.

---

[1] See Carol L. Marks, general introduction to Thomas Traherne, *Christian Ethicks* (Ithaca: Cornell University Press, 1968), xv.

[2] The attribution question has never been resolved definitively, but it is generally agreed that Richard Allestree is the author. For a thorough discussion, see Paul Elmen, "Richard Allestree and *The Whole Duty of Man*," *The Library*, 5th ser., 6 (1951): 19–27.

[3] Traherne, *Christian Ethicks*, 3. All further references to this work will be cited by page number in the text with the abbreviation *CE*.

My thesis is that *Christian Ethicks* has more in common with *The Whole Duty of Man* than has been historically acknowledged. This is generally evident by the short but significant passages that Traherne drafts directly from Allestree's text into his own without citing the source. Gladys Wade believes that Traherne's ostensible failure to give acknowledgment is likely a printer's error, given the author's scrupulous annotations in *Roman Forgeries* and elsewhere in *Christian Ethicks*.[4] And yet she indebts Traherne no further to *Whole Duty* than to ascribe to it "the stimulus of irritation."[5] C. J. Stranks is more forgiving in his assessment of the work's value to Traherne, citing the praise he accords it in the preface to *Christian Ethicks*, but remarks that Traherne quotes it "apparently unconsciously," as if the author's ethics were loath to descend to common understanding.[6] Carol L. Marks and Stanley Stewart have been similarly reluctant to attribute to *Whole Duty* more than a negligible hand in the formulation of Traherne's ethical outlook.[7]

There is a certain danger, I feel, in overstating the degree of separation between works designated for "popular" and "elite" audiences, a case that has been made convincingly of late by scholars of early modern culture.[8] The level of intellectual interchange brought to bear upon early modern life by way of the written word — and the sheer volume of materials made available through print — are substantial enough to warrant joint consideration of works ostensibly aimed at different readerships. Traherne, though he announces the departure of *Christian Ethicks* from its popular predecessor, never follows through on his stated intention. By summoning *The Whole Duty of Man* to participate in his own intellectual labors, consciously or otherwise, Traherne puts the stamp of popular recognition

---

[4] Gladys I. Wade, *Thomas Traherne* (Princeton: Princeton University Press, 1944), 142 n. 67. The extracts from Allestree that Wade locates in *Christian Ethicks* are from the first partition of *The Whole Duty of Man*, items 29, 33, 36, 37, and 38.

[5] Wade, *Traherne*, 142 n. 67.

[6] C. J. Stranks, *Anglican Devotion* (London: Camelot Press, 1961), 124. Stranks is the first critic I am aware of who gives serious consideration to the parallelisms between the ethical views of Allestree and Traherne.

[7] See Stanley Stewart, *The Expanded Voice: The Art of Thomas Traherne* (San Marino: Huntington Library, 1970), 50–51, 220 n. 39; Marks, gen. introd. to *CE*, xxv–xxvi.

[8] See Roger Chartier, ed., *The Culture of Print: Power and the Uses of Print in Early Modern Europe*, trans. Lydia G. Cochrane (Princeton: Princeton University Press, 1989); idem, *The Order of Books: Readers, Authors, and Libraries in Europe Between the Fourteenth and Eighteenth Centuries*, trans. eadem (Stanford: Stanford University Press, 1994); Adam Fox, *Oral and Literate Culture in England, 1500–1700* (Oxford: Clarendon Press, 2000); Tessa Watt, *Cheap Print and Popular Piety, 1550–1640* (Cambridge: Cambridge University Press, 1991); Nigel Wheale, *Writing and Society: Literacy, Print and Politics in Britain, 1590–1660* (London: Routledge, 1999).

upon his own work and legend. This aspect of his ethics needs to be recognized. In considering Traherne's ideas as not opposed but rather indebted to the popular orientation emblazoned in *The Whole Duty of Man*, we may see in *Christian Ethicks* a model of ethical reasoning that is as socially inclusive as it is intellectually rigorous.

In *The Expanded Voice: The Art of Thomas Traherne*, Stanley Stewart suggests that Traherne's intense focus on virtue and seeming disregard for matters of duty or conduct may be explained by his resistance to the emergent trend toward secularism in ethics, spearheaded in the seventeenth century by the writings of Hugo Grotius and Thomas Hobbes. "After all," Stewart holds, "conduct is the potential meeting place of that dubious triumvirate of humankind: 'Custom, Action, [and] Desire.'"[9] Where a writer like Hobbes might assert that men's incentive to live peaceably is driven chiefly by fear of death and desire for material comforts — with reason serving mainly to suggest "convenient articles of peace, upon which men may be drawn to agreement"[10] — Traherne will not abide reasoning that has men coerced into recognition of virtue's intrinsic worth by social expedients. "[S]ome are so blind as to deny there are any [virtues] existent in Nature," he observes: "But yet it may, and will be made easily apparent, that all the *Peace* and *Beauty* in the World proceedeth from *them*, all *Honour* and *Security* is founded in them, all *Glory* and *Esteem* is acquired by them" (*CE*, 4). Herein is issued an unambiguous challenge to the materialist conception that virtue "consisteth in comparison."[11] For Traherne, it falls manifestly upon the individual to recognize virtue's excellence. "No other man (at least) can make us so," he insists, "without our own willingness, and endeavour to do it" (*CE*, 6).

Realistically, it is doubtful that the Restoration layperson would put his or her own moral code to the same philosophical test. The social and political climate of the latter century is not hospitable to the level of religious experimentation that is prevalent during the Cromwell regime. Censorship regulates the body politic; science and reason are called upon to fill social needs, not fuel individual speculation.[12] C. John Sommerville acknowledges that the best-selling religious works of the era show an increasing concern with exploring human

---

[9] Stewart, *Expanded Voice*, 51.

[10] Thomas Hobbes, *Leviathan*, ed. Richard Tuck (Cambridge: Cambridge University Press, 1991), 90.

[11] Hobbes, *Leviathan*, 50.

[12] See Christopher Hill, "'Reason' and 'Reasonableness'," chap. 4 in idem, *Change and Continuity in Seventeenth-Century England* (Cambridge, MA: Harvard University Press, 1975), 103–23. Hill's long thesis is that the "irrationalisms" of the sixteenth century accelerated the eventual movement toward the "new reason" of experience and common sense that broadly characterizes the culture of late seventeenth-century England.

emotions — but he detects no accompanying progression toward a theology centered around man. "Attention to both God and Christ rose slightly," he finds, "while that toward man remained constant from the early to the later best sellers. But the works with a constant popularity were higher in attention to all three subjects, while neglecting social and philosophical questions."[13] Another observer is more succinct in her appraisal of the period's subdued intellectual curiosity: "Obedience, not individual experimenting, suited the mood of the burnt child."[14] A nation grown weary of the controversies of mid-century, by this account, would not respond sympathetically to a work so enflamed with religious zeal as *Christian Ethicks*.

And still, the model of ethical reasoning presented in the work seems not so overwhelming as to elude modest capabilities: the speech is plain, the language native, the allusions manageable for the reader with some knowledge of scripture. Comparably rigorous works, such as Jeremy Taylor's *Holy Living* and *Holy Dying* (1650, 1651), achieved enormous popularity in the latter part of the century; the Taylor volumes appeared in a total of seventeen editions by century's end, despite being written in a language steeped in classical and patristic sources.[15] That *Christian Ethicks* sees only limited circulation by comparison — and is doomed to an eventual two and a half centuries of obscurity — likely stems as much from its radically anthropocentric philosophy as from the material circumstances surrounding its publication. The author selects for his work an obscure publisher, Jonathan Edwin, whose printed output consists of a scant thirty-eight books over eight years (1671–1679).[16] Then in October 1674, two months after submitting *Christian Ethicks* to be published, Traherne dies. With no reliable authority left to oversee the preparation of the manuscript for publication, the book is subject to irretrievable errors in composition.[17] The printer's request that the

---

[13] C. John Sommerville, *Popular Religion in Restoration England* (Gainesville, FL: The University Presses of Florida, 1977), 78 n. 25.

[14] Wade, *Traherne*, 141.

[15] P. G. Stanwood, in the general introduction to his critical edition of *Holy Living* and *Holy Dying* (Oxford: Clarendon Press, 1989), notes the appearance of a condensed volume of the works in 1701 by Edward Stacy. Stacy, an Anglican minister, prefaced his version by stating that Taylor's original was too difficult and too expensive for the common reader. Stanwood dismisses the claim on the basis that Stacy's "wretched paraphrase is a commercial venture dependent on Taylor's continued popularity" (lv).

[16] Wade, *Traherne*, 132.

[17] George Robert Guffey, textual introduction to *CE*, 1i–1ii. Guffey notes that the portion of the 1675 text set by "Compositor A" (sigs. A, a, Aa–Qq) is competently handled, while that set by "Compositor B" (sigs. B–Z) contains the majority of the errors. Lynn Sauls, in "The Careless Compositor for 'Christian Ethicks'" (*Papers of the Bibliographical*

reader "pardon those few Errata's which have escaped in the Printing by so sad an occasion," included in the 1675 edition of *Christian Ethicks*, is a fitting epitaph for a work — and career — that would languish in neglect for years to come.

Absent a longstanding critical tradition through which to trace the significance of *Christian Ethicks* — or more seriously, documented reactions to the work from Traherne's historical contemporaries — its standing in relation to the religious culture of the period remains distressingly uncertain. Carol Marks, searching the text for clues as to what audience the work may have attracted, determines that Traherne was writing neither for plebeians nor scholars but rather for educated laymen, with whom Traherne came into regular contact in his service as chaplain to Sir Orlando Bridgeman, Lord Keeper under Charles II. Coupling the evidence provided by the text with that suggested by the character of Bridgeman, himself a man of sizable religious curiosity, Marks speculates that the work most likely would have been read by "an educated, intelligent person playing an active role in an increasingly secular world, a thoughtful person seeking a pragmatic ethic based upon eternal and immutable morality."[18]

The advantage of reading *Christian Ethicks* through the complexion of its ideal reader is clear: it ameliorates the pressure of trying to penetrate the psychology of the author, and initiates the crucial (if imperfect) process of socializing the work. Moreover, it is a fair approach to apply to a treatise that, we presume, went largely unread. Still, in all likelihood, the truth of how *Christian Ethicks* was received in its time would fall short of the profile envisioned by Marks. She admits having to hypothetically sever Bridgeman from his contradictory political attachments in order to preserve his exemplary status; his latitudinarianism, in particular, ill suits Traherne's High Church loyalties.[19] Profiling an ideal reader for *Christian Ethicks* inevitably diminishes the true-to-life circumstances that might have governed the relationship between the work and its individual readers. And it leaves little idea as to the viability of Traherne's ethical model across social or philosophical divisions. The treatise stands, much to our frustration, as a genuine artifact of cultural history that has precious little material history to speak of.

To fill in this history, so to speak, *The Whole Duty of Man* is especially deserving of attention. In order to determine where Traherne's views stood in relation to the lay discourse of ethical reasoning — and how he may have represented them accordingly — *Whole Duty* can at minimum serve as a barometer of

---

Society of America 63 [1969]: 123–26), contends that Compositor B, in fact, is truer than Compositor A to the manuscript original, and therefore "helps us get a glimpse of Traherne at his writing desk" (126).

[18] Marks, gen. introd. to *CE*, xxxi.

[19] Marks, gen. introd. to *CE*, xxvi–xxxi.

the ideas and attitudes circulating in that discourse. The status of the work as a touchstone for popular ethics is beyond question: the book sustains its popularity from the time of its initial publication through the eighteenth century, appearing in numerous editions, translations, and adaptations.[20] Henry Hammond's prefatory remarks, heralding the work's "Condescension to the meanest capacities, but with all, *That* weight of Spiritual Arguments wherein the best proficients will be glad to be assisted," suggest its potential for diverse and far-reaching application.[21] Precisely how far it might condescend to the least literate members of English society is a matter for further investigation. The demonstrable social demand for *Whole Duty* should not lead us to imagine that such a work could effectively redeem the English population for the written word, particularly in a culture still beholden in large part to its oral counterpart.

Recent studies dealing with the relationship between literacy and social class in early modern England shed considerable light on the seeming ability of *The Whole Duty of Man* to cut across varying levels of proficiency. The advent of print plays a key role in facilitating the interchange of ideas among different segments of English society, a view that is substantiated in such studies as Tessa Watt's *Cheap Print and Popular Piety, 1550–1640* and Nigel Wheale's *Writing and Society: Literacy, Print and Politics in Britain, 1590–1660*. Watt examines the least expensive printed wares available to readers in post-Reformation England — ballads, chapbooks, and woodcuts — and finds no evidence to suggest that the cheapest of works were read only by the humblest of readers. Wheale confirms that in "this pre-industrial, largely pre-urban society, not yet driven by large-scale consumption," the borders between different social strata were remarkably permeable where reading preferences were concerned.[22] Whatever target audience may have been conceived for modestly inclined works, they ultimately made their way beyond that audience and interacted with authorized cultural values in such a way as to find readers of diverse means, beliefs, and literacy levels.

Admittedly, the notion that fully educated persons frequently read works below their level of sophistication is a reasonable one to begin with. More daunting

---

[20] Sommerville, citing the appearance of three of Allestree's books among the best sellers of the era, regards him "the favorite author of his age" (*Popular Religion*, 38).

[21] Richard Allestree, *Whole duty of man* (London, 1658), sigs. A5v–A6r. This is the uniform title by which the work was regularly recognized; the complete title reads, "*The practice of Christian graces. Or The whole duty of man laid down in a plaine and familiar way for the use of all, but especially the meanest reader. Divided into XVII. chapters, one whereof being read every Lords Day the whole may be read over thrice in the year. With private devotions for several occasions; viz. for morning evening. Sacrament. The sick, &c. Times of pub. calamities.*" Subsequent quotations from this work shall be cited in the text with the abbreviation *WD*.

[22] Wheale, *Writing and Society*, 86.

is the task of reclaiming quantifiably unpopular works — such as *Christian Ethicks* — for consideration underneath the banner of "practical literature." Wheale contends that religious texts had especially strong crossover potential, given the inclination of pious individuals to reach beyond their intellectual grasp.[23] A more ambitious hypothesis is suggested by Adam Fox, who argues that the sixteenth and seventeenth centuries witnessed "the literary restructuring of popular culture."[24] Fox, taking issue with the arbitrary distinction between "oral" and "literate" culture that until very recently has been the standard for literacy studies and popular culture, concludes that the relationship between the two modes of communication in early modern England was seldom less than dynamic. Reading aloud was customary, and those who could not read usually lived within proximity of someone who could. As a result, the market for printed works, especially the Bible, expanded to multiple tiers of society, not merely the learned. Subjects historically disseminated by word of mouth, such as local laws, current events, and songs and jokes, were written down (via script or print) with increasing frequency. As these texts circulated back into the culture, Fox explains, they came to exert a tremendous influence over patterns of speech, language, and social organization. "In almost every aspect of contemporary culture," he asserts, "the permeation of the popular vernacular stock by learned and literary sources is evident," and even the least literate members of society fell under their sweep.[25]

We should be careful, still, not to overestimate the impact of literacy in galvanizing religious sentiment across the population. The growing influence of the written word in the social arena gradually communicates the desirability of becoming literate, but systematic educational reforms to that end do not come about until the nineteenth century. Until then the drive toward literacy is more limited in its success, as David Cressy explains in *Literacy and the Social Order*. Cressy appropriates the language of "push and pull" dynamics to evaluate the incentives toward becoming literate in Tudor and Stuart England. As he describes it, those who sought after literacy were alternately "pushed" into it by ideological imperatives, and "pulled" into it by more basic economic or pragmatic needs. But their numbers were few, particularly those reacting to externally imposed ideals. The religious push toward literacy, led in the Restoration period by the likes of Richard Baxter and other nonconformists, did not meet with widespread success. It was the rare occasion, Cressy notes, that religious propaganda would inspire the individual to seek out instruction in reading and writing, the Protestant drive toward self-edification notwithstanding. While this sort of propaganda was frequent

---

[23] Wheale, *Writing and Society*, 87.
[24] Fox, *Oral and Literate Culture*, 19.
[25] Fox, *Oral and Literate Culture*, 410.

and abundant in English society, it never consolidated into a formidable presence. "The stream of rhetoric in favour of reading and writing," Cressy writes, "was swamped in the welter of pluralistic opinions which surged and frothed in renaissance England, and the government, which might have been persuaded to sponsor a programme for mass literacy, was by no means convinced that popular education would serve its interests."[26]

That *The Whole Duty of Man* served those interests with such precision — sounding the Anglican call to conformity in the digestible language of practical guidelines for living — confirms the rhetorical efficiency of the work but contests its "popular" credibility. Only through the inability of literacy to achieve penetration beyond pockets of the population could the best-selling religious work of the period double as a manifesto for the enshrinement of High Church orthodoxy. Historians of seventeenth-century religious culture, by and large, are given to agree that the advent of Protestantism did not instantly revolutionize the behaviors and belief systems of the English laity. "Popular *ir*religion," to borrow Patrick Collinson's phrase, was still the doctrine of choice for the majority of individuals in post-Reformation England.[27]

In light of this knowledge, it is important that we qualify the term "popular" as we use it to assess the religious sensibilities of the period, and it is equally important to question the motivations of written works laying claim to that designation. *The Whole Duty of Man* clearly fits this mold, with its prefatory disclaimer, "*THE only intent of this ensuing* Treatise, *is to be a short & plain direction to the very meanest* Readers, *to behave themselves so in* this *world, that they may be* happy *for ever in the* next" (*WD*, sig. a1r). Critics have rightly seen through the modest intentions declared by the author, pointing to the book's emphasis on obedience over faith and the legalist overtones of its title as evidence of its strong ideological bent.[28] Sommerville suggests that the work would have been of offense to dissenters mainly "in

---

[26] David Cressy, *Literacy and the Social Order* (Cambridge: Cambridge University Press, 1980), 186.

[27] Patrick Collinson, *The Religion of Protestants: The Church in English Society 1559–1625* (Oxford: Clarendon Press, 1982), 195. For further discussions of the relationship between religion and popular culture in Renaissance England, see Keith Thomas, "Religion and the People," chap. 6 in idem, *Religion and the Decline of Magic* (New York: Charles Scribner's Sons, 1971), 151–73; Christopher Hill, "Puritans and 'the Dark Corners of the Land'," chap. 1 in idem, *Change and Continuity in Seventeenth-Century England*, 3–47; Barry Reay, "Popular Religion," in *Popular Culture in Seventeenth-Century England*, ed. idem (New York: St. Martin's Press, 1985), 91–128.

[28] The title of Allestree's work is taken from Ecclesiastes 12:13: "Fear God, and keep his commandments: for this is the whole duty of man." This sentiment is also echoed in the 1662 Book of Common Prayer Catechism.

its guise as a spiritual manual,"[29] while Isabel Rivers deems it specifically anti-Calvinist. Citing its association with Hammond's *Practical Catechisme* (1644), which forthrightly stated the case for salvation through action, Rivers reads in Allestree's work an implicit critique of the Calvinist vogue for "spiritual darkness and afflicted consciences."[30] This critique, she suggests, would have been recognized readily by the more knowledgeable of the book's readers. The rest would value it for its practical advice.

For the readers who lacked even basic reading skills, the influence of the work was still felt. *Whole Duty*s abounded in the universe of late seventeenth-century print, capitalizing on the name recognition of the original.[31] A representative example of how Allestree's work was adapted further to accommodate the lower reaches of the population is provided by *The Art of Catechising: or, The Compleat Catechist* (1692), an anonymous book that announced itself "Fitted for the meanest Capacitites, the weakest Memories, the plainest Teachers, and the most un-instructed Learners."[32] The work is divided into four sections, the first three of which consist of routine exercises in Prayer Book instruction: yes-or-no questions, plain explication, and scriptural proofs, respectively. The fourth section repeats the catechetical model of the first with *The Whole Duty of Man* as its subject, condensing the liturgical exposition of Allestree's original into simple questions asking rote adherence to its precepts. All responses, upholding the function of the official Prayer Book catechism, systematically reinforce the authority of the Church, which stresses the recollection of truths from the collective wisdom of its teachings and discourages the incursion of individual judgments.[33] As such,

---

[29] Sommerville, *Popular Religion*, 38–39.

[30] Isabel Rivers, *Reason, Grace, and Sentiment: A Study of the Language of Religion and Ethics in England, 1660–1780*, 2 vols. (Cambridge: Cambridge University Press, 1991), 1:23.

[31] See Marks, gen. introd. to *CE*, xxiii; Stranks, *Anglican Devotion*, 148.

[32] The full title is *The art of catechising: or, The compleat catechist. In four parts. I. The church-catechism resolved into easie questions, to be answered only by yes or no. II. An exposition of it in a continued, full, and plain discourse. III. The church-catechism resolved into Scripture-proofs. IV. The whole duty of man reduced into questions, to be answered by a single yes or no. Fitted for the meanest capacities, the weakest memories, the plainest teachers, and the most un-instructed learners. Imprimatur. Feb. 4. 1690/1. Z. Isham, R.P.D. Henrico Episc. Lond. à sacris*, 2nd ed. (London, 1692).

[33] Ramie Targoff, *Common Prayer: The Language of Public Devotion in Early Modern England* (Chicago: University of Chicago Press, 2001), illustrates that the roots of Prayer Book theology ran deeply in the devotional poetry and practices of the sixteenth and seventeenth centuries. Targoff argues that the Book of Common Prayer exerted a more powerful resistance to the reformist emphasis on self-defined worship patterns than has been previously acknowledged.

only questions posed in the negative may elicit responses in the affirmative; those posed directly may seldom tolerate the same burden of affirmation. When asked, for instance, "May a Christian give divine Worship to a Saint or Angel, or to any Image?", the reader must answer an unequivocal 'No': but when pressed "Is it not Idolatry to do so?", he or she may then concede in the affirmative, as if summoning knowledge that the Church has long since bequeathed to its followers.[34]

The formal methods of instruction deployed in *The Art of Catechising* are unremarkable. What distinguishes the work from its prototype is the transparency with which it establishes its ideological aims. The author directs his work specifically toward the youthful and the ignorant as well as to the preachers in their service; "proficients" are unregarded. He establishes the necessity of catechizing on grounds that are dedicated unswervingly to the preservation of the English Church: "*For the numerous Enemies of the best establish'd Church in the World, are all at work, and with united Voices crying,* Down with it, down with it, *to the Ground.*"[35] Remarkably, no attempt is made in the work to obscure the less agreeable elements associated with catechizing. The ultimate service it performs is more important,

> *whatever Self-denial, or Pains, or Difficulties, or Humility, or Condescension, or letting down of our selves, it cost us.*
>
> *I have found by my own Experience, that to do it well and conscionably has more of all these in it, than Preaching it self; and when all is done, it shall please much less.*
>
> *But when I consider that my Business is to please God and not Man, and that my Hopes and Consolations, will at last result from my having with Purity of Intention, designed the Former, more than the Latter: . . . I find I can be content with that Contempt and Scorn, those Pains and Difficulties, that Self-denial and humble Condescension, which will most times accompany the conscionable Discharge of this very useful, and very necessary Duty.*[36]

Such comments, within the context of late-century religious polemic, sound a note of complaint common among segments of the population who viewed catechizing as a necessary adjunct to preaching. Clergy perceived as being neglectful of the former practice while zealous of the latter drew frequent and oftentimes strident criticism in local parish communities.[37] Yet the sentiment expressed in

---

[34] *Art of catechising*, 145.

[35] *Art of catechising*, sig. A3r, quoting Psalm 137:7 (BCP).

[36] *Art of catechising*, sigs. A3r–A4r.

[37] I. M. Green, *The Christian's ABC: Catechisms and Catechizing in England c.1530–1740* (Oxford: Clarendon Press, 1996), 130. My discussion of catechizing is informed heavily by chapter 3, "Catechizing in Theory and Practice: In Church," in which Green gives an invaluable overview of how the public dimensions of this important tradition evolve during the early modern period.

The Art of Catechising is more pointed than that: the writer charts a course of intense personal sacrifice that will be necessary to uplift the "useful" and "necessary" duty of catechizing from the debased condition into which it has lapsed. Set against the comparatively impersonal nature of the sermon and its rapid absorption into public affairs in the decades following the Restoration, the survival of the catechism comes to embody the hope that the forces of secularization are indeed repressible. Preaching welcomes the imposition of aesthetic standards; catechizing puts them off.[38] Accordingly, when in *The Art of Catechising* the author professes "to please God and not man" — the same reference used in Joseph Glanvill's *An Essay Concerning Preaching* (1678) to defend a plainer style of pulpit oratory[39] — he means it not at all in the homiletical sense. His focus is to reform the discipline of devotion, not the style; citing John 21:15–17, he maintains that God's sheep must be fed before they may be contented.

Allestree, presumably writing during the Interregnum, excludes overt reference to theological opponents in *The Whole Duty of Man*. The widespread success of his work has usually been attributed to the skill with which it asserts an Anglican program of devotion while effacing its doctrinal affinities. In this regard it bears out the assessment of critics who view Anglican claims to moderation with skepticism. Richard Ashcraft, examining the political motives behind the latitudinarian platform of comprehension, categorically rejects the notion that talk of incorporating dissenters into a Broad Church establishment signified a fundamental shift in the theological outlook of the church. On the contrary, he asserts, the policy of comprehension was wielded by clergy to frustrate — not further — the cause of toleration, and nonconformists, by and large, were alert to this fact. Accordingly, advises Ashcraft, any measure of "doctrinal consensus" eventually brought about between dissenters and the Anglican establishment should be seen not as the product of growing latitude within the Episcopal ranks; more likely, it was wrought of the need to present a broad mandate for the execution of ecclesiastical powers. Consensus serves the interests of authority; latitudinarianism, in its efforts to build that consensus, can be seen as the "acceptable face of the persecution of religious dissent."[40]

---

[38] W. Fraser Mitchell, part III of *English Pulpit Oratory from Andrewes to Tillotson* (New York: Russell & Russell, 1962), 347–402. Mitchell observes the increasing conformity of preaching to prose theories over the course of the seventeenth century: "The sermon, therefore, may be regarded not only as itself providing a species of prose, but as a kind of index of what men were likely to attempt or applaud in contemporary literature" (382).

[39] Joseph Glanvill, *An Essay Concerning Preaching* (1678), 23, cited in Rolf Lessenich, *Elements of Pulpit Oratory in Eighteenth-Century England (1660–1800)* (Cologne: Böhlau, 1972), 14.

[40] Richard Ashcraft, "Latitudinarianism and Toleration: Historical Myth Versus Political History," in *Philosophy, Science, and Religion in England, 1640–1700*, ed. Richard Kroll, idem, and Perez Zagorin (Cambridge: Cambridge University Press, 1992), 151–77, here 155.

Allestree's High Church credentials are secure; there is no reason to suspect that his is the voice of enlightened reason. Nevertheless, the success of *The Whole Duty of Man* in distilling the fineries of Anglican theology into "*one* general *duty* preparatory *to all the rest*" (*WD*, sig. a1r) speaks just as vividly as its Broad Church counterparts of the need to consolidate opposition to sectarian rumblings, and of the wisdom of using discretion to silence dissent. Inasmuch as the work invites disputation, it does so in ways that primarily would excite the preoccupations of evangelical extremists, not the Presbyterian moderates that the Church saw fit for conforming.[41] Noticeably absent from *Whole Duty* are extended inquiries into the doctrine of divine grace, an issue that would have been of decisive interest to the conscientious dissenter. Allestree's resolution not to dwell upon the issue of grace — focusing instead on what man must *do* to ingratiate himself with the Almighty — made safe its philosophical distance from Baptists, Congregationalists, and other sects that would have no conditions besides faith put upon election and justification. This is not to imply that Allestree's work disparages grace, but that it abstains from making a theoretically vigorous case for the Arminian point of view that would eventually define the conformist identity in Restoration England. The program of moral instruction that it takes up — and the issues of doctrine it leaves behind — make the case strongly enough.

To the extent that church catechizing experiences the level of neglect described in *The Art of Catechising*, it stands to reason that *The Whole Duty of Man*, which soars in popularity during the same period, is to some degree associated in that decline. The humbler work applies itself to what many conservative Anglicans would see as the nobler cause: the restoration of catechizing to the center of Anglican spiritual practice. However readily the internal logic of Allestree's work might lend itself to catechistic treatment, and however categorically it might defend public catechizing itself,[42] the greater social trend to which it speaks is of a waning emphasis on the practice. *Whole Duty* comes to prominence during a period when lay opposition to clerical authority is varied and extensive: in addition to complaints of parents and masters not sending their children and servants to be catechized, the most frequent complaint among clergy "was that [adults]

---

[41] Rivers, *Reason, Grace, and Sentiment*, 1:96.

[42] Allestree apologizes for including only private devotions with his treatise, and emphatically asserts the continued importance of public devotion: "*I must answer for my self, that it was not from any opinion, that God is not as well to be worship'd in the Family, as in the Closet; but because the providence of God and the Church hath already furnish'd thee for that purpose, infinitely beyond what my utmost care could do. I mean the* PUBLICK LITURGY, *or* COMMON-PRAYER, *which for all publick addresses to God (and such are family-Prayers) are so excellent and useful, that we may say of it as* David *did of* Goliah's *sword,* I Sam. 21.9. There is none like it" (*Whole Duty*, 561).

were reluctant either to be catechized themselves, in public or private, or that they refused to conduct catechizing in their own households."[43] With the Bible, Prayer Book, and *The Whole Duty of Man* comprising a veritable curriculum in Anglican devotion unto themselves — and enjoying print runs in unprecedented numbers — the work of religious instruction increasingly could be conducted as capably in the privacy of the individual household as in the authorized setting of the parish. This is not meant simply to imply a collective transfer of religious energies from the public to the private arena but rather an increase in alternatives to religious learning by priestly intervention. Catechisms, the effectiveness of which had long been the subject of debate in educational circles, retain their place as the most common aids to religion in seventeenth-century print.[44] But they are pressed into an exceedingly defensive role after 1689, coming more strongly to represent resistance to the slackening of ecclesiastical hierarchy and swelling of religious pluralism that take place under the Toleration Act. Once rights of assembly are extended to the majority of Protestants, the pressure toward attending church services is mitigated for Dissenters and Conformists alike; catechizing, insofar as it had served the cause of outward conformity, sees its fortunes suffer in turn.

To unearth a last gasp of High Church conventionality from the most inauspicious of genres — the catechism — is perhaps not surprising. Yet to hear it reassert the importance of the tradition with such stalwart conviction, while the popular standard-bearer of Anglican conformity dissembles its orthodox affiliations within the rhetoric of common sense, forms a striking study in contrasts. *The Whole Duty of Man* by far is the more popular work, but *The Art of Catechising* is more steadfast in its defense of Anglican theology, more skeptical in its treatment of homiletics, and ostensibly more knowing with regard to the facility of public devotion in conforming the multitudes to the good of the nation. It wears on its sleeve the high politics that its source is unwilling to avow, all the while yielding itself to practice of the lowliest sort.

The Art of Catechising provides a useful illustration of the types of use for which a work such as *Whole Duty* might be taken up. The two works, considered alongside one another, bear witness not only to timely debates at work within lay and clerical circles, but also to the stake held by popular culture in shaping those debates. It is impossible to gauge the precise influence wielded by works such as *The Art of Catechising* that appealed forwardly to the core audience that *Whole Duty* found in its original form. But collectively, the proliferation of such works refutes the perception that *Whole Duty* occupied the lowest tier of late Restoration devotional works. All we know for certain with respect to the popularity of *Whole Duty* is that it sold well. Its resonance across the ideological spectrum is

---

[43] Green, *Christian's ABC*, 132.
[44] Collinson, *Religion of Protestants*, 232–33.

too densely entangled in religion, politics, and social custom for us to know positively much more.

The level of uncertainty hanging over *Christian Ethicks* is even more pronounced: there is no record of its reception to speak of. When Traherne makes reference to *The Whole Duty of Man*, thus, he favors us with a provisionary acknowledgment of the wider social context in which both works might have been understood. The popular cachet of *Whole Duty*, of course, does not tell the whole story of its usefulness to Traherne. In order to flesh out that story, it is necessary to observe both Traherne's specific interactions with the work, and the way he refracts them through the conceptual macrocosm of *Christian Ethicks*.

Traherne's direct appropriations of *Whole Duty* are concentrated exclusively in chapter XVIII of *Christian Ethicks*, "Of Charity toward GOD," where he demonstrates the difference between love and charity. The difference is one of degree, not of substance. Love, he observes, is generically applied to all objects in Heaven and Earth, dead or alive. "But there is another sort of Love," he continues, "towards *Living Objects,* Divine and reasonable, which we call *Charity*" (*CE*, 134). Following a sequence of scriptural invocations through which Traherne gradually insinuates the divine nature of charity, he reveals it all at once to be the product of a fully formed eschatology:

> It is the End of the very Creation of the World, of all Gods Labors and Endeavours, of all his Ways in all Ages, all the faculties and powers of the Soul, the very End of the Redemption of Mankind, the End of the Jewish Oeconomy under the Law, the End of all the Dispensations of Grace and Mercy under the Gospel; the End of our Saviours coming down into the World, the End of all his Miracles, Tears, and Blood, the End of the Holy Ghosts appearing upon Earth, the End of all the Means of Grace, and in some sort the very last End of all Rewards and Punishments whatsoever. (*CE*, 135)

It is important for Traherne to establish the prototype of charity toward God in completed action, in the safe knowledge of God's will having been done, such that it shows love drawn irresistibly to virtue, not simply driven by vagaries of circumstance. Traherne deduces that if love indeed is the end to which all of God's dispensations are directed, then "there must be something in its Nature Equivalent to all these Transcendent Undertakings, to justifie the *Wisdom* that selected Love for its Sovereign Object" (*CE*, 136). In its pure, unadulterated form, love is no arbitrary undertaking but rather the surest route to perfection. Wisdom, upon finding it, is relieved of the need to negotiate mean for end in assuring the best outcome for one's earthly travails. In charity is manifest the assurance that negotiations have been settled, and thus that love has been perfectly calibrated to receive God's gifts.

Traherne's concern with differentiating charity from less exalted applications of love should be seen within the context of the stages, or "estates," into which he divides the spiritual progress of humankind. In chapter IV of *Christian Ethicks* these are identified as innocence, grace, and glory, each connoting a corresponding set of virtues whose work is to incline human actions and affections toward supreme happiness while fulfilling the laws and ordinances of God.[45] The first estate, innocence, is especially significant for Traherne, as it anticipates the logic through which he is ultimately able to collapse the distinctions of virtue he introduces and exonerate duty of the material burden it accumulates in passing through the different estates. The virtues that apply in all estates — knowledge, loving, righteousness, holiness, goodness, and wisdom — he describes as having been "enjoyned in the Estate of Innocency, without any need of a positive Law, by the very nature of GOD and the Soul, and of things themselves" (*CE*, 31). These virtues are so fundamental to human happiness that they need no external backing; they are the means "whereby even GOD himself doth enjoy his Felicity" (*CE*, 30) and thus occupy a position of rare privilege in the ethical order that Traherne sets up.

The advent of sin, however, gives birth to virtues unforeseen in the first estate — and Traherne is noticeably ambivalent about the belief that honorable duties can derive from such base origins. In regard to those virtues occasioned by the Fall, among which Traherne lists meekness, repentance, patience, fortitude, and resignation to the divine will, he claims: "THEY are but an *Æquivocal* Offspring of the Fall: Sin could never beget such beautiful Children . . ." (*CE*, 33). Traherne is at a loss to assign a divine author for virtues brought about solely by the passing of human history into a fallen state; they are children not sired by God, and yet remain precious in his sight. Traherne resolves that they be viewed "not as Food, but Physick" (*CE*, 33), as providing short relief to the afflicted soul but no sustenance, and certainly not the means by which God partakes of his own happiness.

With virtue resigned in large part to surrogate status in the fallen world, Traherne stresses the need to reinstate the innocence that first ensured the human birthright to felicity. Such a goal demands separation from worldly attachments, understandably, but also from certain agencies of understanding that bear distinct marks of a divine lineage. According to Traherne, reason required no expedients at all, godly or otherwise, before the entry of sin into the world:

---

[45] In his preface to the reader Traherne alludes to another estate, misery, between innocence and grace, but when he begins the work of detailing the classifications in chapter IV, the framework remains nominally threefold. Traherne recognizes the estate of misery, but hesitates to link it with virtue.

There had been no *Faith* in the *Incarnation* of the Son of God, because no occasion for that Incarnation; no Ceremonial *Law of Moses*, no *Baptism*, nor *Lords Supper*, because there were no supernatural Mysteries to be Typified, but the clear Light of a Diviner Reason, and a free Communion with God in the Right discharge of those Vertues, Divine and Moral, which naturally belong to the Estate of Innocency. All which Original and Primitive Vertues ought now to continue, as it were the Face of Religion beneath that *Mask* or *Vizor* of Ordinances and new Duties, which Sin and Corruption hath put upon it . . . (*CE*, 34)

The fallen state, it appears, has not only bastardized virtue but convoluted the elemental logic through which its goodness may be understood. Traherne, in drawing attention to all we have had to learn of God by inference, simultaneously brings to light all we have been denied of him by our flawed intuition.[46] We are implicated with the Israelites at Mount Sinai, for whom the divinely illumined face of Moses was too much to bear and had to be veiled before his law could be dispensed.[47] Since the loss of innocence, the divine light of nature has dimmed within ourselves.[48] Faith is now required to recognize God's grace manifest in the body of Christ; the sacraments must intervene to unravel "supernatural Mysteries" whose wisdom was once known. The virtues that dispose reason to such service are commendable in their own right, but their necessity underscores how estranged human beings have become from the purity of apprehension into which they were born. Whatever success fallen man has achieved in repairing his damaged faculties — in donning the "*Mask* or *Vizor* of Ordinances and new Duties" — this cannot overcome the deep-seated realization that there once was an easier way.

Traherne entertains the possibility that there may yet be, albeit not without some equivocation as to where and when this expectation may be fulfilled. By

---

[46] In his diagnosis of the postlapsarian intellect, Traherne recalls Milton's description of the separation between human and divine reason in Book V of *Paradise Lost*. Raphael instructs Adam that the human race is relegated to applied, or "discursive" reasoning, whereas angels are entitled to the immediate, or "intuitive" kind (5.488). Where Traherne departs from the Miltonic model is in his insistence that the pure intuition enjoyed in the innocent estate may be recaptured on Earth. The fate Raphael wishes for Adam is also optimistic, but more measured:
>   Meanwhile enjoy
> Your fill what happiness this happy state
> Can comprehend, incapable of more. (5.503–505)

[47] See Exodus 34: 28–35.

[48] The concept of the "light of Nature" is particular neither to Traherne nor to his Neoplatonic leanings. Allestree invokes it to stress the duties to which human beings are naturally disposed irrespective of their exposure to Scripture (*Whole Duty*, 2).

the end of the fourth chapter of *Christian Ethicks*, Traherne is able to project with confidence a point when the virtues that have sustained human reason during its banishment from perfect enjoyment of God have run their course. "For all these Occasional Vertues are but Temporary," he maintains, but

> when our Life, and this present World are past and gone as a Dream, Love, and Joy, and Gratitude will be all that will continue for ever . . . Repentance shall be gone, and Patience cease, Faith and Hope be swallowed up in fruition, Right Reason be extended to all Objects in all Worlds, and Eternity in all its Beauties and Treasures, seen, desired, esteemed, enjoyed. (*CE*, 35)

Officially the replacement of "Occasional Vertues" by "Right Reason" occurs in death, in the passing of the soul to a state of unbounded glory. Yet Traherne offers no formal indictment of the mortal world, none as we see in Allestree's description of the glorious estate. Allestree, who shares Traherne's expectation of finding eternal glories left in our name, insists that *"all things here below should seem* vile *and mean to us"* before we may lay claim to the blessed inheritance (*WD*, sig. a7v). *"Our* duty *herein,"* he explains, *"is to be exceeding* careful, *that we forfeit not our* parts *in it, which we shall certainly do, if we continue* impenitent *in any sin . . ."* (*WD*, sig. a7r). Traherne, meanwhile, has little use for being careful or penitent: his view is teleologically driven, like Allestree's, but not for the promise of a final reprieve from mortal suffering. He warns against valuing religion for its restorative attributes, imploring readers instead to seek out

> the Hidden Manna, the substantial Food underneath, the Satisfaction of all Wishes and Desires, the true and Cœlestial Pleasures, the Causes of Love, and Praise, and Thanksgiving founded in the Manifestations of Gods Eternal favour, especially in the Ends, for the sake of which all Helps and Remedies are prepared. (*CE*, 35)

Where Allestree had cautioned his readers to set their sights "on things above & not on things on the earth" (*WD*, sig. a7r), Traherne stirs them to plumb the depths. With each potentiality that Traherne uncovers from beneath religion's surface, he moves progressively closer toward purifying reason of its accrued contaminants; the hermeneutic mediating our understanding of the divine is simplified such that we are made to seek one thing and one thing alone: God's eternal favor. Inasmuch as the virtues conferred upon us in innocence belong to eternity, they should be at our service — and we at theirs — now and forever. Traherne, in step with this view, ceases the business of contriving divine preparatives to help us through the time we have left on Earth. Rather than concern himself over the distance between us and the glorious estate to come, Traherne induces the effects of that estate for direct and immediate application.

Meanwhile, the misbegotten rigors of the fallen state continue to weigh heavily on the ethical course charted in *The Whole Duty of Man*, a fact which draws into question Traherne's decision to adopt portions of that text for *Christian Ethicks*. That *Whole Duty* is summoned to take part in the task of defining charity toward God — a virtue that in that work is subsumed under the larger heading of "Christian love"[49] — suggests minimally that Traherne's intellectual aspirations have their limits, that moving beyond the "ordinary" treatment of virtue does not entail disavowing it altogether. More seriously, it gives us pause to consider if Traherne has not staked his claim to the estate of innocence prematurely. It is clear that Traherne aims after an ethics whose substance is comprised solely of virtue. However, the elementary dynamic provided by pairing it with vice translates more readily to rules of practice than the finely-tuned divisions to which virtue by itself is subject in the unfallen state. Traherne's theology — and certainly his poetics — can accommodate these divisions comfortably, but his ethics threaten an abstraction without the benefit of contrasting materials.[50] The vice-virtue paradigm is not inevitable for Christian ethics. But when the better part of those ethics is dedicated to the protection of free will, they can maintain their integrity only by heeding pressures imposed from the outside. The will needs an object to define itself against for its freedom to persevere.

It is tempting, then, to conclude that *The Whole Duty of Man* provides a practical counterpart to the more quixotic propensities of *Christian Ethicks*, a nominal ethical dimension to mitigate Traherne's demonstrable lack of concern with the everyday business of conforming one's will to God. This assessment is not altogether untrue: *Whole Duty* is a resolutely practical work, and would have been recognized by readers as such. However, the suggestion that *Christian Ethicks* lays a path for thought, not action, is mistaken. Paul Cefalu offers a useful corrective to this line of thinking in opposing the customary attribution of Traherne's conception of felicity to Neoplatonic mysticism, a trend perpetuated historically by the prominent inclusion of excerpts from Ficino, Henry More, and Hermes Trismegistus in the author's Commonplace Book.[51] Breaking with this

---

[49] Allestree associates the term "charity" primarily with neighborly service and almsgiving, deferring discussion of this duty to the end of *Whole Duty* (partitions 16 and 17).

[50] For a full discussion of the methods through which Traherne's theology informs his poetics, see Barbara Lewalski, "Thomas Traherne: Naked Truth, Transparent Words, and the Renunciation of Metaphor," chap. 11 in eadem, *Protestant Poetics and the Seventeenth-Century Religious Lyric* (Princeton: Princeton University Press, 1979), 352–87.

[51] Paul Cefalu, "Thomistic Metaphysics and Ethics in the Poetry and Prose of Thomas Traherne," *Literature and Theology* 16 (2002): 248–69, here 248. Cefalu acknowledges the mystical and Platonic elements of Traherne's writings, but asserts that "With respect to questions of human psychology and cognition, moral philosophy, and the nature of God, Traherne is a neo-scholastic who makes use of Platonic imagery and concepts, not a Platonist who sometimes invokes scholastic terminology" (249).

trend, Cefalu locates Traherne's moral philosophy in the Aristotelian-Thomistic tradition of ethical habituation, through which the individual undertakes a program of rigorous worldly training with the eventual hope of achieving "perfect actuality" (as manifest in God's essence). Cefalu contends that "Traherne's scholastic and empirical preoccupation with the processes by which potency realizes actuality further displaces whatever purely mystical and contemplative elements are introduced in a given work."[52] To let these elements dictate our approach to Traherne's mode of thought forgets the simple fact that his ethics will not allow inactivity. Traherne himself underscores this point: "I am not so Stoical," he claims, "as to make all Felicity consist in a meer Apathy, or freedom from Passion, nor yet so Dissolute, as to give the Passions all their Liberty" (*CE*, 17). On the contrary, his ethics run a decidedly middling course:

> THAT which I desire to teach a man is, How to make a Good use of all the Advantages of his Birth and Breeding; How in the Increase of Riches and Honors, to be Happy in their Enjoyment: How to secure himself in the temptations of Affluence, and to make a man glorious in himself, and delightful to others in Abundance: Or else if Affliction should arise, and the State of Affairs change, how to triumph over *adverse* Fortune, and to be Happy notwithstanding his Calamities. How to govern himself in all Estates so as to turn them to his own advantage. (*CE*, 17)

Traherne strategically poises himself between the behavioral extremes represented by stoic and libertine approaches, delivering a statement of purpose that is as practically minded as most anything we see in *Whole Duty*. Traherne does not retreat from questions of right conduct; his "felicity," rather than scale grandiose heights of emotion, stays comfortably grounded in the language of quantifiable enjoyments and afflictions. Philosophically, it is impossible that his ethics be anything *but* practical, with or without the intermediary presence of *Whole Duty*. The interpolation of Allestree's text into *Christian Ethics* may have augmented the "practical" sensibility for the reader who recognized it, but its usage in the work as a whole is too limited for us to conclude that Traherne was making a nakedly popular appeal. It is more feasible, and certainly more useful, to consider that Traherne utilizes *Whole Duty* in much the same way he does all knowledge: not to condescend to the hypothetical "common reader" but rather to elevate his petition with the expectation that a truly reasonable argument need not make itself clearer. Traherne, in this regard, casts himself as a rhetorical centrist, with *Whole Duty's* prosaic manner lending itself at once to be chastened by the exactitudes of right reason and to indulge Traherne's characteristic forays into more ecstatic territory.

---

[52] Cefalu, "Thomistic Metaphyics," 260.

Traherne's treatment of contentment is especially valuable as a measure of the author's concern with bringing felicity to earth and presenting it in a manner suitable for application. Contentment occupies a peculiar place in Traherne's ethical scheme; he neglects to mention it in chapter III of *Christian Ethicks*, where the different classifications of virtue are detailed, but then introduces it extemporaneously in chapter XXVII: "THOUGH we have not named it, in our first distribution of Vertue into its several kinds, yet the commendation which Contentment hath in Scripture, imports it to be a Vertue" (*CE*, 216). The discussion of contentment immediately precedes a sequence of chapters on the "less principal" moral virtues of magnanimity, modesty, liberality, and magnificence (chapters XXVIII–XXXI), described as such not because they are unimportant but because "they are more remote, and less Avail in the Way to Felicity, and are more confined in their Operations" (*CE*, 24). While Traherne does not specifically assign contentment to this category, he begins the chapter on magnanimity by stating that the two virtues "are very near allyed, like Brothers and Sisters" (*CE*, 224), suggesting that the service Traherne has in mind for contentment is a specialized one.

Indeed, he cannot bear it in a more extended application: when the subject of contentment is first broached in chapter VIII, it is entangled with the burdensome legacy of pagan Stoicism:

> BUT however familiar, and near, and easie these Great and evident Truths appear, it so happened, that the Heathen Philosophers were Blind unto them, and in the midst of their Searches after Felicity, failed of the Discovery; they became vain in their Imaginations, placing felicity in a meer Apathy, or conceited Ἀυτάρκεια, a self-sufficiency, or in a brave Contempt of all misfortunes, in a forced Contentment Dark and empty . . . (*CE*, 60)

The "Great and evident Truths" yielded by recognizing God as the soul's object and end are lost upon the heathens, according to Traherne. Aristotle gets right the internal schematics of virtue but not the entirety of its potential; Seneca, who takes the crucial step of entering God into the ethical equation, does little to show that he has made good use or sense of this development. It is not the appreciation of virtue for its intrinsic excellence to which Traherne objects; this, after all, is the very project that inspires *Christian Ethicks*. Rather, it is the irreversible fulfillment of purpose implied by contentment, the deadening effect it has on the erstwhile restless spirit, that he has trouble reconciling with his ethic of activity.

To some degree, this ambivalence explains the curious treatment that contentment receives in *Christian Ethicks*. For all that Traherne finds fault with in the heathens and the Stoics, they chanced upon knowledge that is central to his own understanding of felicity. Even a reformed contentment, advocating not rigorous self-discipline but *"the full satisfaction of a Knowing Mind"* (*CE*, 216), seems disconcertingly sedentary to Traherne without further qualification. Allestree, in contrast, finesses the passivity problem handily. Though he essentially shares Traherne's understanding of contentment, viewing it more as a cheerful discipline than a studied contempt, Allestree bypasses the corollary task of rationalizing its precise nature as a virtue. Such speculation, it is probable, would be of little use to *Whole Duty*'s modestly inclined readers. Alternatively, Allestree establishes the merit of contentment by "rule of contraries" (*WD*, 159): since it naturally opposes and conquers vices such as murmuring, ambition, and envy, its worthiness needs no further elaboration.

Allestree does, however, dilate upon the subject more comprehensively in another treatise, *The Art of Contentment* (1675). The later work slants toward a more learned readership, and thus intellectually shows itself a fit subject for comparison with *Christian Ethicks*. In *The Art of Contentment* Allestree confronts the same dilemma that had troubled Traherne in treating contentment: how to recognize self-sustaining properties in virtue without killing off human desire — and more importantly, God himself — in the process. And again, the Stoics are incriminated with derailing human happiness through their erroneous application of internally sound principles: they correctly understood the divine attributes of self-sufficiency but mistakenly believed that achieving it endowed them with godly dimensions. "But abating the insolent blasphemy of an independent felicity," Allestree continues, "Christianity acknowledges a material truth in the assertion: and St. *Paul* declares of himself, that having *learnt how to want and how to abound, and in whatever state he happens to be in, therewith to be content. . . .*"[53] Like Traherne, Allestree finds a way of giving backhanded praise to his heathenish predecessors as he redeems them for nobler purposes. But ultimately he fears God too mightily to raise himself to the storied heights of Traherne's felicity. *The Art of Contentment* is so committed to reinforcing the absolute sovereignty of God that contentment, as a human attribute, is scarcely allowed to approach on anything divine. We have been struck with godly impressions, Allestree admits, but are so confounded in applying them that we have now become the "unhappiest of the creatures."[54] Our wills must be broken entirely, our pride mortified, before we may resign ourselves to contentment. Indeed, the language of resignation comes to prevail decisively over Allestree's treatment of contentment, culminating in a qualification of residual Stoicism more delicate than was ever necessary for Traherne. "I do not here propose such a Stoical insensibility as makes no distinction of events," he maintains. "I mean only such a superiority of mind as raises us above our sufferings, tho

---

[53] Allestree, *The art of contentment. By the author of The whole duty of man, &c* (Oxford, 1675), 5.
[54] Allestree, *Contentment*, 9.

it exemt us not from the sense of them."[55] The art of contentment, it appears, has become ever the assiduous one.

With apparent resolve to avoid such an end, Traherne proceeds to disarm the stoic claim of virtue through self-denial. Pausing upon two very tangible effects of contentment — security and power — Traherne exults in the audacity of experience into which the contented spirit compels the individual. True contentment, he argues, secures us from evil with *"the whole Armour of GOD"* (*CE*, 221); it empowers us to undertake action that does not deny the self but re-creates it many times over:

> He that is secure, and he that hath enough, is independant, and *bold as a Lion:* And besides all this he has a certain lustre in his Actions, that gives him authority and power over others, to intercede and prevail in his requests, to live in honour and good esteem, and to make many subservient to his best occasions. He is great in Heaven, and whatever he asks of his eternal Father in his Sons Name, with Wisdom and Piety, shall not be denied him. (*CE*, 222)

Traherne compensates for the self-effacing qualities of "forced Contentment" with an overdetermination of presence. The contented spirit is strong like a soldier, bold like a lion, as ready to offend as it is to fend off. Self-sufficiency is rendered in the language of exponential privilege.

By the chapter's finish, the tone shifts. Traherne retreats from the crusading spirit with which he had seized contentment from the grip of Stoic doctrine, gently advising the reader to take care in harvesting the fruits of his labor, for "Thou hast no charge over any other than thine own *Vineyard*" (*CE*, 223). The sudden shift away from the rhetoric of heroic conquest to that of domestic industry underscores the author's unspoken allegiance to the practical treatment administered in *The Whole Duty of Man*. Ethically, that work identifies more strongly with *Christian Ethicks* than does *The Art of Contentment*, despite the intellectual compatibility of the latter two. In *Whole Duty*, contentment is praised for its ability to subdue several vices at once, as it is in *Christian Ethicks*. The stress on resignation, which in *The Art of Contentment* is cited as the very cause of contentment, is effectively muted in *Whole Duty*: there is work to be done, and the psychology of suffering need not interfere. Traherne, for his part, has internalized this particular knowledge already, and is thus at liberty to express loftier ambitions for his own work. Yet he also recognizes the danger of leaving to chance the particulars of applying theoretical knowledge. Thus for him, the premier service rendered by a work like *Whole Duty* is to temper his own idea of happiness lest it fail to issue into action.

---

[55] Allestree, *Contentment*, 202.

The Art of Contentment is stranded between thought and action, its insistence on compulsory happiness undermined by its elevation of duty into an art form.

The purpose of triangulating these three works is not to undercut the utility of distinguishing written works along popular lines. *Christian Ethicks* and *The Art of Contentment* catered specifically to literate, well-educated audiences; *Whole Duty* was proudly expansive in its reach. These truths affirm the existence of different readerships — popular and elite, we may even call them — and thereby hint at a legitimate demographic model of inquiry through which to diagnose the intellectual complexion of late Restoration England. It is in relying upon these differences to connote corresponding ideological persuasions where the model threatens to rupture. *Whole Duty* may be understood as a declaration of popular piety, *Christian Ethicks* as its high-minded apologia: but their shared ethics disallow them from having altogether distinct applications. Ultimately both works are drawn to the common ground of activity, a ground that excludes neither the ignorant nor the learned, the vulgar nor the pious. As such, cerebral though it may be, it is infeasible to consign Traherne's work to the rarefied territory of "meta-ethics"; the sheer force of his intellect sends him crashing into practice, with *Whole Duty* guiding the way.

Still, in order to inquire pointedly into the qualitative association between *Christian Ethicks* and *The Whole Duty of Man*, it is necessary to examine those passages in which Traherne appropriates Allestree's text directly. Traherne commences this process by availing himself — quite generously — of the text's division of the effects of loving God into two categories: the desire to please and the desire to enjoy. The scheme is Allestree's, and initially Traherne models his text closely after it. As both authors begin discussion of the desire of pleasing, the resemblance is unmistakable:

> For the *first* 'tis known by all, that he that *loves* any person, is very desirous to *approve* himself to him, to do whatsoever he thinks will be *pleasing* to him; and according to the degree of *love*, so is this *desire* more or less; where we love *earnestly*, we are very *earnest*, and *careful* to *please*. (*WD*, 16)

> For he that Loves, is very desirous to approve himself, and to do whatsoever he thinks will be grateful to his Beloved. According to the Degree of Love, the desire is more or less. Where we Love Earnestly, we are extreamly Earnest and Careful to please . . . (*CE*, 141)

Immediately thereafter, though, Traherne moves beyond his source, as if sensing that the immensity of love's effects has not yet been captured in full:

> But *infinite* Love! It is impossible to declare what favour and Zeal it will produce. If we love GOD, we shall keep his Commandments with a Tenderness and Desire so extreme, that no Joy will be so great as the Observation

of his Laws; It will be with us, as it was with our Lord Jesus Christ, it will
be *our Meat and Drink to do the Will of our Father which is in Heaven*. (*CE*,
141–42)

Allestree will go so far as to implore that we love God "as much as is *possible* for
us" (*WD*, 17), but not so fervently that we exceed that which is ordained by our
nature. But Traherne pushes further: through a single interjectory phrase — "But
infinite Love!" — he unsettles the logic of degree and proportion that inscribes
love's effects within a relativistic framework. Infinity has no degree; the intensity it effects in the individual whose love is blessed with it cannot be declared.
In acknowledging a love of such expanse, Traherne looks back to the glories of
the first estate, when the observation of God's will, he believes, was conditioned
by a natural desire for happiness, not by "any need of a positive Law" (*CE*, 31),
and virtue to the soul was not "Physick" but the very "*Meat and Drink*". Sin and
misery long since having bereft reason of its clarity of vision, Traherne puts faith
in the ability of the utmost heights of religious intensity to restore to the simple
act of obedience its prelapsarian delight. His dedication to this vision, in turn, is
so clear that within it the punitive and the pleasing aspects of choosing God over
man become scarcely distinguishable:

> The measure of our Love will not infuse some slight and faint Endeavours
> of Pleasing, but put us on the most painful and costly Duties, make us will-
> ing to forsake our own Ease, Goods, Friends, yea Life it self, when we can-
> not keep them without offending our Creator. (*CE*, 142)

The identification of "Duties" here — in a passage embedded between extracts
from *The Whole Duty of Man* on the dual effects of love — seems a conscious gesture on the part of Traherne to release the term from the debilitating reverence
that Allestree shows it. Love is pitched so high in Traherne's rendering that it
does not merely stir the soul into pleasing action: it compels it to embrace its godly duty with absolute disregard for human comfort. At its height Traherne imagines the desire to please as an inversion of *contemptus mundi*, an extrication of the
self from the interests of the world so complete that it infuses the world ever more
perfectly. And the benevolence it shows can scarcely be second-guessed; its motives are perfectly transparent.

The negation of worldly duty implied by Traherne brings him discernibly
closer to Calvinist territory, however, and shortly thereafter he resumes his sub-
ordination to Allestree's text. After having described the desire of pleasing, both
authors proceed into the second of the effects of love: the desire of enjoying.
And again, Traherne borrows liberally from his source, adhering to Allestree's
scheme of distinguishing "imperfect" from "perfect" enjoyments of God. The
former of these Allestree locates in earthly acts of "conversation" with God, "in his

ordinances, in *praying*, and *meditating*, in *hearing* his *word*, in *receiving* the *Sacrament*, which are all intended for this purpose, to bring us into an *intimacy*, and *familiarity* with *God*, by *speaking* to him, and *hearing* him *speak* to us" (*WD*, 18). Traherne proffers a description of the imperfect enjoyments of God that is nearly identical,[56] but on the "perfect" enjoyments — the quality of communion with God to be experienced in the life to come — he once again diverges from his source text. Allestree renders perfect enjoyment in terms that are purely temporal; he envisions a *"perpetual* enjoying" of God that may prolong itself *"continually* without *interruption*, or breaking off" (*WD*, 19). Invoking the Biblical example of Jacob, for whom the fourteen years spent to win Rachel's hand in marriage seemed *"but a few dayes"* (*WD*, 20), Allestree trusts that a lifetime of servitude to God on earth shall seem negligible in comparison to the rewards it yields in the afterlife. Traherne, on the other hand, dispenses with contractual expedients: for him it is evident that the exchange of intermittent for continuous pleasure is an inadequate testament to the glories incarnate in godly perfection. It bespeaks a Creator whose scope is unconscionably estimable, whose love has been corroded by the dull imagination. Traherne, then, must take it upon himself to imagine communion without mediation:

> And for as much as there is another Enjoyment of GOD which is more compleat and perfect, we shall groan earnestly, *desire to be dissolved and be with Christ*, where we may see no more in a Glass, but Face to Face, and Know as we are Known. For Love is strong as Death, many Waters cannot quench Love, neither can the floods drown it. Affliction, Persecution, Sickness, any thing that will bring us to Heaven, will be acceptable and Delightful. (*CE*, 142)

There is no concession made to intermediary agencies in Traherne's conception of "perfect enjoyment": he has it so fully ingrained within the body of Christ itself as to annul the need for substitutive pleasures. Accordingly, Traherne finds his own biblical antecedent to model the progress to such perfection; citing Philippians 1:23, he trades in the equivocations of Jacob for the evangelism of Paul, even modifying the scripture to have the speaker not "depart" (as in the Authorized Version) but rather "be dissolved" with Christ (as in the *Vulgate*'s *"dissolvi"*).[57]

---

[56] The corresponding passage in *Christian Ethicks* reads, "Here upon Earth we desire to converse with him in his Ordinances, in Prayer, Meditation, hearing his Word, in receiving the Sacrament, which are intended all for this purpose, to bring us into a neerer Intimacy, and familiarity with GOD by speaking so to him, & hearing him speak, and shew himself to us" (142).

[57] Marks, commentary on *CE*, 349.

And the adversities that he locates en route to perfect enjoyment — "Affliction, Persecution, and Sickness" — again oppose duty to utilitarian considerations. Traherne does not discount such considerations altogether, but he is continually wary of their potential to beget a habit of mind that prizes hardship solely for the implicit promise it holds of greater things to come. In his view, to think and act in deference to the hope of divine consolation for earthly tribulation is to rationalize God on man-made terms — and it certainly fails in showing love's full effects. To rush toward suffering — and be unable to distinguish it from delight — is the true test of a love born of reason.

Conceding the irreconcilability of such a sentiment with the practical ethics of *The Whole Duty of Man*, it is not unreasonable to conclude that the work's vestigial presence in *Christian Ethicks* serves chiefly as a negative example, a terse reminder that God is non-negotiable. Where this conclusion falters is in quarantining Traherne's ethics in proverbial wisdom: it treats *Whole Duty* as a theoretical expedient, nothing more, forgetting the work's verifiable conduciveness to practice. *Whole Duty* traffics in the miserly language of contract, but not so inveterately as to unseat ethics from its godly foundations. This fact is not lost on Traherne. Perhaps there is no more revealing indication of the mutual duty shared by the two works than when Traherne first inducts Allestree into his network of reference materials. Traherne, seeking to express the station of humankind in relation to the magnitude of God's goodness, settles on the image of waters flowing back and forth between the ocean and smaller streams:

> [T]here is nothing Good in the world, but what hath received all its Goodness from Him. His Goodness is the Ocean, and all the Goodnesses of Creatures little Streams flowing from that Ocean. Now you would think him a Madman that should say the Sea were not greater then a trifling Brook: and certainly it is no less folly to suppose that the Goodness of GOD doth not as much (nay infinitely more) exceed that of all the Creatures. (*CE*, 140)

The circulation metaphor is characteristically Traherne, and has been documented as such.[58] Hence upon locating virtually the same passage in *Whole Duty* — a work we might imagine to be resolutely linear in its figurative expanse — the effect is positively uncanny:

---

[58] Traherne uses similar imagery in his poem "The Circulation." See Marjorie Hope Nicolson's discussion of the poem in *The Breaking of the Circle: Studies in the Effect of the "New Science" on Seventeenth-Century Poetry*, rev. ed. (New York: Columbia University Press, 1960), 139. A patristic source for this concept is Augustine, *City of God* 12.12. See also Marks, commentary on *CE*, 326–27.

> [T]here is nothing *good* in the world, but what hath received all its *goodness* from *God*: His *goodness* is as the *Sea*, or *Ocean*; and the *goodness* of all *creatures*, but as some *small streames*, flowing from that Sea; now you would certainly think him a mad man, that should say the *Sea* were not greater then some little brook, and certainly it is no less *folly* to suppose, that the *goodness* of God doth not as much (nay *infinitely* more) *exceed* that of all *creatures*. (*WD*, 13–14)

It is not only the love between God and humankind that has come full circle; it is the very debt owed one author to the other. Traherne alludes to *Whole Duty* for the apparent purpose of modulating the pitch of his felicity, and in doing so here sounds like no one so much as his amplified self. He cuts off the allusion when it proceeds to describe God's creatures as "*imperfect* and mixt with much evil" (*WD*, 14), but the glimpse we catch of contrary sensibilities merging into a seamless oneness is indelible. In its formal essence, to be sure, *Christian Ethicks* remains a near-perfect utterance of resistance to the staid, workmanlike ethics of record in the latter seventeenth century. However, when we put Traherne's treatise into conversation with the single most popular ethical manual of the time and deign only to hear antithesis, we deny all manner of resonance generated by the two works in tandem. When we listen instead for similarity in difference, difference in similarity — and for the occasional note of fortuitous correspondence — we make the whole duty of Traherne's ethics more abundantly clear.

Language and the Fall:
The Quest for Prelapsarian Speech in the Writings of Thomas Traherne and his Contemporaries

Cynthia Saenz
Cabrillo College

Recent Thomas Traherne scholarship has helped modern readers better position the poet within a Restoration context as well as appreciate his unique sensibility which utilizes varying, even disparate, elements of religious and philosophical thought. For instance, scholars have demonstrated that Traherne aligns himself with political conformists, sanctioning religious and political unity under the Anglican Restoration settlement, while simultaneously assimilating nonconformist and even radical religious thought into his imaginative ideal.[1] Traherne advocates the liturgical practice of the newly restored Church,[2] but nevertheless the personal voice in his poetry and prose holds an ecstatic tone which seems to run counter to the conformists' aim to quell disruptive individualism. Traherne's philosophy with regard to language reform however, has not been explored extensively.

---

[1] Traherne was a political conformist despising the "wickedness of Ignorant Zealots! Who contemn thy mercies and Despise the union the Beautifull union of my Nationall church" (*Select Meditations*, ed. Julia Smith [Manchester: Carcanet Press, 1997], 1.85). (All references to *Select Meditations* are taken from this edition and will henceforth be cited in the body of this text using the abbreviation *SM.*) However, he was still critical of King Charles II. For a detailed study demonstrating that Traherne held critical views differing from a staunch royalist position, see Nabil Matar, "The Political Views of Thomas Traherne," *Huntington Library Quarterly* 57 (1994): 241–53. Also see Julia Smith, "Thomas Traherne and the Restoration," *The Seventeenth Century* 3 (1988): 203–22. This study posits that Traherne was concerned with contemporary politics; however, "[i]t was not the purpose of spiritual vision to formulate political reform, but it was the case that contemporary events enriched his spiritual and theological perceptions" (219).

[2] Traherne pays homage to the central text of the restored church, the *1662 Book of Common Prayer*, with his own work *The Church's Year Book*.

Investigating a selection of Traherne's poetry and prose writings as well as his theological encyclopedia *Commentaries of Heaven* reveals that he was indeed aware of the myriad language debates of the age. These debates focused upon such issues as how to convey word definitions, whether or not to employ metaphor in religious writing, and how to write in a clear "plain" style to convey religious truth. These disputes were themselves indicative of the deep conflicts between conformist and nonconformist ideals. To address this topic would require a book-length study. For the purposes of this chapter, I limit my investigation to one particular area: Traherne's view of language and the Fall of Adam, and the seventeenth-century quest for prelapsarian speech.[3] The first section of this essay discusses the prevailing views of Adam's language; generally these views were uniform throughout the spectrum of beliefs held by conformists and nonconformists. For the most part, Traherne agrees with biblical commentators like Andrew Willet and George Hughes in assessing the qualities of Edenic speech. The second section describes the importance of infants and children in Traherne's works, thereby illustrating that the poet is part of a Latitudinarian and Pre-Nicene tradition, which became increasingly prominent towards the latter half of the century. The movement maintained that the prelinguistic state of infancy as well as that of early childhood was akin to Paradise in Eden. The final section analyzes Traherne's attitudes towards what may be called the second linguistic Fall, the Tower of Babel. Traherne offers a unique view of this episode by seeing multiple languages as a *felix culpa*; he celebrates blessed diversity rather than laments humankind's differing modes of discourse. The chapter demonstrates not only that Traherne is a thinker with an "eclectic intellect"[4] who embraces contrarieties as part of the divine scheme of infinite variety and inclusion, but also that solipsistic individualism and social communion, silence and speech, innocence and experience are all incorporated in his vision of felicity.

Whether or not modern man could recapture prelapsarian speech or create a new philosophical character incorporating the attributes of such a language was a topic of great concern for numerous groups and individuals. The Garden of Eden, Adam and the Fall, the Tower of Babel, and indeed all the hexaemeral texts were central topics of contention for both conformists and nonconformists.[5]

---

[3] See Umberto Eco, *The Search for the Perfect Language*, trans. J. Fentress (Oxford: Blackwell, 1995).

[4] Carol Marks, "Thomas Traherne and Cambridge Platonism," *PMLA* 81 (1966): 521–34, here 521.

[5] The hexaemeral texts are specifically Genesis, and sometimes more generally the first five books of the Bible. In the first part of the century commentaries on these books were numerous, and in particular "commentaries on Genesis . . . [occupied] a central position in the intellectual life of the Renaissance" (Arnold Williams, *The Common Expositor: An Account of the Commentaries on Genesis 1527–1633* [Chapel Hill: University of North Carolina Press, 1948], 9).

To the seventeenth-century mind holding a deep concern for early human history and language, they provided a way to understand humanity's fallen condition as well as a possible remedy for the religious and linguistic confusion of the times. After the turbulent years of the Civil War and Interregnum followed by the momentous Restoration of the crown in 1660, it was commonplace for people to believe that the nation had fallen from divine grace and awaited reparation for its sinfulness. For conforming royalists, the Restoration was a joyous rebirth after the sinful years of the Protectorate; conversely, for nonconformists such as John Milton, it was another Fall due to the failure and impurity of the Commonwealth. Regardless of a given political and religious position, a general consensus was that finding the perfect mode of communication was one answer to the turbulent upheavals of the age, for it would simultaneously improve commerce, eradicate religious controversy, and aid science. A reformed language that had the attributes of Edenic speech would, according to philologist and Royal Society member John Wilkins, facilitate communication and "contribute much to the clearing of some of [the] Modern differences in Religion, by unmasking many wild errors."[6] To be sure, individuals had different views of what this language would look like, but almost universally they harked back to Genesis searching for a model for guidance and inspiration. Yet unlike most language reformers, Traherne embraced linguistic diversity, the post-Babel condition.

1. Adam's Prelapsarian Speech

Biblical stories of the hexaemeral tradition — Adam naming the animals, the creation of Eve, the Fall from Paradise — served as historical sources for the projects of language reformers. Sometimes they inspired individuals to revive the original prelapsarian language which was widely assumed to be Hebrew; other times they provided the imaginative impetus for creating a wholly new "philosophical character," or artificial language, as seen in the projects of certain scientists and language planners. For instance, the language planners of the Oxford Circle, and later the Royal Society, were largely responsible for promoting linguistic reform through their experiments with philosophical language schemes. John Wilkins and his group of fellow philologists began their inquiries into language reform at Oxford during the 1650s. This was precisely the time when Thomas Traherne was beginning his undergraduate studies at the university.[7] In

---

[6] John Wilkins, *An Essay towards a Real Character and a Philosophical Language* (1668), A Scolar Press Facsimile (Menston: Scolar Press, 1968), Epistle Dedicatory, sig. br.

[7] We do not know if Traherne knew Wilkins or his works, but it is reasonable to assume that he was aware of the push for language reform by these prominent university

his *Essay towards a Real Character and a Philosophical Language* (1668), Wilkins ruminates over the origins of speech. He acknowledges that "There is scarce any subject that hath been more throughly scanned and debated amongst Learned men, than the *Original* of *Languages* and *Letters*." He maintains that "'tis evident enough that the first Language was con created with our first Parents, they immediately understanding the voice of God speaking to them in the Garden."[8] In chapter three of the first part of his *Essay*, Wilkins further addresses the question of the origin of letters. He suggests that there is a deeply spiritual element that went into the invention of them.

> the Invention . . . was a thing of so great Art and exquisiteness, that *Tully* doth from hence inferr the divinity and spirituality of the humane *soul*, and that it must needs be of a farr more excellent and abstracted Essence then mere Matter or Body, in that it was able to reduce all articulate sounds to 24 *Letters*.[9]

He goes on to say that although there is no scriptural evidence for it, he believes that Adam invented the ancient Hebrew character. Though Wilkins and his colleagues did not try to revive Hebrew as a linguistic solution, the fact that there had been a perfect language in human history was enough to encourage and inspire their attempts to create a new artificial language such as the one found in the *Essay*.[10]

In addition to inspiring the imagination of scientists and philologists, hexaemeral texts were the subject of discussion and meditation. Various biblical commentators focused on one passage in particular, the animal-naming episode from the Book of Genesis: "And out of the ground the LORD God formed every beast of the field, and every fowl of the air; and brought them unto Adam to see what he would call them: and whatsoever Adam called every living creature, that was the name thereof" (Gen. 2:19).[11] The commentators typically addressed three main topics: Adam's profound knowledge of his surroundings, his subsequent dominion over the creation due to this knowledge, and his need for human companionship. For instance, the seventeenth-century commentator Andrew Willet

men. For a longer discussion about Traherne and the language planners see Cynthia Saenz, "Thomas Traherne's View of Language in Restoration England" (D.Phil. diss., University of Oxford, 1997), chap. 1.

[8] Wilkins, *Essay*, 2.

[9] Wilkins, *Essay*, 10.

[10] For a more thorough discussion of Traherne and the language movements see Saenz, "Thomas Traherne's View of Language in Restoration England."

[11] *Bible*, Authorized King James Version (Nashville: Thomas Nelson Publishers, 1972). All quotations from the Bible will be taken from this text and cited in the body of this chapter.

says that one reason the animals were brought before Adam was so "that mans authority and dominion over the creatures might appeare."[12] The Presbyterian minister George Hughes believed that Adam had been granted authority over the Creation, for if one could name one could control the thing named.[13] Numerous other commentators echoed these sentiments, and linguists harked back to this idyllic time when man had an intimate understanding of all things and could assign names to them, thus achieving a perfect relationship of verisimilitude between objects and words, or signified and signifiers.

The naming episode is frequently linked to the creation of Eve and to Adam's societal needs; in knowing the true nature of each creature, Adam realized that they were not fit companions for conversation. We are familiar with the episode in Milton's *Paradise Lost* when Adam feels acutely the absence of one with whom he may commune:

> I named them, as they passed, and understood
> Their nature, with such knowledge God endued
> My sudden apprehension: but in these
> I found not what me thought I wanted still. . . . (*Paradise Lost*, 8.352–355)[14]

Milton links Adam's linguistic purity with innate knowledge and the inherent need to communicate with a suitable partner.

Traherne shares many of the commentators' views, positing in both his prose writings and poetry, that: first, Adam had a special understanding of the creation; second, he had dominion over the creation; and third, he had an intense desire to communicate with other humans.[15] In addition, Traherne highlights a

---

[12] Andrew Willet, *Hexapla in Genesin That Is a Sixfold Commentarie upon Genesis* (1605) (London, 1632), 29.

[13] George Hughes, *An Analytical Exposition of the Whole First Book of Moses Called Genesis* (London, 1672), 22.

[14] John Milton, *Paradise Lost*, ed. Alastair Fowler (London: Group UK Ltd., 1971). Hereafter, all quotations from *Paradise Lost* will be taken from this edition and cited in the body of this chapter.

[15] Since 1932, Traherne has been associated with *Meditations on the Six Days of the Creation*, a work which is part of the hexaemeral tradition. However, since its authorship is still in dispute, the piece will not be treated extensively here. For further information see George Robert Guffey, ed., *Meditations on the Six Days of the Creation* (1717), Augustan Reprint 119 (Los Angeles: Augustan Reprint Society, 1966); Catherine Owen, "The Authorship of the 'Meditations on the Six Days of Creation' and the 'Meditations and Devotions on the Life of Christ'," *Modern Language Review* 56 (1961): 1–12; Saenz, "Thomas Traherne's View of Language in Restoration England"; Gladys Wade, *Poetical Works of Thomas Traherne* (London: P. J. and A. E. Dobell, 1932), xvi–xx; and eadem, *Thomas Traherne* (Princeton: Princeton University Press, 1944), 145–56.

fourth topic; praising God, or "prizing" the Creation, was the goal of prelapsarian speech or perfected speech. The entry "Adam" from his theological encyclopedia *Commentaries of Heaven* illustrates these four points. Traherne explains that Adam understood nature and had an intimate knowledge of the essence of all things. Moreover, the poet describes Adam's mastery over the creation, for "the World was his House, and he the Lord and End for which it was made, in which respect he was infinitely Greater, and Higher than the Heavens. He was Crowned with Glory and Honor, and had Dominion over all the Creatures" (*Commentaries of Heaven*, fol. 37v.1).[16] Traherne emphasizes the importance of Eve's society and conversation. She is "His Superadded Treasure" (*CH*, fol. 37v.1–2) who offers him enjoyment and pleasure through her conversation: "In Eve he had a New Delight and in all his posterity, with whom he was to converse in a sweet and heavenly maner" (*CH*, fol. 38r.1). He expresses similar views in *Christian Ethicks* when speaking of Charity as "natural and Easie in the Estate of Innocency."[17] Adam's natural love for Eve includes having conversation with her:

> He had a Noble Creature made in the Image of GOD for him alone! Her soul was far more excellent in Beauty than her Face, a Diviner and more Glorious Object than the whole world. Her Intelligence and Vivacity, Her Lofty and clear Apprehensions, Her Honour and Majesty, Her Freedome of Action, her Kindness of Behaviour, her Angelical Affections, Her fitness for Conversation. . . . (*CE*, 145)

Part of the unfallen state included a natural desire for society and persons with whom to commune. Notably, the above passage emphasizes Eve's intelligent mind that animates her conversation and in turn enriches Adam by adding a variety of thoughts to his experience. Traherne's desire to celebrate the great variety within the creation is commonplace in all of his works. By meditating upon Adam's "Illustrious children, more than the Stars of Heaven in Multitude" (*CH*, fol. 37v.1), he finds another opportunity to convey his enthusiasm for human diversity.

Despite this celebration of human community and conversation in the *Commentaries of Heaven*, Traherne also conveys an intense solipsistic vision in his writings, maintaining that solitude is important to the individual. This solipsism

---

[16] Thomas Traherne, *Commentaries of Heaven*, London, British Library, MS. Additional 63054, fol. 2r. All references from this manuscript will henceforth be cited in the body of this chapter using the abbreviation *CH*. Also, I give folio number, followed by recto or verso and a period. The folios are further divided into two columns, which I indicate by using the numerals 1 or 2.

[17] Traherne, *Christian Ethicks*, ed. Carol Marks and George Guffey (Ithaca: Cornell University Press, 1968), 144. Henceforth all references to this work will be taken from this edition and cited in the body of this chapter using the abbreviation *CE*.

runs counter to his position that Adam needed, and indeed all humans need, to communicate with others. In the *Centuries of Meditations* Traherne celebrates the solipsistic individual who is isolated from society by entreating his audience to realize that each one of them is the "Heir of all the World" (*CM*, 1.35). In *Christian Ethics* everyone is the "Sole heir" of God's kingdom (*CE*, 55). In the entry "Adam" from *Commentaries of Heaven* he explains why it is sometimes necessary to focus entirely on the individual, why originally Adam was created alone:

> . . . it was expedient he should be alone: That all Eys might see the Univers was made for one. Nay rather, becaus the Univers was made for one; and for him alone. The former being a shady, this a substantial Reason. For GOD Creating the World for one; intended to Exalt him to the utmost Height of all possible Exaltation as the only Object of his Eternal Love. And designing to give the World peculiarly for him, out of him made a Creature more Excellent than the World, and gave her to be his. . . . (*CH*, fol. 38v.1)

The passage highlights the supremacy of the individual and suggests that the paradox of everyone being a "Sole heir" is not problematic for the Divine. In his entry "Alone" from *Commentaries of Heaven* Traherne acknowledges the complexity of the human psyche, craving both solitude and company:

> There is a Property in the soul of man, wherby he cannot endure to be alone, and yet loves to enjoy a Kingdom or a Crown by himself, abhorring Rivals Sharers and Competetors, as much as Desolatness and that as much as Death and Desert Solitariness. Both these Inclinations in him are natural and yet incompatible. . . . Neither of them Springs from corruption, but primitive and pure nature. Either is to be indulged, neither is to be Crucified, both are to be filled, and in both nature it self is to be Gratified. For the uniting of such contrary Interests doth more Glorify the Wisdom of God, and as both these were on purpose given us, that we might have more Capacities to be replenished, so he whose Bounty infinit is, is All-sufficient, as well able as willing to perfect these opposit Inclinations, with their full Enjoyments. Their warfare shall be converted into an Amicable Agreement conspiring to further the perfection of our Bliss and Glory. (*CH*, fol. 79v.1)

The passage offers an astute understanding of human nature, maintaining that both propensities can replenish the spirit if experienced appropriately. Adam is created perfectly in solitude; nevertheless, he feels so much pleasure in the creation that he must communicate it to Eve and their posterity (*CH*, fol. 38r.1). This is a situation not only true for prelapsarian man but also for all humans after the Fall. Numerous times in his writings Traherne claims that human love, gratitude, and enjoyment of heavenly treasures are so immense that they must overflow into recipients, or other humans, through simple conversation:

for the Joy of Communicating and the Joy of receiving maketh perfect Happiness. And therfore are the Sons of Men our Greatest Treasures, because they can giv and receiv: Treasures perhaps infinit as well as Affections. But this I am sure they are our Treasures. And therfore is Conversation so Delightfull becaus they are the Greatest. (*CM*, 4.18)[18]

The above passage celebrates the exchange of ideas through verbal communication. It is not enough to express one's thoughts; one must also understand other views and other languages because "Man is . . . a Sociable Creature, of all other Creatures the most capable of Company and most desiring it, Speech is given him on purpose for Communication, He delights to see and bee seen, he can hear and understand anothers Language" (*CH*, fol. 79v.1). And yet Traherne fluctuates back and forth, celebrating solitary solipsistic states, to highlight the singular importance of an individual, as well as society, to celebrate the infinite variety available for humans to experience. Both hold a place in the prelapsarian world as well as one after the Fall.

In addition to commonplace interpretations of Genesis 2:19 — Adam's knowledge, his dominion, and his need for conversation — Traherne addresses a fourth topic when analyzing the nature of prelapsarian speech: the theme of "prizing", or first understanding the essence of the creation and second praising God for it through appropriate language. Traherne links the naming episode to one of his basic tenets about human apprehension — humans are great "Spectators" (*CM*, 1.41) who are capable of prizing, or apprehending correctly, the whole of the creation. In order to prize the creation, Adam must be able to understand its value and weigh it precisely, for it is his duty to God.[19] For Traherne, poetry is a means of prizing God and his creation. In the poem "Sight" he speaks of a pure "Infant-Ey" which has "Two Sights." One is from his two physical eyes, while the other and more important one is from an interior Eye. This Eye moves into "New Regions" beyond physical restraints towards an "Infinit Space." It sees the visible world and prizes it spiritually. In the fifth stanza of the poem, the interior Eye is

---

[18] Traherne, *Centuries, Poems, and Thanksgivings*, ed. H. M. Margoliouth, 2 vols. (Oxford: Clarendon Press, 1958). All references from the *Centuries, Poems*, and *Thanksgivings* are taken from this text and will henceforth be cited in the body of this chapter.

[19] An example is found in *Commentaries of Heaven*: "His Duty and His pleasures were one . . . Right reason required Him to Prize all the Blessing he had so newly received. And not only to prize them but according to right. That is to say to prize nothing over or under its value, but evry thing according to the measure of its goodness, justly and truly. in doing which His Happiness was Enjoyed. Which GOD commanded which Gods Lov to him required. . . ." (*CH*, fol. 37v.2).

> A Looking-Glass
> Of signal Worth; wherin,
> More than mine Eys
> Could see or prize,
> Such things as Virtues win,
> Life Joy, Lov, Peace, appear'd: a Light
> Which to my Sight
> Did Objects represent
> So excellent;
> That I no more without the same can see
> Than Beasts that have no tru Felicity. ("Sight," 51–60)

Without the penetrating capabilities of the inward Eye which sees the "Light," the speaker could not truly prize his environment. He would be just like animals, devoid of Felicity.

The act of prizing also appears numerous times in Traherne's prose, such as the *Centuries of Meditations*. In the first Century he explains that the human ability to "prize" actually makes us godlike because "we are like Him when our Minds are in Frame. our Minds are in Frame when our Thoughts are like his. And our Thoughts are then like his when we hav such Conceptions of all objects as God hath, and Prize all Things according to their value" (*CM*, 1.13). A subsequent meditation goes so far as to say that prizing correctly places one in Heaven while failing to do so places one in Hell: "To have Blessings and to Prize them is to be in Heaven: To hav them, and not to Prize them, is to be in Hell, I would say upon Earth: To prize them and not to hav them, is to be in Hell" (*CM*, 1.47). The sentiment is reminiscent of Milton's views that heaven and hell are interior states of mind. Repeatedly in *Paradise Lost* Satan intimates that no matter where he goes physically, hell reigns inside him (*Paradise Lost*, 4.74–78). A passage from *Select Meditations* links prizing the Creation with Justice (*SM*, 4.59). Giving something or someone its "Due Esteem" is evaluating it correctly. When one does this, not only does it honor God, but also it enlarges the self:

> we Transfer our selves into them whom we Prize as our selves, and are Seated there, are there affected, feel and receiv, do the work of nature and Delight, are by them received. But Justice Extendeth further. Inanimat creatures are capable of it. We ought to do Right to the Sun and Sea and Stars, to the skie the Earth Beasts and Trees. to value the Services which they already do us, which are by being Prized all Enjoyed. To them also do we giv our selves (in Pondering their Excellencies) and in them to God Almighty. Justice is a Kind of Bartering of ware, a commutativ vertue Exercised in giving and receiving, to the Common Benefit and Good of all. we are Enlarged in the Sun while we are there Esteeming it, becaus each of them are our Second Selves in God Almighty, becaus He is more. (*SM*, 4.59)

Fully comprehending elements of the cosmos — the sun, sea, stars, sky, earth, beasts, trees — will allow humans to appreciate them, take joy in their creation, and share in their wonder. A reciprocal energy develops and all the prized objects reflect back towards the observer.

Traherne's notion of prizing also underlies his linguistic theory insofar as it promotes the idea that humans can understand the essence of things, assign words to them, and communicate using a perfected language (perfected not by changing the language, but by changing one's understanding of things which the language represents). Traherne's massive theological encyclopedia, *Commentaries of Heaven*, purports to open the "Mysteries of Felicitie" through word definitions, which will in turn reveal "ALL THINGS" to be "Objects of Happiness" (*CH*, fol. 2r). The poet's notions of linguistic clarity, plainness, and veracity — stated aspirations of the language movements of the seventeenth century — all rest upon his doctrine of Felicity. Readers of Traherne will be familiar with the doctrine that states that Felicity is paradise on earth. It is a condition linking the infinite capacity of humans for obtaining knowledge with the ability to perceive and apprehend clearly and perfectly things within the world, and with the understanding that the world was created expressly for human enjoyment. When discussing the role of prelapsarian Adam (who may be seen as a representative of all humans), Traherne maintains that the triad "Right Reason, GOD and Happiness" require Adam to perform his "Duty." This duty is to "prize" the Creation, that is, to achieve a perfect understanding of all things, organize them into a particular "order," and finally praise God for them. Fulfilling this duty will bring Felicity, for Adam's "Duty and His pleasure were one" (*CH*, fol. 37v.2).[20] Instead of creating a new philosophical character, Traherne attempts to reform English by endorsing a change in mental perception. The soul first penetrates then apprehends the centers of things. Afterwards, a word can be assigned to them. The entry for the word "Abridgement" is itself concerned with the defining of words. For Traherne, the word "Abridgement" is used synonymously with "word." In the following passage the poet celebrates the ability of the soul to understand objects and to provide significations for words,

> Concerning Abridgement I shall speak but little: Observing in it only the Glory of the Soul, that can frame an Abridgement; and instructing men how to use it. . . . [the soul] can draw all these into a little Abstract, and lodg them in fit and convenient Repositories, even in a Centre, containing in it self Rooms Enough wherin to Dispose them, in Clear Light, in fair Treasuries, in Distinct Accessible Orders, so that it can Approach and make a familiar use of them. . . . (*CH*, fol. 7v.1)

---

[20] Compare the essay by Laam in this volume, above, 37–63.

Traherne believes that a word itself does not require change, but rather that human perception regarding what the word signifies must be altered. Perception is a crucial part of appreciating the nature of objects and purifying language.[21]

Taking one of his most radical positions and echoing nonconformist thought, Traherne insists that humans should assign value to the creation. God needs spectators to enjoy and give value to his works, thus a symbiotic link exists between Himself and humans.[22] The results of his theology are audacious expressions such as the following from the poem "The Demonstration":

> The GODHEAD cannot prize
> The Sun at all, nor yet the Skies,
> Or Air, or Earth, or Trees, or Seas,
> Or Stars, unless the Soul of Man they pleas. (43–46)

Traherne magnifies man's stature until he appears to be nearly equal with God.[23] These sentiments seem more characteristic of nonconformist or even radical religious thought that focused upon inward inspiration of individual consciences.

Although he did not agree with puritan John Bunyan's predestinarian theology, Traherne's writings nevertheless resemble his sentiments with regard to Adam's ability to both name and create. Bunyan's commentary on the book of Genesis, *An Exposition on the First Ten Chapters of Genesis and Part of the Eleventh,* differs slightly from other commentaries in its emphasis upon the act as one of creation. Before discussing Genesis 2:19, Bunyan explains why Adam is an image of God. He is an image in part through the human soul, and an image "together" through the body and soul combined. Bunyan maintains that man is a shadow of Christ: "In this Adam was a lively type of the Lord Christ's sovereigne and glorious power over all flesh. . . ."[24] Adam reflects the hypostasis of Christ for his soul holds the rational and ethereal qualities of the divine.[25] And yet his body makes him human. Man has dominion over the flesh (for example, the animals) because he is able to name them. But this naming goes beyond mere control, for it is both a judgement and a creative act:

---

[21] For a further discussion of *Commentaries of Heaven*, see Saenz, "Thomas Traherne's View of Language," chap. 1; and Allan Pritchard, "Traherne's *Commentaries of Heaven,*" *University of Toronto Quarterly* 53 (1984): 1–35.

[22] Robert Uphaus, "Thomas Traherne: Perception As Process," *University of Windsor Review* 3 (1968): 19–27, here 20.

[23] John Carey, "Seventeenth-Century Writers: Bacon, Burton, Browne, Herbert, Vaughan, Crashaw, Traherne," lecture series, St. Cross Building, Oxford, 27 Nov. 1996.

[24] Bunyan, *An Exposition on the First Ten Chapters of Genesis and Part of the Eleventh,* in *The Whole Works of John Bunyan,* ed. George Offor (London, 1862), 2:427.

[25] John Bunyan, *An Exposition,* 422.

So Christ nameth the world; whom he will he calleth saints; and whom he will he calleth the world, 'ungodly,' 'serpents,' 'vipers,' and the like. 'I pray for them, I pray not for the world' (John 17.9).

'And whatsoever Adam called every living creature, that *was* the name therof.' Even as Christ passes sentence, so shall their judgement be.[26]

Bunyan links the Genesis episode with the naming of the Elect, or saved souls: a creature is named, created, and judged. Traditionally, human agency has no part in the Election, but here Bunyan is speaking of prelapsarian man and he allows for Adam's active role in the creative process. Adam is the one who supplies the names; he does not merely discover names which the Divine has already assigned.

The above discussion illustrates that there was general consensus that Edenic speech was informed by knowledge, veracity, and enriching communication between humans. But how did seventeenth-century thinkers hope actually to regain the prelapsarian language? Showing the views of a representative few illustrates that there were numerous approaches. As mentioned above, philosophical language planners, such as John Wilkins, began various schemes in the middle and latter part of the century. They hoped to invent a new character that would function like Adam's speech — words would actually mirror reality perfectly, thus eliminating all verbal ambiguities. Such a character could be the panacea for the turbulent religious disputes as well as help to promote the advancement of science.

The Quakers used a different method of returning to linguistic purity that included the eroding away of societal hierarchies within their native tongue of English. Believing that honors conferred by formal address were a form of pride and the work of the devil, they employed informal words such as "thee" and "thou" in their discourse. Worldly honors were inconsequential and speech which conveyed them degenerate. By taking away honorific words which human custom had created, the Quakers helped to eradicate postlapsarian speech and return to a purer form of communication. Hugh Ormsby-Lennon states that

the Society's testimony on oaths was not primarily intended as a challenge to the legitimacy of government — ready to affirm, Friends were denied the opportunity — but was designed to recall folk to standards of veracity obtaining in Eden, upheld by Christ, and appropriate for England's Last Days.[27]

---

[26] Bunyan, *An Exposition*, 427.
[27] Hugh Ormsby-Lennon, "From Shibboleth to Apocalypse," in *Language, Self and Society*, ed. Peter Burke and Roy Porter (Cambridge: Polity Press, 1991), 72–112, here 78.

In addition to theological concerns, Quakers also had political ones and asserted their autonomy through refining their style of speech.

As previously mentioned, some linguists believed that the pure language which Adam spoke was Hebrew, and the revival of this language would return man to his Edenic estate. Additionally, radical groups of the 1640s and 50s devoted much time to Hebraic studies and were intent upon exploring possibilities of obtaining prelapsarian speech.[28] As the millenarian attitude of the Puritans gained momentum people expected the imminent return of the Jews to England and their subsequent conversion to Christianity. The study of Hebrew was to prepare for and help precipitate this momentous occasion. In addition, they viewed Hebrew as being the closest language to the original one spoken by Adam. By returning to it for both prayer and preaching, one was moving back to a purer form of communication, and in turn was reforming or perfecting oneself.

Traherne believed that Hebrew was the original language of man. In the entry "Babel" from the *Commentaries of Heaven* he says that without Babel "Hebrew had been the Tongue / Of all the World" (*CH*, fol. 192r.1). Also, as both Christopher Hill and Nabil Matar point out, he was aware of millenarian views which maintained that the Jews would be converted.[29] Nevertheless, Traherne's own enterprise for linguistic reform did not entail a revival of Hebrew. We are uncertain to what extent he knew the language; he appears to use it only when quoting from the seventeenth-century Hebraist Theophilus Gale. Traherne cites Part II of Gale's *The Court of the Gentiles* in three entries from the *Commentaries of Heaven* — "Amendment," "Aristotle's Philosophie," and "Astrology."[30] He also copied passages from Part II into his *Commonplace Book*, which Carol Marks claims

---

[28] A. P. Coudert, "Five Seventeenth-Century Christian Hebraists," and J. P. Rosenblatt, "John Selden's *De Jure Naturali*," in *Hebraica Veritas?: Christian Hebraists and the Study of Judaism in Early Modern Europe*, ed. eadem and J. S. Shoulson (Philadelphia: University of Pennsylvania Press, 2004), 286–308, 102–24 respectively.

[29] Christopher Hill, *Writing and Revolution in Seventeenth-Century England* (Brighton: Harvester Press, 1985), 231; and Nabil Matar, "The Anglican Eschatology of Thomas Traherne," *Anglican Theological Review* 74 (1992): 289–303. In "Thanksgivings for the Beauty of his Providence," Traherne prays for the restoration of the Jews: "Restore them, O Lord! / That as we have obtained Mercy / Through their unbelief, / So they by our Mercy (and our Faith prevailing) may obtain / Mercy" (373–377). While describing typological references in *Commentaries of Heaven*, Traherne recalls a time when he himself converted a Jew stating that "Moses and the Prophets writ of our Saviour, so, that it is the Easiest thing in the World to convince and confound a Jew, as I my self have done, out of the books of the Old Testament" (*CH*, fol. 139v.1).

[30] Pritchard, "Traherne's *Commentaries*," 5.

"originated as a container for extracts from Gale."[31] However, Traherne's citations do not focus upon Gale's passages about Adam and the original language,
nor does he posit that a revival of Hebrew is necessary for linguistic reform.

Prelapsarian speech inspired many thinkers to create or recapture the perfect language. For Wilkins it was an impetus for embarking on the huge project
of the *Essay*. The Quakers maintained that the original tongue had been devoid
of worldly vanities and therefore used an informal method of address in order to
return to a pre-Fall simplicity. Hebraists such as Gale believed that simply using
Hebrew was the answer to the linguistic fall. For Traherne there were two conditions under which one might achieve the Edenic estate. One was in regenerate
adulthood, when one is able to prize the world correctly; the other was during the
pre-linguistic and isolated purity of infancy.

2. Language and Infancy

Traherne talks about each person's personal experience of paradise, or potential
for experiencing it. One of his hallmark ideas is celebrating the human potential
for goodness and consequently the ability to achieve Felicity while on earth. He
carries the optimism of the Platonists, the Latitudinarians, and the Pre-Nicene
tradition espoused by St. Irenaeus. His writings prompt the question, if all men
are like Adam in Eden or have the potential to achieve that state, then is it possible to obtain a perfect language? An answer depends on what phase of development the human is in: the prenatal state, infancy and childhood, or adulthood.
This section investigates Traherne's views of language at these different human
phases and their relationship to the individual falls which everyone experiences.

In the latter half of the seventeenth century, some religious thinkers exhib-
ited an increasingly positive view of human nature. Members of the Latitude
movement attacked the Calvinist doctrine of innate depravity and promoted the
idea that each individual had the ability to become like the unfallen Adam. [32]
They also championed other causes ranging from an endorsement of religious
toleration and comprehension of nonconformists to rationalism in religion. Isabel
Rivers describes two generations of Latitude-men. The first consisted primarily
(but not exclusively) of students, fellows, and heads of colleges at Cambridge before the Civil War. The second generation was students, mostly from Cambridge,
during the late 1640s and early 1650s. They were influenced by and overlapped

---

[31] Carol Marks, "Studies in the Reading of Thomas Traherne" (B.Litt. thesis, University of Oxford, 1962), 157.

[32] Isabel Rivers, *Reason, Grace and Sentiment: A Study of the Language of Religion and
Ethics in England 1660–1780* (Cambridge: Cambridge University Press, 1991), 1:28–29.

with the first generation. The emphasis of the earlier part of the movement — led by such men as Benjamin Whichcote, Henry More, John Smith, and Ralph Cudworth — was a repudiation of predestination theology.[33] Traherne shares their views in rejecting Calvinism and celebrating the human potential for goodness.

In *The Transformation of Sin*, Patrick Grant points out the connection between Irenaean theodicy and Traherne's views of human nature.[34] Grant posits that the pre-Nicene father St. Irenaeus greatly influenced the poet as well as the Latitudinarians with such notions as universal salvation, which promoted a vision of church unity by overcoming doctrinal differences.[35] In making the comparison between Irenaeus and Traherne, Grant notes that Adam is both the archetype and "everyman" in the poet's works.[36] Irenaeus viewed the fall of man in Genesis as being less serious than the repeated transgressions of contemporary man. Sin results from bad moral choices and is essentially a misevaluation of things. Irenaeus also believed that Adam was created with child-like innocence and needed to grow to maturity, as well as that the creation should be utilized by humans.[37] We find similar beliefs in Traherne's work. The "I" of a poem or prose piece is used interchangeably with "Adam," indicating that the experience of moving from purity and innocence to the state of a degenerate individual is common to all humans and not just one incident in history.

In Traherne's writings, particularly some of his well-known poems and meditations, the infant shares similar characteristics to those of Adam; however, one primary difference is that for Adam language becomes corrupt after he falls, while the mute infant is pure until he is infected with postlapsarian speech. The infant or young child has dominion over his world-view, and he feels possessive: "The Skies were mine, and so were the Sun and Moon and Stars, and all the World was mine, and I the only Spectator and Enjoyer of it" (*CM*, III.3). In this meditation, we see that the infant/child knows the essence of things, for he has pure, unencumbered vision enabling him to apprehend and thereby enjoy the creation before he is corrupted by "the Dirty Devices of this World" (*CM*, III.3).

---

[33] Rivers, *Reason, Grace and Sentiment*, 1:5–30.

[34] Traherne refers to Irenaeus of Lyons in his entry "Antiquitie" from the *Commentaries of Heaven* (fol. 106v.1). In this entry he quotes from Irenaeus in order to discredit the Church of Rome. He also refers to Irenaeus in *Roman Forgeries*: "*Irenæus*, one of the most Ancient Fathers, scholar to S. *Polycarp*, S. John's Disciple, in his Book against Heresies, giveth us four notable marks of their Authors . . .": *Roman Forgeries* (London, 1673), An Advertisement to the Reader.

[35] Patrick Grant, *The Transformation of Sin* (Montreal: McGill-Queen's University Press, 1974), 177.

[36] Grant, *Transformation of Sin*, 170–197.

[37] Grant, *Transformation of Sin*, 181.

The poem "Innocence," a retrospective look at infancy, also illustrates this well as the speaker declares he was once perfect: "I felt no Stain, nor Spot of Sin" (4). In infancy or childhood one's vision and apprehension are perfect and the soul is pure, as stated in the poem "Eden":

> Those Things which first his Eden did adorn,
>   My Infancy
> Did crown. Simplicitie
> Was my Protection when I first was born.
>   Mine Eys those Treasures first did see,
> Which God first made. The first Effects of Lov
> My first Enjoyments upon Earth did prov. . . . (36–42)

In the above stanza his simplicity and ignorance of worldly matters protect his pure vision and apprehension. Two other qualities characterize Traherne's infant: he is ignorant as well as solipsistic. The infant is ignorant of adult boundaries and inhibitions, and Traherne frequently praises this condition:

> A learned and a Happy Ignorance
>   Divided me,
>   From all the Vanitie,
> From all the Sloth Care Sorrow that advance,
>   The madness and the Miserie
> Of Men. No Error, no Distraction I
> Saw soil the Earth, or overcloud the Skie. ("Eden," 1–7)

Here Traherne praises the infant's condition that leaves him ignorant of adult boundaries and inhibitions. Echoing his famous vision from *Centuries of Meditations* 3, Traherne further describes the infant in the entry "Adam" from *Commentaries of Heaven*: "No Hedges and Ditches did bound his possessions, nor did the fields and mountains yeeld him any other Revenews beside their Beauties" (*CH*, fol. 37.v.1).[38] The infant is solipsistic to the extent that he fuses his own consciousness with the things around him. Because he does not draw any boundaries between himself and the empirical world, he is "unable to distinguish between objective reality and his own mental creations."[39]

---

[38] Leah Marcus draws a comparison between Traherne's views and Jeremy Taylor's. Taylor praised ignorance and went so far as to say that since knowledge removed Adam from Paradise, ignorance would help him regain it. See Leah Marcus, *Childhood and Cultural Despair* (Pittsburgh: University of Pittsburgh Press, 1978), 177. Compare also the essay by Greenberg in this volume, above, 21-35.

[39] Marcus, *Children and Cultural Despair*, 180.

Although the infant's ignorance allows for special vision and a fusion between himself and his surroundings, Traherne does not advocate adult ignorance. In fact, in the *Centuries of Meditation,* he insists that Christians must grow up:

> And till we see into the Beauty and Blessedness of Gods Laws, the Glory of His Works, the Excellency of our Souls &c. we are but Children of Darkness, at least but Ignorant and imperfect: neither able to rejoyce in God, as we ought, nor to liv in Communion with Him. (*CM*, 4.4)

Indeed, Traherne says, "evry man ought to spend his time, in studying diligently Divine Philosophy" (*CM*, 4.3). Just as he vacillates between the benefits of solitude and society, so too does Traherne vacillate between the "Happy Ignorance" ("Eden," 1) of the infant and the learnedness of the Christian philosopher.

If everyone experiences Adam's unfallen state in his or her own infancy or childhood, then presumably there is a time when he or she has perfect speech. However, this is not always the case in Traherne's writings. True, he is optimistic about the reform of language and in a project like *Commentaries of Heaven* conveys his belief in the power of words to capture reality. But he also disparages human speech, particularly when it is vain with fanciful metaphors, as seen in his poem "The Author to the Critical Peruser."[40] Moreover, he has a curious position regarding the infant and speech, one that vacillates between celebrating dumbness[41] and celebrating the introduction of language. His views can be analyzed by looking at a selection of his poems and the entry "Babe" from the *Commentaries of Heaven.*

In the poem "The Salutation," a work contemplating the pre-natal state, Traherne celebrates not only the fusion of mind and body, but also the infant's future ability to speak with his tongue. The work anticipates an awakening or birth and subsequently a jubilant revelry over the senses. Conversely, silence in the poem signifies chaos: "When silent I, / So many thousand thousand yeers, / Beneath the Dust did in a Chaos lie" (7–9). While Traherne celebrates the organ of

---

[40] A central debating point in the mid-seventeenth century was whether or not to use metaphor to describe spiritual truth. Conformists and nonconformists took adamant stances, the former disparaging metaphor, the latter claiming it helped convey the divine message. Traherne contributes to this debate in this poem and positions himself with the conformists showing his concern over the use of metaphor, the "idle Fancies, Toys, and Words" (61–62) which cloud the "naked Truth" (1). However, like his fellow conformists, he often uses figurative speech while claiming to write and speak with a "plain" style. For a discussion of Traherne and metaphor, see Saenz, "Thomas Traherne's View of Language."

[41] Compare the essay by Mintz in this volume, above, 1–20.

speech in "The Salutation," he nonetheless depicts the introduction of language as a linguistic fall from infant purity in "Dumnesse," a poem depicting the time shortly after birth. In this poem the perfect state of infancy is characterized by speechlessness, a state conducive to meditation:

> ... he
> Might in himself profoundly Busied be:
> And not vent out, before he hath t'ane in
> Those Antidots that guard his Soul from Sin. (5–8)

The infant, in his dumbness, is in an incubatory state where he builds up immunities before moving into the outside world: "Thus was I pent within / A Fort, Impregnable to any Sin" (53–54). The incubator cuts out sound:

> Wise Nature made him Deaf too, that he might
> Not be disturbd, while he doth take Delight
> In inward Things, nor be depravd with Tongues,
> Nor Injured by the Errors and the Wrongs
> That *Mortal Words* convey. For Sin and Death
> Are most infused by accursed Breath. . . . (9–14)

This baby is not literally deaf, but he is unable to "hear" because he doesn't understand a spoken language. Breaking silence in the poem, or learning to speak, is equated with leaving the blissful state: "I *then my Bliss did, when my Silence, break*" (20).

Yet in "Dumnesse" Traherne's perfect "silence" is curiously auditory. The "fair Face / Of Heav'n and Earth" (18–19) speaks to him before he is corrupted. This "Face" uses the "Pulpit in my Mind," "Temple," "Teacher," and "Text" to instruct (57–59). All of these imply auditory or written instruction and therefore a kind of language. The poet insists that "No Ear, / But Eys them selvs were all the Hearers there" (59–60). In this poem there is clearly a great deal that the infant is subject to hearing, for the Heavens are an oracle, the Earth is a Priest, and all things have a voice. It seems that only the "Human Words" of line 21 and the speaker's Tongue in line 67 are corrupt and begin killing these benevolent "Voices." Man starts as a listener, but his own speech and the words of other men corrupt his infant purity.

Both Traherne and John Bunyan see the ear as a vulnerable spot. Positive forces — in Traherne's poem the voices of the "fair Face of Heav'n" such as the "Pulpit," "Temple," "Teacher," and "Text" — can enter as well as negative ones. In Bunyan's *The Holy War* the King's army attacks Mansoul through Eargate in order to regain it from the Diabolonians. Realizing that this place has potential weaknesses, Lord Willbewill assigns Mr. Prejudice to the Gate. Mr. Prejudice protects the Gate with the help of Deafmen, "men advantageous for that service."[42] In this episode deafness works negatively against Mansoul because it helps to block out the good words of the King's army. Ultimately, however, the positive forces of the King's army penetrate Eargate:

> Now when the Captains saw the answer of the great ones, and that they could not get an hearing from the old Natives of the Town, and that *Mansoul* was resolved to give the Kings Army Battel: they prepared themselves to receive them, and to try it out by the power of the arm. And first they made their force more formidable against *Eargate*. For they knew that unless they could penetrate that, no good could be done upon the Town. This done, they put the rest of their men in their places. After which they gave out the word, which was, *ye must be born again*. Then they sounded the Trumpet, then they in the Town made them answer, with shout against shout, charge against charge, and so the Battel began.[43]

While Traherne believed that deafness and dumbness were part of the solipsistic purity of the infant, John Bunyan depicts deafness in another light in his theological allegory.

The entry "Babe" from the *Commentaries of Heaven* also suggests that speech corrupts the infant. At first the babe knows only himself and the wonders of the world around him; he is all apprehension and can see the beauty and glory of nature. But language destroys this and introduces human inventions which distract the babe from the wonders of the creation:

> But when he begins to speak, he ceases to be a Babe, and is infected with the Corruptions and Customs of Men, taken off from all the Works of God, and entertained as a child with Hobby horses and Rattles, a leading Inducement to all other Pomps and vanities. (*CH*, fol. 191r.2)

How does one account for the difference in attitude in "The Salutation" in which the speech organ is celebrated, and "Dumnesse" and the entry "Babe," in which language is a corruptive force? One explanation may be that Traherne speaks of pre- and postpartum stages of childbirth. "The Salutation" talks about a preexistent state just as the mind and body merge within the womb, while "Dumnesse"

---

[42] Bunyan, *The Holy War*, ed. Roger Sharrock and James Forrest (Oxford: Clarendon Press, 1980), 50.

[43] Bunyan, *The Holy War*, 50.

and "Babe" are about the infant. In the former Traherne celebrates the "Speaking Tongue" and the potential for language. The latter two look at a fall from a perfect, isolated, incubatory state of an infant.

The poem "Silence" conveys an adult experience, but also shares similar sentiments to those found in the poem "Dumnesse" and the encyclopedia entry "Babe." Silence is an ideal state where the meditative faculties may flourish. Traherne opens by talking about a "quiet Silent Person" that can achieve "All that is Great or High in Blessedness" (2). The inward realm can hold the highest perfection: "The Inward Work is the Supreme: for all / The other were occasioned by the Fall" (2–3). Thus the "Idle" man, or silent one, may do the "Greatest Business" (6) which is similar to Adam's prelapsarian actions (7). Yet this "silence" is not without sound or even speech, for the person has an internal voice: "Within, is better than an Empty Voice" (30) which produces a sweet melody that is better than an organ, lute, or harp. Traherne shows some ambivalence when discussing the silent person, for silence in his poems often entails a great deal of sound which comes from an interior voice. Both the mute infant and the silent adult are in a protective enclosure, and the voices they hear are pure and benevolent. This "ideal" situation is solipsistic in nature, and at first glance there appears to be no place for communication with others and the outside world.[44]

However, in the poem "Silence" Traherne also mentions the "outward Busy Acts" (9), which are not found in the silent introspective person. In the following lines one would expect him to list all kinds of undesirable events resulting from "outward" human action; but this is not the case, for he lists virtuous ones: the building of churches, giving to the poor, administering justice, and preaching are a few of them (10–20). All these virtuous acts are necessitated by sin, and in his writings Traherne views them as a *felix culpa*, a beneficial expansion of the human experience. In *Select Meditations*, we can see that Traherne believed that man's Fall and his potential to win back paradise on earth add "Victory and Triumphs" to his estate, for without sin

---

[44] Although Traherne reprimands Thomas Hobbes for his "Ignorant *Leviathan*" in *Christian Ethicks*, nevertheless a parallel may be drawn between their views of language, for they both look at it in relationship to a solipsistic condition as well as talk about the expansion of the individual. Hobbes's solipsist is a floating mind, which he believed was capable of having a working language (see Richard Tuck, *Hobbes*, Past Masters Series [Oxford: Oxford University Press, 1989], 41–42). Traherne's is the infant or adult of the above poems and the entry "Babe." His version of the floating mind is found in such poems as "My Spirit" and "The Salutation."

there had been no Punishments: no Patience no Longsuffering no meekness no contrition no Penitent sinners, no Incarnation of Jesus christ,[45] no Redemption, no new obligations, no Heights and Depths and Enlargments of soul in the Abisses of misery and the Heights of Blessedness seen at the same time. No victory and Triumph infinitly Sweeter than Quiet Possession, no miracles, no Revelations from Heaven no use of patriarchs Prophets and Apostles. (*SM*, 3.52)

Sin allows all of the above redemptive moments to occur, which surpass the original Fall of human nature.

Some of Traherne's writing calls for silence and inwardness, and yet there is a time for breaking this silence. Speech corrupts the individual, but if sin can bring new "Heights and Depths and Enlargments" to a person, perhaps a fallen language can be beneficial. The ambiguity expressed in the poems indicates that this may be Traherne's position. Irenaeus posits that the child must mature, which is also true in Traherne's writings. Although the child grows and learns about the "Churlish Proprieties" (*CM*, 3.3), he nevertheless overcomes these spiritual boundaries and enlarges his soul. Traherne anticipates the growth of the infant's comprehension and suggests that silence may no longer be necessary or preferred at later stages in life. The tone in "The Salutation," where the speaker looks at the preexistent phase of human life before the soul merges with the body, is one of anticipation for human language. The disembodied speaker recounts his birth into bodily sensations, and the acquisition of a "Speaking Tongue" (6). Before this, he is in a silent chaos; his latent energies poised to experience "New Burnisht Joys" (19) and presumably to use the "Speaking Tongue."

In the poem "Shadows in the Water" the child has outgrown the protective confinement of the incubator and silence is no longer desired. True, he has clear vision, but this is no longer enough without additional knowledge. Although the poem holds a tone of wonder and self-discovery as a child looks at his reflection in a pool of water, it also carries a plaintive tone that conveys a degree of incommunicability: "I call'd them oft, but call'd in vain; / No Speeches we could entertain" (33–34). It is not enough to be a simple "Ey" focusing on inward things as in "The Preparative," another pre-natal poem. The growing child in "Shadows in the Water" requires answers to his many questions:

---

[45] This was an ancient patristic controversy: would the Second Person of the Holy Trinity have become incarnate even if Adam had never sinned? Some church fathers thought so and others did not.

What *Secret* borders on those Ends?
    Are lofty Hevens hurl'd
    'Bout your inferior World?
    Are ye the Representatives
    Of other Peopl's distant Lives? (68–72)

According to Traherne, the manner in which one perceives things determines their value.[46] Attaining true Felicity as an adult amounts to overcoming boundaries; seeing the true nature of the creation; and finally, prizing and in turn praising God. In his work *Commentaries of Heaven*, Traherne calls for this same mental transformation in every individual in order to bring about linguistic reform. This does not require one correct way of speaking, or even one language, but rather spiritual awareness to appreciate the Divine's complex world.

3. The Tower of Babel

For seventeenth-century philologists and religious thinkers, the story of the Tower of Babel was an actual historical event, its consequences being the multifarious languages, and a "curse" causing strife among different peoples. Those who attempted to reform language harked back to a time of imagined peace and harmony before this linguistic Fall. For instance, the language planners such as John Wilkins believed that reversing the consequences of Babel — finding a common universal character — would eliminate religious and political strife. Biblical commentators such as Willet and Hughes, who give multiple reasons for the building of the Tower, frequently discuss the Babel episode of Genesis 11. They explain that it was intended as a place of refuge against another flood or fire, or represented a desire to achieve domination and unification. They claimed it was a memorial to human strength. The commentators also provide reasons why these were nefarious acts — humans attempted to reach a God-like status, they wanted to achieve worldly fame, and they were proud of human endeavors. God's punishment was to confuse the languages and thereby frustrate human ambition. Andrew Willet gives several reasons why the Babylonians built the tower: the endeavor was inspired by "the ambitious desire of dominion" and impulse "to maintain society" so humans "might dwell together, and not be scattered here and there."[47] He argues that the

---

[46] Marcus summarizes this idea: "But his writings give strong and consistent emphasis not to things in themselves, but to things as they are perceived. By seeing the world about him as Eden and his own body as beautiful and pure, the child makes them so; and by failing to perceive evil, in effect he uncreates it" (*Childhood and Cultural Despair*, 182–83).

[47] Willet, *Hexapla in Genesin*, 108.

people of Nimrod attempted to "get them a name," or reputation, thereby ensuring that their "*houses* [would] *endure for ever.*"[48] Because of their pride and refusal to be dispersed, God gave them a linguistic punishment. A common language has a unifying force, the confusion of language a dispersing effect.

The political theorist Thomas Hobbes, offering his own commentary, sees the confusion at Babel as divine reparation for human rebellion:

> But all this language gotten, and augmented by *Adam* and his posterity, was again lost at the tower of *Babel*, when by the hand of God, every man was stricken for his rebellion, with an oblivion of his former language. And being hereby forced to disperse themselves into severall parts of the world, it must needs be, that the diversity of Tongues that now is, proceeded by degrees from them, in such manner, as need (the mother of all inventions) taught them; and in tract of time grew every where more copious.[49]

Babel is usually seen as a "curse of confusion" tarnishing the linguistic purity of the first language. In his project, *An Essay Towards a Real Character, and a Philosophical Language*, Wilkins frequently mentions the "Curse": "It cannot be denied, but that the *variety* of *Letters* is an appendix to the Curse of *Babel*, namely, the multitude and variety of *Languages.*"[50] His main goal is to amend the problem of multiple forms of communication with his philosophical character. Uniformity and precision are crucial for returning to the prelapsarian condition where knowledge was conveyed perfectly, "[s]o that if men should generally consent upon the same way or manner of *Expression*, as they do agree in the same *Notion*, we should then be freed from that Curse in the Confusion of Tongues, with all the unhappy consequences of it."[51] The consequences he refers to are religious disputes and "*wild errors*"[52] in relaying scientific discoveries.

Traherne's view of Babel fluctuates. In "The Author to the Critical Peruser" he mentions "*Babel-Hell*" with derision. He evokes Babel's negative connotation when describing the corruptions of a man-made world:

> Truly there are two Worlds. One was made by God, the other by Men. That made by GOD, was Great and Beautifull. Before the Fall, It was Adams Joy, and the Temple of his Glory. That made by men is a Babel of Confusion: Invented Riches, Pomps and Vanities, brought in by Sin. (*CM*, 1.7)

---

[48] Willet, *Hexapla in Genesin*, 108.

[49] Thomas Hobbes, *Leviathan*, ed. Richard Tuck (Cambridge: Cambridge University Press, 1996), 25.

[50] Wilkins, *Essay*, 13.

[51] Wilkins, *Essay*, 20.

[52] Wilkins, *Essay*, Epistle Dedicatory, sig. br.

However, Babel is not always seen as a curse. Unlike the language project of Wilkins, for instance, Traherne's *Commentaries of Heaven* does not propose to undo its consequences. In his entry "Babel" he acknowledges the common beliefs surrounding the episode but reinterprets them in a unique way. He begins by making thematic links with the entry "Babe" which initially suggest that Babel is a fall from linguistic purity:

> Many Difficulties are introduced into the World to the great Disorder and Trouble of Infants, which nature in it self never intended. When we enter first upon the yeers of Discretion, we find ourselves Babes still to the Forrein Nations and Kingdoms on Earth: for by reason of the variety of Languages we are dumb (as it were) to all men but those of our own Country. . . . (*CH*, fol. 191v.1)

He draws a parallel between an infant's confusion over the introduction of speech and an adult's confusion over a foreign language. However, rather than seeing the episode as only a contamination of a pure incubatory space, the Confusion is also shown in a positive light. In the entry "Babe" the infant is "infected" by the introduction of speech, but in "Babel" Traherne softens this assessment calling speech merely a "difficultie" which can trouble an infant. The infant is associated with adults who are unable to understand foreign languages, suffer for this, but ultimately obtain "a vaste Advantage" when overcoming the language barrier and knowing "the Wisdom and the Beauty of other nations" (*CH*, fol. 191v.1).

At another point Traherne links the two entries. In "Babe" the infant inherits "Hopes" from its parents that in turn rescue it from original sin, or "the Miserie of their first Parents." "Babel" talks about inherited sinfulness as well as benefits from parents: "Children are by nature Subject to the Errors and miscarriages of their parents; as they are by nature also capable of their Advantages. Their condition is such, that their Interest is interwoven: They are joynt partakers of the same Benefits, and of the same miseries" (*CH*, fol. 191v.1). Though language has an initial corrupting influence, Traherne maintains that this will not always be the case. With Babel, the infusion of languages into a previously perfect space (humankind with one language) can be a beneficial occurrence depending on one's perspective:

> Whether Babel be an object of Bliss, or miserie, may much to be disputed, especialy by men not well acquainted with the nature of Bliss: but by men of a discerning Spirit may easily be decided. For they that Know, that all Things are objects of Miserie to the Wicked, and of Bliss to the virtuous can easily divide to evry man his Share in Babel also, which is a woe to the one, and a Joy to the other. (*CH*, fol. 191v.1)

As mentioned above, silence, solipsism, and inwardness can be seen as a perfect condition, but there is a time for sound and language. In the poem "Silence" there is a distinctly auditory quality present, and the "outward Busy Acts" suggest a beneficial verbal action present in the fallen state.

Traherne characteristically celebrates the great variety in the creation and infinite expanse of the cosmos. Expansion and possibility are ideals that frequently stimulate his theological vision, despite his longing for religious and political unity. This is true of his attitude toward the multiple languages resulting from the Tower of Babel. The confusion, the appearance of several languages, and the subsequent dispersion are all celebrated because they contribute to the variety in the world. Traherne employs the image of a fountain to relay the effusive effects of Babel:

> Babel is a Fountain of Great Alteration, and has occasioned many changes in the World. The Eternal Continuance of which changes flowing from a few in the Beginning of the World, and Spreading abroad in such a maner show us two Things of considerable Importance. (*CH*, fol. 191v.2)

One positive result is free will. All the major events relating to the degeneration of humankind are the result of human actions. Traherne says that "the Hearts and Actions of men are the great Stars that overrule the world for no Conjunction of the Planets begot the Confusion of Languages, no more then it did the Fall of Man, or the Deluge itself, or the Destruction of Paradise" (*CH*, fol. 191v.2). Another thing of "considerable Importance" is "the Diffusive nature of evry Object" (*CH*, fol. 191v.2). The poet sees all actions as having ever-expanding consequences. Babel, for instance, touches all ages and transforms them. The vibrant activity of free choice resulting in ever-expanding consequences is a phenomenon that should be celebrated. Later in the entry he states: "The variety of Languages is a marvellous Ornament and Beauty to the World: which maketh Babel the more fit to be enjoyed" (*CH*, fol. 192r.1). Traherne says that Pentecost answers the Confusion:

> As Mount Sion answereth Mount Sinai which is in Arabia, and the crucifixion[53] of Christ, the Giving of the Law: so doth the Coming down of the Holy Ghost upon the Apostles, the Confusion at Babel. For, for evry man to speak all Languages, or all men but one, is the same in Effect; except it be more glorious to be acquainted with all. (*CH*, fol. 191v.2)

---

[53] The manuscript reads "crucififixion" at this point.

Traherne assumes that in speaking several languages the Apostles also under-stood them, and thereby negated the effects of the Confusion. Traherne views human "falls" as being *felices culpae* because of the multifarious possibilities they create. Having one prelapsarian language is good, but not as wonderful as over-coming the Confusion and understanding multiple languages which were occa-sioned by the Tower of Babel and dispersion of the people.

Traherne is not alone in seeing Pentecost as a remedy for Babel. Edward Sparke contemplates the "Cloven Tongues" of the Apostles and their resulting ability to convert the Nations:

> They spake with divers tongues, as, &c. these tongues then betokened the *Gift of Languages*, wherby they were enabled to perform that great taske Christ had set them, *Go forth and teach, &c.* See, God never giveth a bur-then, but withall strength to bear it: if he will have them teach, he will fur-nish them with Tongues. . . .[54]

Similarly, Anthony Sparrow, in *Rationale Upon the Book of Common-Prayer*, says that the multiple tongues of the Apostles were a divine gift.[55] Traherne cites the works of both authors in his *Church's Year Book*. However, he differs from these writers in associating the gift of tongues with the Babel episode itself; for Tra-herne, the Confusion is a blessing.

Looking at another facet of the "vaste Advantage" of learning new languag-es, Traherne dramatically depicts the moment when two people meet and find they can communicate. In the poem at the end of the entry he enacts the Babel episode:

> They feel no Hurt; and yet they all complain.
> There's nothing seen in all the troubled Throng,
> But Hurrying and Confusion: Crowding here,
> And scattering there! A Blasted Facultie
> Is the Sole cause of all their miserie. (*CH*, fol. 192r.1)

Amidst this terrifying confusion two people meet and find they have the same language: "At last some one or two meet; that conceiv / What either speaks; then all the rest they leav" (*CH*, fol. 192r.1). Communication becomes the pri-mary link replacing blood ties, as the people at Babel leave their families and join with those who have the same language. This new discovery is made all the more sweet having been preceded by loss and confusion: "This sad Distress made noth-ing else so Sweet, / As the Convenience of a Soul to meet" (*CH*, fol. 192r.1).

---

[54] Edward Sparke, *Scintilla Altaris* (London, 1652), 167.

[55] Anthony Sparrow, *Rationale Upon the Book of Common-Prayer* (London, 1655), 198.

Traherne's interpretation of the Babel episode gives us insight into his definition of perfection. Diffusive energy and ever-expanding possibilities excite the poet and surmount initial restrictions found in a given act, in this instance a linguistic Fall. He acknowledges that there may be a debate amongst language reformers as to whether or not Babel is an object of bliss or misery, but the outcome depends upon one's perspective. His entry "Babel" in the *Commentaries of Heaven* depicts both sides of the issue, the negative and the positive interpretation of Babel. The entry's concluding poem beginning with the ambiguous words, "A Spiritual Stroak upon the Tongue, / Is now the Object of my Dubious Song" (*CH*, fol. 192r.1), alerts Traherne's reader to the two interpretations of the Babel episode. Though he ultimately celebrates the resulting variety of languages, he is not oblivious to the strife between different countries due in part to the difference in language:

> There had no English been,
> No French, no Spaniards, no contest between
> The Dutch and France: Hebrew had been the Tongue
> Of all the World, nor had I made this Song.
> Well then may Babel be a Joy to me
> Tho tis to some perhaps a miserie. (*CH*, fol. 192r.1)

Above he alludes to the wars of religion between Protestant Netherlands and Catholic France. He also suggests that his own song in English would not have existed without Babel.

St. Irenaeus posits that sin is essentially a misevaluation of things, a philosophy that Traherne ultimately adopts. Being acquainted with Bliss, he sees Babel as a glorious occurrence. The project of the *Commentaries of Heaven* is to reveal all things as objects of happiness. The commonplace and miserable may be reevaluated to reveal Felicity. Thus he shows the Confusion unfolding into blissful diversity. We have seen Traherne fluctuating between varying points of view — the benefits of Adam's solitude and the necessity of Eve's conversation; solipsism and communal living; silence and speech; the curse of Babel and the blessing of multiple languages. Though he was a political conformist, celebrating unity under one monarch and one national church, this unity did not necessitate sameness or uniformity in his theological outlook. This sentiment is found throughout the poet's works as he insists on marrying contrarieties into his vision of Felicity.

Tuning the World:
Traherne, Psalms, and Praise

Raymond-Jean Frontain
University of Central Arkansas

Reformation purification or simplification of communal ritual, and the corresponding intensification of emphasis placed upon the individual's interior state, challenged seventeenth-century Christians to reset the balance between private and public prayer, between the spiritual needs of the self and those of the community.[1]

---

[1] Stanley Stewart summarizes a major ideological conflict between dissenting and establishment clergy at Oxford during Traherne's undergraduate days at Brasenose College during the last eight years of the Cromwellian protectorate. University members who had broken with the Anglican communion "argued that the thrust of the Reformation was toward reliance on the self rather than on church hierarchy, and away from the established liturgy toward spontaneous prayer and praise." But faculty and students who continued to adhere to the Church of England "perceived in the Puritan emphasis on the individual's reading of Scripture a kind of *hybris*, a self-centered quality with far-reaching religious and political implications. If every man were equally qualified to read and understand Scripture, and if that understanding alone could guide him to the sole salvation, what would become of the holy church?" (*Expanded Voice: The Art of Thomas Traherne* [San Marino, CA: Huntington Library, 1970], 8).Traherne's attempt to create a "circle of praise" in *Centuries* should be read in the light of this tension between the individual and the congregation, between private and public acts of devotion.

Throughout I am indebted to Louis Martz's analysis of Traherne's reliance upon Augustinian techniques and Bonaventurean spirituality as he "sought a way toward God without the help of the old ecclesiastical establishment" following "the collapse of ancient institutions in the middle of the seventeenth century" (*The Paradise Within: Studies in Vaughan, Traherne, and Milton* [New Haven: Yale University Press, 1964], 37).

Ramie Targoff's recent analysis of the language of public devotion in early modern England offers important, and oftentimes surprising, qualifications to traditional understandings of Catholic and Protestant paradigms of religious behavior. Nonetheless her work illustrates how difficult it was in the seventeenth century to set the balance between public and private prayer, between communal and individual devotion. See Ramie Targoff, *Common Prayer: The Language of Public Devotion in Early Modern England* (Chicago: University of Chicago Press, 2001).

One response to this challenge was the renewed emphasis placed upon the ecclesiastical custom of communal psalm-singing, David and his supposedly spontaneous ejaculations in the Psalms serving as a biblical model for individual devotion put to communal use. The seventeenth-century lyric poet or meditational writer discovered in David a model by which one person's praise of God inspires others to perform the same, private prayer having a ripple effect that expands through the community and unites the earthly and heavenly choirs in a circle of praise that tunes the world, bringing it closer to its prelapsarian harmony.[2]

The ecstatic voice of religious praise sounds in Thomas Traherne's *Centuries of Meditation* (circa 1670–1674), which — excepting John Bunyan's *Pilgrim's Progress* (1675) — is the last great work of English Reformation literature. In his epigraph Traherne reveals that he has written his book for "the friend of my best friend," Mrs. Susanna Hopton, his beloved sister in Christ, "That she may write my Makers prais therin / And make her self therby a Cherubin."[3] And in his pivotal *Third*

---

[2] John Donne — a poet who, like Traherne, is often associated with the metaphysical or "private" mode of devotion rather than with "social" concerns — also tried to work out the balance between private and public prayer. "Christ loves not singularity; he called not one alone," Donne reminded his auditors in St. Paul's Cathedral (*The Sermons of John Donne*, ed. Evelyn M. Simpson and George R. Potter, 10 vols. [Berkeley: University of California Press, 1953–1962], 2: 280). Elsewhere he stresses the efficacy of public, communal prayer for the private individual:

> Whilst thou art a member of that Congregation, that speaks to God with a thousand tongues, beleeve that thou speakest to God with all those tongues. And though thou know thine own prayers unworthy to come up to God, because thou liftest up to him an eye, which is but not withdrawne from a licentious glancing, and hands which are guilty yet of unrepented uncleannesses, a tongue that hath but lately blasphemed God, a heart which even now breaks the walls of this house of God, and steps home, or runs abroad upon the memory, or upon the new plotting of pleasurable or profitable purposes, though this make thee thinke thine own prayers uneffectuall, yet beleeve that some honester man then thy selfe stands by thee, and that when he prayes with thee, he prayes for thee; and that, if there be one righteous man in the Congregation, thou art made the more acceptable to God by his prayers. . . . (*Sermons* 7: 233)

On Donne's being inspired by the psalms to create a "circle of praise" such as the one that Traherne creates in *Centuries*, see Raymond-Jean Frontain, "Translating Heavenwards: 'Upon the Translation of the Psalmes' and John Donne's Poetics of Praise," *Explorations in Renaissance Culture* 22 (1996): 103–25.

[3] Thomas Traherne, *Centuries, Poems, and Thanksgiving*, ed. H. M. Margoliouth, 2 vols., corrected ed. (Oxford: Clarendon Press, 1972), I.2. Subsequent citations are from this edition. Citations note the volume by roman, and page number by arabic, numeral. I distinguish citations of Traherne's *Centuries* by the abbreviation "*CM*" preceding the Century and section number.

Century Traherne emphasizes that he himself learned his lyric exuberance from David. That is, Traherne, having learned from David how to praise God, shares his private meditations with Mrs. Hopton in order that she might herself learn how to praise her Creator and transform herself spiritually: *Centuries* forms the critical link in a chain in which the gift of praise that has been made by David to Traherne is in turn passed along to Mrs. Hopton. An additionally curious feature of the text is that, although it was not published in Traherne's lifetime or apparently intended for circulation beyond Traherne's immediate devotional circle, the general reader of the printed text, projected from profane to sacred time by the cyclical structure of each "century" of hundred meditations or years, is, like Mrs. Hopton, called upon to complete and thus perfect the fragmentary fifth century. The print reader is thus drawn into a series of circles in which praise ripples outward from God at the center, to David and his psalms, and finally to Traherne and his meditations; the reader who is inspired to praise God after reading Traherne's *Centuries* creates a new ring, expanding that circle further.

Traherne's *Centuries* thus posits a complex literary and spiritual operation, one intended to create an ever-expanding interpretive community. The individual devotion recorded in a holograph manuscript possesses the potential to recreate the Christian community; a private voice hopes to stimulate and reform public worship; and the ecstatic voice of the poet in his private meditation sounds as part of a cosmic harmony. The inspiration for, and instigation of, such a complex operation is David's praise of God in the Psalms.

Psalm-Singing and Tuning the World

That the Psalms served as a model for the seventeenth-century religious lyric has been noted, among others, by Lily Bess Campbell, Harold Fisch, Anthony Low, and Barbara K. Lewalski.[4] But the Psalms made available to the devotional poet more than a lyrical model. Psalm-singing, and particularly the action of praise associated with psalm-singing, was seen by both the church fathers and the Protestant Reformers as an important agency for wide-scale spiritual renovation, allowing the individual Christian the means of participating in the "tuning" of the world.

---

[4] Lily Bess Campbell, *Divine Poetry and Drama in Sixteenth-Century England* (Cambridge: Cambridge University Press, and Berkeley: University of California Press, 1959); Harold Fisch, *Jerusalem and Albion: The Hebraic Factor in Seventeenth-Century Literature* (London: Routledge and Kegan Paul, 1964); Anthony Low, *Love's Architecture: Devotional Modes in Seventeenth-Century English Poetry* (New York: New York University Press, 1978); and Barbara Lewalski, *Protestant Poetics and the Seventeenth-Century Religious Lyric* (Princeton: Princeton University Press, 1979).

For the Reformers and early Christians alike, the biblical commandment regarding psalm-singing was clear. "And be not drunk with wine, wherein is excess," Paul admonished the Ephesians, "but be filled with the Spirit; speaking to yourselves in psalms and hymns and spiritual songs, singing and making melody in your heart to the Lord."[5] By reciting the Psalms, Athanasius explained in his influential *Letter to Marcellinus*, the prayerful man "becom[es] himself a stringful instrument" and allows the Holy Spirit to play upon him; his perverse will is emptied and he "may obey in all his members and emotions, and serve the will of God. The harmonious reading of the Psalms is a figure and type of such undisturbed and calm equanimity of our thoughts."[6] It is for this reason that the Psalms were thought to possess a remarkable therapeutic power.[7] As Diodore of Tarsus noted, they "calm carnal passions, . . . [and] evil inclinations[;] chase demons away[;] . . . they heal the wounds that life has struck."[8] Hymns drawn from the Bible, counseled Milton in *The Reason of Church Government* (1642), "are of power . . . to allay the perturbations of the mind and set the affections in right tune."[9]

---

[5] Eph. 5: 18–19 (King James Version). The theme is continued in the Apocrypha, the wise man in Ecclesiasticus encouraging his followers to "lift your voices in song, / praising the Lord for all he has done. / Ascribe majesty to his name / and give thanks to him with praise, / with harps and the singing of songs" (Ecclus. 39: 14–15; see also 39: 35); I quote the Apocrypha from *The Oxford Study Bible* (New York: Oxford University Press, 1992). Ecclesiasticus insists that it is the duty of humankind to sing praise for whatever comes, trusting that at the appropriate moment God's purpose will be revealed.

[6] *Athanasius*, ed. and trans. Robert C. Gregg, Classics of Western Spirituality (New York: Paulist Press, 1980), 124. Important statements concerning the Psalms are collected in J. M. Neale and R. F. Littlefield, *A Commentary on the Psalms from the Primitive and Medieval Writers; and from the Various Office-books and Hymns of the Roman, Mozarabic, Ambrosian, Gallican, Greek, Armenian, and Syriac Ritual*, 4th ed. (London: Joseph Master, 1884; repr. New York: AMS Press, 1976); and Edward A. Gosselin, *The King's Progress to Jerusalem: Some Interpretations of David during the Reformation Period and Their Patristic and Medieval Background* (Malibu: Undena Publications, 1976). Martin Luther, "Preface to the Psalms" (1528), in *Martin Luther: Selections from His Writings*, ed. John Dillenberger (Garden, City, NY: Doubleday-Anchor, 1961), 37–41; and George Wither, *A Preparation to the Psalter (1619)*, Spenser Society 37 (New York: Burt Franklin, 1967) are two important Reformation discussions that make many of the same claims about the Psalms' power as Dante, Milton, and Donne make.

[7] Recitation of the Psalms was in fact a principal part of the monastic office.

[8] Quoted in Eric Werner, *The Sacred Bridge: The Interdependence of Liturgy and Music in Synagogue and Church during the First Millennium* (New York: Columbia University Press, 1959), 148.

[9] John Milton, *Complete Poems and Major Prose*, ed. Merritt Y. Hughes (New York: Macmillan, 1957), 669. Subsequent citations of Milton's works are from this edition. Richard Rolle similarly praises the Psalms as a "medicyne of wordes":

The Psalms' ability, in Richard Rolle's estimation, "To stirre to more deuo-cyowne"[10] — that is, to deepen devotion in those who hear the songs sung — makes a world in which they are regularly sung one of spiritual equanimity.[11] Jerome painted such a scene of life in fourth-century Bethlehem for his friend Marcella, who had remained in Rome:

> In Christ's humble cottage there is only rustic simplicity; except for the chanting of psalms, silence is perfect. Wherever you go, the husbandman sings the alleluia over his plough; the toiling harvester refreshes himself with the psalms; the vine dresser prunes his vine to a song of David. These are the popular songs of this country; the love songs of the shepherd's whistle; the lyrics of the farmer as he tills the soil with devotion.[12]

Grete haboundance of gastly comfort and ioy in god comes in the hertes of thaim at says or synges deuotly the psalmes in louynge of ihesu crist. Thai drope swetnes in mannys saule and hellis delite in thaire thoghtis and kyndlis thaire willes with the fyre of luf, mankand thaim hate and brennand withinen, and faire and lufly in cristis eghen. And thaim that lastes in thaire deuocioun, thair rays thaim in til contemplatyf lyf, & oft sith in til soun & myrth of heuen.

Quoted in Michael P. Kuczynski, *Prophetic Song: The Psalms as Moral Discourse in Late Medieval England* (Philadelphia: University of Pennsylvannia Press, 1995), 12–13.

[10] Quoted in Kuczynski, *Prophetic Song*, 16.

[11] As Kuczynski notes, in early Christian and medieval communities liturgical repetition of a psalm was thought to increase the poem's "authority as a form of morally prophetic utterance, because its affective power is thereby enhanced," making the recitation "more likely to provoke a powerful sense of identification in others" (*Prophetic Song*, 57). What is more, for Augustine and the commentators who follow him, "psalmody is a private practice with a profoundly public significance and effect. It is a form of personal prayer and social action" (67):

> "Augustine . . . insists in his sermon that his congregation recite the words of Psalm 50 not only for themselves, but for all those who are absent — that is, for the entire Christian community. The individual or private significance of David's example and psalm meditation, for him, must always be connected with their communal or public aspect. Experiencing the moral benefits of David imitation entails the responsibility of actively distributing these fruits to others, in the form of psalm-based language and actions. . . . For him, private Davidic imitation is useless if it does not generate new forms of social behavior: patterns of ethical speech and activity based in [sic] David's example and the language of the Psalms" (66).

[12] *The Homilies of Saint Jerome*, Vol. 1, trans. Sister Marie Liguori Ewald (Washington: Catholic University of America Press, 1964), xi–xii (Letter 46.11, PL 22.491).

Psalm-singing replaces the singing of idle, lascivious songs among people whose seriousness of spiritual purpose is most clearly indicated by their transforming the most ordinary of daily tasks into acts of devotion. Jerome's vision of heaven on earth exercised a powerful influence on many of the Reformers. Will the Dreamer spends his time at the loom reciting psalms in Langland's *Piers Plowman*,[13] and in his *Paraclesis*, Erasmus notes how happy he would be if

> the ploughman holdynge the plough dyd synge somwhat of the mystycall Psalmes in his owne mother tonge[;] yea and yf the wever, syttyng at his worke, dyd synge somewhat of the gospell, for his solace and comforte in his labours[;] & moreover yf the mayster of the shyppe, syttyng faste at the sterne, do synge also somewhat of the same[;] and for to make an ende yf the wedded wyfe, when she sytteth at her dystaffe, have some companyon, or kynneswoman nere unto her which doth reade and reherse somewhat herof unto her.[14]

The desire to realize Jerome's ideal motivated Reformers to make metrical versions of the Psalms available in the vernacular. In the introduction to his *Ghoastley Psalmes and Spirituall Songes*, for example, Miles Coverdale expresses his hope that

> Yea, would God that our minstrels had none other thing to play upon, neither our carters and ploughmen other thing to whistle upon, save psalms, hymns, and such godly songs as David is occupied withal! And if women, sitting at their rocks, or spinning at their wheels, had none other songs to pass their time withal, that such as Moses' sister, Glehana's wife, Debora, and Mary the mother of Christ, have sung before them, they should be better occupied with *hey nony nony, hey troly troly,* and such like phantasies. . . . For truly, as we love, so sing we; and where our affection is, thence cometh our mirth and joy.[15]

This was also the avowed purpose of Clément Marot in providing a French metrical psalter. As he exclaims in the Preface to the 1543 edition:

> O bien heureux qui voyr pourra
> Florir le temps que l'on orra

---

[13] See Kuczynski's discussion both of the importance of the Psalms to Langland (*Prophetic Song*, 189–90), and of "the ideal Christian community" described by Langland's Conscience in which everyone is engaged in psalm recitation (213), which is strikingly similar to Jerome's.

[14] Quoted in Campbell, *Divine Poetry and Drama*, 18–19.

[15] Quoted in Charles A. Huttar, "English Metrical Paraphrases of the Psalms, 1500–1640" (Ph.D. diss., Northwestern University, 1956), 84.

Le labourer a sa charrue,
Le charretier parmy la rue,
Et l'artisan en sa boutique,
Avecques un Pseaume ou Cantique,
En son labeur se soulager.[16]

So widespread was Jerome's vision of a psalm-singing New Jerusalem that William Slayter, "in the introduction to his 1643 edition of the Psalms[,] . . . enumerates the ploughman on land, the shipman at sea, the master at helm, the delver at his spade, the scholar wearied at his studies, etc., all as ardent singers of the Psalms."[17] And even Shakespeare's Sir John Falstaff could swear, when disappointed by an unhappy turn of events, that this is "a bad world, I say. I would I were a weaver; I could sing psalms or any thing."[18]

Liturgically, responsorial psalm-singing was intended to unite the Christian community in heartfelt praise of its creator.[19] Early Christians believed that when

---

[16] Quoted in Huttar, "English Metrical Paraphrases," 41.

[17] Philip von Rohr-Sauer, *English Metrical Psalms from 1600 to 1660: A Study in the Religious and Aesthetic Trends of That Period* (Freiburg: Poppen and Ortmann, 1938), 36.

[18] William Shakespeare, *Henry the Fourth, Part One*, in *The Riverside Shakespeare*, ed. G. Blakemore Evans (Boston: Houghton, 1974), 2.4.132–34. The Ferrars nearly achieved this ideal in their community at Little Gidding. An observer noted that, as a result of Nicholas Ferrar's bribing the village children to memorize psalms, one might hear

the houses, and doores, and Streets Sound out the Sweet Musick of Davids harp in all places and at all times of the day, the weomen hearing and the Children repeating and conning the Psalms with out Book as they Sat a Spinning and Knitting: when as before those Childrens mouths and tongues were exercised dayly . . . in Singing of naughty, leaud, and at least Vain Songs and Ballets. (Quoted in Low, *Love's Architecture*, 16)

Failing to recognize that the theme derives ultimately from Jerome, Stephen Greenblatt (*Renaissance Self-Fashioning: From More to Shakespeare* [Chicago: University of Chicago Press, 1980], 106) adduces the influence of Erasmus upon a variation of this motif in William *Tyndale's Obedience of a Christian Man*.

[19] As Theodor Klauser notes, early Christians continued in their services the synagogue practice of psalm-singing (*A Short History of the Western Liturgy*, trans. John Halliburton, 2nd edition [Oxford: Oxford University Press, 1979], 5). By the end of the fourth century, however, psalm-singing had become "the staple element in prayer, a development which had been effected long before the foundation of the first monasteries" (Klauser, *Short History*, 9–10). But as James Anderson Winn observes, Pope Gregory the Great's promulgation of the melodically uniform chant which continues to bear his name was intended to effect as much a political as a spiritual uniformity in Christendom (*Unsuspected Eloquence: A History of the Relations between Poetry and Music* [New Haven: Yale University Press, 1981], 56–57).

the minister's or choir's chant was answered by the congregation's sung response, the ideal of *koinonia* or "unison" in community was realized, and the imperfect earthly realm was transmuted into the heavenly kingdom on earth.[20] Praising David for writing the Psalms, and through them for inspiring human beings to praise their creator, John Chrysostom exclaimed that David "excites the praises of God . . . , congregating the servants of God into seraphic bands, turn[ing] earth into heaven, and convert[ing] men into angels."[21] Thomas Mace, a seventeenth-century Anglican, described just such a conversion. In *Music's Monument* (1676), he narrates how the inhabitants of York met on eleven successive Sundays in 1644 as Cromwell's army besieged the city:

> the whole congregation sang a Psalm, together with the quire and the organ: and you must know, that there was then a most excellent, large, plump, lusty, full-speaking organ. . . . This organ, I say, when the Psalm was set before the sermon, being let out into all its fullness of stops, together with the quire, began the Psalm. But when the vast-concording unity of the whole congregational-chorus, came, as I may say, thundering in, even so as it made the very ground shake under us: oh the unutterable ravishing soul's delight! in the which I was so transported and wrapt up in high contemplations, that there was no room left in my whole man, viz., body, soul, and spirit, for any thing below Divine and heavenly raptures: nor could there possibly be any thing to which that very singing might be truly compared, except the right apprehension or conceiving of that glorious and miraculous quire, recorded in the scriptures at the dedication of the temple.[22]

Participation in "that vast-concording unity of the whole congregational chorus" was an act of purification for Mace. It joined him in harmony not only with his neighbors in praise of God, but with the biblical community of praise and devotion, and with the angelic choir as well. This sense of being translated heavenwards — of joining with the heavenly choir while still on earth — was the desired result of congregational psalm-singing.[23]

---

[20] Werner, *The Sacred Bridge*, 134.

[21] Quoted in Neale and Littlefield, *A Commentary on the Psalms*, 1–2.

[22] Quoted in John Holland, *The Psalmists of Britain*, 2 vols. (London: R. Groombridge, 1843), 1:52–53.

[23] The phrase "translating heavenwards" comes from John Donne's "Upon the translation of the Psalmes," in *Complete Poetry*, ed. John T. Shawcross (Garden City, NY: Doubleday-Anchor, 1967), 388–90. See my reading of this poem (Frontain, "Translating Heavenwards"), from which I adapt here the section on "Psalm-Singing and Tuning the World." Book 5, chapters 37–39, of Richard Hooker's *Of the Laws of Ecclesiastical Polity*

Milton's "At a Solemn Musick" summarizes the musical "myth" that relates language to religious worship and spiritual reform.[24] In the prelapsarian, song-filled universe, angels sang "Hymns devout and holy Psalms," for to obey God is to sing his praise. "Disproportion'd" sin, however, struck everything out of tune.[25] After Satan's rebellion, there are in heaven only those faithful angels whose song may inspire men on earth to sing with them. Spiritually astute persons attempt to put the world back in tune and aid in its redemption by overcoming their sinful natures and remaining obedient to divine law; thus, in *Paradise Lost* prelapsarian Adam and Eve awaken every morning and sing spontaneously their Maker's praise, a litany in which all creation joins (5.144–208). This is the power of psalms and hymns for Milton: when men sing "at a solemn musick" they renew the world, joining "Voice" to "Verse" in the creation of a hymn of praise, and uniting human with angelic voice in a harmonious praise of their joint Maker.[26]

(ed. A. S. McGrade and Brian Vickers [New York: St. Martin's Press, 1975]) answer Puritan objections to singing or antiphonally reciting psalms by recalling the history of, and emphasizing the harmony that results from, the practice.

[24] The poem appears in Milton, *Complete Poems*, 81–82.

[25] Clement of Alexandria notes that the musical voice of God "composed the universe into melodious order, and tuned the discord of the elements to harmonious arrangement, so that the whole world might become harmony." David, according to Clement, imitates that divine process of creation by making himself the instrument on which the Holy Spirit plays: "And He who is of David, and yet before him, the Word of God, despising the lyre and harp, which are but lifeless instruments, and having tuned by the Holy Spirit the universe, and especially man — who, composed of body and soul, is a universe in miniature — makes melody to God on this instrument of many tones" (quoted in S.K. Henninger, Jr., *Touches of Sweet Harmony: Pythagorean Cosmology and Renaissance Poetics* [San Marino, CA: Huntington Library, 1974], 212–13). John Donne similarly summarizes creation and salvation history in terms of harmony and dissonance: "God made this whole world in such an uniformity, such a correspondency, such a concinnity of parts, as that it was an Instrument, perfectly in tune: we may say, the trebles, the highest strings were disordered first; the best understandings, Angels and Men, put this instrument out of tune. God rectified it all again, by putting in a new string, *semen mulieris*, the seed of the woman, the *Messiah*. . . . Gods hand tun'd it the second time. . . ." (*Sermons* 2: 170).

[26] In his translation of Francesco Giovanni Loredano's *The Ascents of the Soul* (1681), Henry Lord Coleraine observes how the unified understanding or apprehension allowed by the psalms models the unification of heaven and earth: "I have fancied the whole Piece [Loredano's *Ascents*] to be a sketch of *Jacob*'s Vision, and *David*'s Psalter, like *Israel*'s Scale, reaching to the Divine Throne, whereon devout Spirits have scope to run descant up and down, and by the various Motions of their Piety, (as by the several Degrees of their Understandings) they make better Music than the imagin'd Spheres could ever be supposed to do: For surely, thereupon is grounded the best Harmony of Heaven and Earth" (quoted in Stewart, *Expanded Voice*, 99–100).

This confluence of angelic and human praise implies a circular dynamic in which one choir inspires the second to sing, the end result being that harmony is reestablished throughout the cosmos, if only for the moment of song. The circle, of course, images perfection, and it is through such a "circle of praise" that the broken world is returned closer to its original prelapsarian harmony. The function of the human poet in such a system is to set off a chain reaction, his praise of a superior being inspiring others to begin singing praise as well. What is more, there is something spiritually self-righting about reciting praise of another (especially of God) in that it functions as an erasure of ego, as the performance of humility before a superior power, as the acquiescence, even, of one's will to a superior will. Praise, thus, contributes to the reharmonization of the world.

Praise in *Centuries*

"O that I were as *David*, the Sweet Singer of *Israel*! / In meeter Psalms to set forth thy [Christ's] Praises," exclaims Traherne in *The Thanksgivings* (2.223). Traherne's emulation of David, Michael Ponsford has argued, aims at "the spiritual fusion of his own personality with that of David."

> The discovery of David is really the discovery of a second self, allowing their personalities to merge. This is, perhaps, a "metaphysical" seeking of unity in diversity, but it has little in common with the troubled awareness of self that characterizes the work of the metaphysical poets. It is part of the larger theme of communication, as David's communication with God eventually becomes a communion, which Traherne, in his emulation of David, is himself capable of sharing.[27]

Ponsford astutely points to Traherne's imitation of David as an attempt to ascend towards felicity by emulating "the sublimity of the poetry of David."[28] Such imitation, however, serves a wider purpose, the spiritual "tuning" or reharmonizing of the world. Ponsford intuits this when he speaks of Traherne's move toward coherency, of combining two in one. But he overlooks how essential the action of praise is to achieving this coherency. For, humbled by his consciousness of the gifts that he has received from his Creator, Traherne can respond only in praise. Aware, however, that his praise can never prove adequate recompense for

---

[27] Michael Ponsford, "Men after God's Own Heart: The Context of Thomas Traherne's Emulation of David," *Studia Mystica* 9 (1986): 3–11, here 10.

[28] Ponsford, "Men after God's Own Heart," 6.

God's extraordinary gifts, Traherne aspires to be as sublime a poet as David, the purported author of the biblical Book of Psalms; for, if the function of poetry is to praise God, then the great model of poetry is the Psalms. Significantly, as becomes clear in the *Centuries*, the first step towards praising God is praising David for having led the way and taught others how to do so themselves. And by "becoming" David, Traherne in turn positions himself as a model for "the friend of my friend," the spiritually earnest Mrs. Hopton. Traherne's identification with David re-initiates a process of praise and imitation intended to reawaken the understanding of others and, thus, spiritualize the world.

The process is made clear in *Centuries* 3:70 where Traherne, narrating how he came to understand the significance of that creation which led him as a child to his first experience of felicity, explains that

> When I saw those Objects celebrated in His [David's] Psalmes which GOD and Nature had proposed to me, and which I thought chance only presented to my view: you cannot imagine how unspeakably I was delighted, to see so Glorious a Person, so Great a Prince, so Divine a Sage, that was a Man after Gods own Heart by the testimony of God Himself, rejoycing in the same things, meditating on the same and Praising GOD for the same. For by this I perceived we were led by one Spirit: and that following the clew of Nature into this Labyrinth I was brought into the midst of Celestial Joys: and that to be retired from Earthly Cares and fears and Distractions that we might in sweet and heavenly Peace contemplat all the Works of GOD, was to live in Heaven and the only way to becom what David was a Man after Gods own Heart. There we might be enflamed with those Causes for which we ought to lov Him: there we might see those Viands which feed the Soul with Angels food [Psalm 78:25]: there might Bath in those Streams of Pleasure that flow at His Right Hand for evermore [Psalm 16:11].

Enjoyment of felicity initially risked isolating the young Traherne, who thought that "chance only presented [the glories of Nature] to *my* view" (emphasis added). Discovering in David's psalms a similar enjoyment of the created world made Traherne aware that a creator, not chance, had put nature before his view, and that nature was created for others as well as for himself.

At issue is the process of "understanding." For Traherne, the world was not created to be possessed physically or exploited economically, but to engage His creatures with their Creator:

> the Way to becom Rich and Blessed, was not by heaping Accidental and Devised Riches to make ourselvs great in the vulgar maner, but to approach more near, and to see more Clearly with the Ey of our understanding, the Beauties and Glories of the whole world: and to hav communion with the Deity in the Riches of GOD and Nature. (*CM* 3.67)

Things that the majority assume will provide greatness are, paradoxically, those which in actuality create spiritual poverty. Rather than thinking about "heaping" or hoarding money, the Christian should meditate constantly upon the great gift of creation and be filled with praise of the divine Donor. And this Traherne claims to have learned from reading the Psalms of David. "You are never truly Great till all the World is yours," Traherne explains in *Centuries* 2.14, "and the Goodness of the Donor so much your Joy, that you think upon it all day long. Which King David, the Royal Man, well understood, when He said; My Lips shall be filled with thy Prais, and thy Honor all the Day [Psalm 71:8 (variant)]." This mention of David as the model of the man who understands the importance of praise — as the "Royal Man" who, rather than expecting to receive the tribute of praise from his inferiors, instead offers praise to his superior — is, significantly, the first reference to him in *Centuries*. David, thus, is introduced as the model of understanding, whose right perception results in praise, "the very End for which the World was created" (*CM* 3.82). David is the single great model of how a creature lives in this world, his Psalms inviting others to "hav a Communion . . . in a Rational Knowledg of the . . . Nature and Excellency" of "Gods Works and Ways and Laws" (*CM* 3.92).

David's praise of the Creator leads Traherne in *Centuries* 3.69 to attempt his own "psalm" in which he praises David for teaching him to praise God.[29] The poem is preceded by Traherne's account in *Centuries* 3.66 of how he discovered, only by reading the Psalms, that his meditations upon God's goodness in creating the world could be accounted prayer. This discovery spurred him to unite his private ruminations in "the Way of Communion with God in all Saints, as I saw Clearly in the Person of David." David delivered him from solipsism, from being enclosed in private thought; because of David, Traherne's private prayer is now part of a larger, cosmic operation. Thus, it is not surprising that in his poem Traherne emphasizes that David's most enjoying himself "when he / Did as a Poet prais the Deitie" (39–40) is evidence of his correct understanding and behavior. David is "a Glorious King" (1) not in the traditional sense of earthly power and might (a subtle rebuke of the restored, pleasure-loving Charles II?), but because, paradoxically, "He before his GOD did kneel" (77). David was transformed by his humility: "Raisd from a Shepherds lowly State" (2), he became not only "a Glorious King" but "A Constantly Heavenly Pure Seraphick Flame" (76–78), singing in the angelic choir while still on earth.

David's song, Traherne emphasizes, was his way of participating in an echoing, responsive universe. "Enflamd with Lov it was his great Desire, / To Sing Contemplat Ponder and Admire" (129–130). Yet when "His fingers touched his Trembling

---

[29] Failing to recognize the importance of Traherne's identification with David, Martz dismisses this poem as "a piece of labored didacticism, where the virtues of David are merely asserted" (*Paradise Within*, 95).

Lyre, / And every Quavering String did yeeld," his song resonated outwardly to fill "all the Jewish Quire / And Ecchoed in the Field" (21–24). His song had a harmonizing affect on "Those that did his Heavenly musick hear," for "every Drop that from his flowing Quill / Came down, did all the World with Nectar fill" (48–50). The sin-soured world is sweeter for the presence of David's song, but David's song also makes his listeners more conscious of the sweetness of God's original creation. And just as his music echoes in the ears of his auditors, so does his personal example. Despite having "Advanced unto Thrones," David sought no more "Sublime Reward" than to "Delight . . . in the Stars" (6–10). Similarly Traherne concludes his poem with an expression of his own new-found ambition: "Oh that I might unto His Throne Aspire; / And all His Joys abov the Stars Admire!" (79–80). As David understood the entirely relative value of earthly kingship and gave himself over to service of the heavenly king, so Traherne aspires to serve the divine poet David. And as David most enjoyed himself in writing poems in praise of the Deity, so Traherne writes a poem in praise of David, further filling the world with song.

The result is the reunification of the sin-splintered world or reharmonization of the disproportioned universe. In stanza 5, David is celebrated for unifying all his roles in praise.

> A Shepherd, Soldier, and Divine,
> A Judge, a Courtier, and a King,
> Priest, Angel, Prophet, Oracle did shine
> At once; when He did sing. (41–44)

What is more, the poem celebrates how David's "Clear Soul and Open Sight" allowed him alone among mortal men to see and hear the celestial harmony, resulting in the paradox that "when He was alone He all became" (65–69). That is, when he was alone in meditation or standing apart from the frenetic crowd, he was most fully united with his Creator and appreciative of His Creation, and thus most able to escape the solipsism that prevents humans from enjoying Felicity. But also, that he alone among humankind was so appreciative of the divine Donor's gifts that he could enter into the cosmic harmony and fully enjoy them all. Appropriately, the poem plays on the paradox of all-in-one, as one activity — praise — allows the Christian access to the All.

Praise of David, who was the original poet to write in praise of God, was a major part of Traherne's vocation. David's inspiration upon Traherne, however, is but part of what is, suggestively, an ever-expanding process. The *Centuries*, Traherne emphasizes at the outset, were intended as a devotional guide for, or spiritual aid to, Mrs. Susannah Hopton, "the friend of my best friend,"

> That she may write my Makers prais therin
> And make her self therby a Cherubin. (2)

David taught Traherne to praise, just as Traherne now teaches Mrs. Hopton. And just as David became through his song an angel on earth, so Mrs. Hopton through praise may "make her self . . . a Cherubin." The world is spiritualized through praise, human voices on earth joining with the angelic choir in heaven in praise of their creator.

Traherne's collapsing of his spiritual identity with Mrs. Hopton's, and of hers with Christ's — in addition to his encouragement of shared authorship — should be considered part of what Stanley Stewart calls "the leitmotiv of dissolving boundaries" in *Centuries*:

> This is the special thematic function of the opening quatrain and the blank leaves left at the end of the text. These pages remain for the original donor of the volume to fill. Presumably this friend, Hopton . . . , is to fill the empty pages with new wonders. The pages are a tabula rasa to be filled with "words," thus imitating the original "Creation" of the "Word." More than a hyperbolic statement of affection and trust, the collaboration is, in effect, a defining act of the speaker's character. In creating his "word," he creates the opening for "her" response ("I send / That she may write"). His love for the friend emerges as thematic and structural evidence of a will to accept — as his — her freedom to create *him* anew, and by this act, to create herself: "And make herself therby a Cherubin."[30]

It is important to emphasize as well, however, how Traherne's insistence upon shared authorship participates in the outward rippling of praise and union, and the extent to which praise is an act of self-creation. Traherne's ambiguous construction "the friend of my best friend" suggests an expanding circle of friendship. Traherne's friendship with Mrs. Hopton imitates Christ's friendship with Traherne, providing in turn a model for Mrs. Hopton's relationship with Christ; Traherne's and Mrs. Hopton's friendships interspeak with and redefine each other, just as David's praise of God originally taught Traherne the value of his own.[31]

---

[30] Stanley Stewart, "Thomas Traherne," in *Seventeenth-Century British Nondramatic Writers, Third Series*, ed. M. Thomas Hester, Dictionary of Literary Biography 131 (Detroit: Gale, 1993), 278.

[31] On the collapsing or conflation of identities in *Centuries*, see Stewart, *Expanded Voice*, 111, 114. One of the most significant conflations, of course, is of Traherne's voice with David's. Stewart astutely notes "the emerging dominance of the psalmic voice in the Third Century. The speaker's personality as well as his voice becomes absorbed in the being of another" (*Expanded Voice*, 132) — that is, David. Martz is equally astute in referring to "a duet of praise" being acted out in *Centuries* 3.71–94, the "lavish quotations from the Psalms providing the melody, while Traherne's commentary brings in the second voice" (*Paradise Within*, 95).

Likewise, this expanding circle of friendship possesses a transformative power similar to that which David's writing of Psalms had, for by writing Traherne's Maker's praise in the book, Mrs. Hopton "make[s] her self therby a Cherubin." Humans may not be able to create the world, but they can re-create themselves by praising God. Praise is Mrs. Hopton's way of imitating the divine act of Creation, and she learns it from Traherne, who learned it from David.[32]

As Traherne cautions in *Centuries* 4.99, "a Limitation of Praises" will lead "to the Endangering of the Perfection of Gods Kingdom." Conversely, among "the strange and Wonderfull Things" that necessarily follow from "the Understanding and Affection of the Soul, Traherne counts: "a Return of infinit Thanksgivings . . . [,] A Fulnes of Joy which nothing can exceed . . . [, and] An Infinit Glory in the Communion of the Saints, Every one being a Treasure to all the Residue and Enjoying the Residue, and in the Residue all the Glory of all Worlds" (*CM*, 4.100). Appreciation of the gifts of Creation leads to thanksgiving for or praise of the Creator, as well as an appreciation of others. Individuals are no longer separate entities but a communion, the glory of this world being joined in the glory of all worlds. A shadow of the prelapsarian unity of the cosmos can be glimpsed, if only for the moment of communion, through praise.[33]

The "circle of praise" that Traherne extends in *Centuries* is similar to the chain of influence that Athanasius attempts to construct in his *Letter to Marcellinus*. In commending his friend's diligence in studying the Psalter, Athanasius offers to report to Marcellinus what an "old man" dedicated to their study once told Athanasius about the Psalms. Commentators rarely accept the existence of this third party and often wonder why Athanasius did not admit that the observations that

---

[32] This equation of making with writing and praising is extended in *Centuries* 1.1 where the empty book is imaged as an infant's soul, and the inscription of praise is equated with growth to adulthood. The speaker's writing praise, not sexual intercourse, is how humans share in the divine act of creation. Inscription is creation, Traherne's *Centuries* being "a Mark" of "the Wisest Love" that he bears for Mrs. Hopton, in emulation of the love that Jesus ("my best friend") bore humankind. The blank pages on which she "may write my Makers prais" being the space on which she makes her "Mark" and thereby fashions herself as a part of the angelic choir. Praise of the Maker is both the mark or sign of the wisest love and the means of spiritual self-transformation.

My thinking concerning the rhetorical operations of *Centuries* is indebted to Stewart's superb reading of Traherne's dedicatory poem to Mrs. Hopton in *Expanded Voice*, 103–5.

[33] Although he is concerned with Traherne's promotion of "gratitude" in *Christian Ethicks*, Malcolm Day reaches a similar conclusion concerning the socio-spiritual dynamic of Traherne's writing. "As Traherne explains, Gratitude is necessary to the perfecting of the creation"; "when the individual soul freely completes the intended circulation of Gratitude back to God, a mutual enhancement takes place among all souls" (*Thomas Traherne* [Boston: Twayne, 1982], 39, 40).

followed were his own. But by claiming that the old man had been influenced by the Psalms, and that he, in turn, had been influenced by the old man, Athanasius creates a chain of influence as he himself writes Marcellinus on the subject. Clearly, his hope was that Marcellinus would in turn be inspired to speak of the Psalms to others, that they in turn would do likewise, and that this ripple effect would make for the gradual reharmonization of the world.[34]

By writing to Mrs. Hopton his praise of David, whose psalms had taught Traherne how to praise God, Traherne hoped to draw her within the circle of praise, further extending the resulting harmony through the world, and turning more humans into songful "Cherubin." "Are not Praises the very End for which the World was created?" Traherne asks rhetorically in *Centuries* 3.82. Yes, the reader might answer, and it is the Psalms of David that teach Christians how and why.

Conclusion: Seventeenth-Century Circles of Praise

In *Centuries* Traherne creates a circle of praise in which the person-in-meditation, inspired by David's praise of the Creator, gives himself over to the ecstasy of praise and provides a model that a reader such as Mrs. Hopton may subsequently imitate. And, although no record exists of Mrs. Hopton's response to her counselor's meditations, Traherne may even have hoped that the enhanced devotion of "the friend of my best friend" would in turn have inspired others in their community to imitate Mrs. Hopton, extending the circle of praise further still. Whatever the historical success of Traherne's effort, three conclusions may be drawn from study of his operation.

The first concerns the traditional categorization of Traherne as a poet of private meditation and the larger assumption that meditation or devotion is a private act. The division between "private" and "social" literary modes was popularized

---

[34] Early commentaries on the seven Penitential Psalms emphasized that just as David's psalms were written in response to the reproof that David received from the prophet Nathan (2 Sam.13), Christians imitate David when they respond to the moral reproof that is contained in his psalms (Kuczynski, *Prophetic Song*, 68). The notion of the Psalms being at the center of an expansive moral universe is, thus, an important element in patristic promotion of psalm recitation. Indeed, Augustine "argues that the process of Davidic imitation, beginning with David's imitation of his own moral teacher, Nathan, continues beyond the walls of the church into the home, where the moral lessons others learn from David's poetry must be translated into the prosaic terms of everyday moral discourse and activity. . . . The entire process is one of translation: of David's sentiments and expressions into one's own, and of one's own Davidic sentiments and expressions into those of the wider Christian community" (Kuczynski, *Prophetic Song*, 76).

by Earl Miner in his influential three-volume history of seventeenth-century poetry.[35] Miner's enormously useful distinctions need to be qualified insofar as they fail to take account of the ambivalent ways in which private discourse easily slips into public discourse, or in which a private action can be completed through a public or printed text. Indeed, a major thrust of recent Renaissance scholarship explores how the manuscript circulation of a text, which is seemingly limited to a private, coterie audience, could be a very public act, while a printed, supposedly "public," text (such as Raleigh's *Ocean to Cynthia*) can harbor an intimate message to a single, highly specific reader. Since Bertram E. Dobell first publicized in 1900 William T. Brooke's discovery of the manuscripts of Traherne's *Centuries of Meditation* and *Poems of Felicity*, discussion of Traherne has framed him as the humble, retiring pastor concerned primarily with his own salvation and that of his small flock. Reading *Centuries* within the tradition of psalm recitation and commentary, however, suggests that he was well aware of the social or communal implications of his seemingly private devotional act. Stewart, for example, notes that Traherne did not, like George Herbert, even arrange on his deathbed for the publication of his meditations, suggesting that Traherne was even less concerned with the world outside his parish than the country parson of Bemerton.[36] But by passing his incomplete *Centuries* to Mrs. Hopton and encouraging her to complete the final round of meditations, Traherne clearly hoped to engineer a different kind of circulation among, and use by, a community. The conclusion that Traherne "failed" to publish his work may indicate more about twentieth- and twenty-first-century readers' misunderstanding of how his text was intended to find and complete, as well as be completed by, his audience, than about Traherne's supposed social and literary reservations.

Second, there is the quintessentially religious nature of the extended rhetorical community intended by *Centuries*. While the religious function of praise in seventeenth-century literature has been explored by Lewalski and Hardison,[37] the poetic maneuver of sounding praise for the praiser in the hope of initiating or extending a circle of praise has not. A trend in recent scholarship has been to reduce the praise sounded in seventeenth-century epideictic verse to venal attempts to secure or repay patronage; thus, John Donne's poem in praise of the translation of the psalms by Sir Philip Sidney and the Countess of Pembroke is seen by Arthur Marotti as an

---

[35] Earl Miner, *The Metaphysical Mode from Donne to Cowley* (Princeton: Princeton University Press, 1969) and *The Cavalier Mode from Jonson to Cotton* (Princeton: Princeton University Press, 1971).

[36] Stewart, *Expanded Voice*, 3.

[37] Barbara K. Lewalski, *Donne's Anniversaries and the Poetry of Praise: The Creation of a Symbolic Mode* (Princeton: Princeton University Press, 1973); and O. B. Hardison, *The Enduring Monument: A Study of the Idea of Praise in Renaissance Literary Theory and Practice* (Chapel Hill, NC: University of North Carolina Press, 1962).

"exercise" to secure "the ecclesiastical preferment he desired."[38] Yet, as my reading of the dynamic of praise in Traherne's *Centuries* suggests, such epideictic gestures may be part of a religious community's attempt to extend the spiritual reformation of the world. For example, Joseph Hall's "To the Praise of the Dead, and the Anatomy," prefaced to the 1612 edition of John Donne's *Anniversaries*, praises Donne for having the perspicacity to praise Elizabeth Drury for showing those Christians remaining on earth how to praise God. Hall's poem in effect extends the circle of praise created by Donne in the *Anniversaries*, which may explain why Donne was disappointed by the reception that his supposedly hyperbolic praise of Elizabeth Drury met with in influential quarters. Criticism might do better to consider the "failure" of Donne's *Anniversaries* to be, rather, the failure of print, a Renaissance medium in which language gradually lost the talismanic power assumed and asserted by oral tradition, a talismanic power that had lingered on in manuscript tradition.[39] I suspect that Traherne preferred not to consign his *Centuries* to print

---

[38] Arthur F. Marotti, *John Donne, Coterie Poet* (Madison: University of Wisconsin Press, 1986), 285.

[39] On Donne's attempts to marshal the oracular powers of oral poetry, see Raymond-Jean Frontain, "Donne, Spenser, and the Performative Action of Renaissance Poetry," *Explorations in Renaissance Culture* 32 [Special Issue in Honor of John T. Shawcross], (forthcoming 2006). Epic poetry, even in manuscript tradition, retains vestiges of the talismanic power of language that inheres in oral poetry. Consider the case of the widening circle of praise as it operates in Dante's *Divine Comedy*. Song is the primary motif of Dante's epic, as is suggested by Dante's dividing his poem into 100 cantos or "songs." It is what the sinners in hell cannot do, their garbled songs proving to be anti-song, a mockery of divine harmony; they curse rather than praise. The psalms sung by the repentant souls as they climb the Mount of Purgatory, however, are intended both to signal their own spiritual transformation and to encourage their fellows in the same task. As Dante comments upon leaving the Seventh Cornice, where the Lustful flagellate themselves as they sing, "And in this way, I think, they sing their prayer / And cry their praise for as long as they must stay / Within the holy fire that burns them there" (*Purgatorio* 35.136–138, in *The Divine Comedy*, trans. John Ciardi [New York: Norton, 1977]). The complete harmony that characterizes Heaven is anticipated in the Earthly Paradise where even plants sing. In Paradise, the souls of the blessed who exist in perpetual praise of their Creator form "that choir whose notes are tuned / to the eternal music of the spheres" (*Purg.* 30.92–93). Just as the celestial "light" of the words of Psalm 92 can "pierce the mists as gather in [Dante's] thoughts" (as Mathilda explains in *Purg.* 28.80–81), the psalms sung by the repentant as they ascend Mt. Purgatory teach Dante how to sing himself. *The Divine Comedy* is Dante's song, designed to lead his reader to repentance.

Paradiso 11–12 offers an excellent illustration of how praise brings forth praise. Although in Dante's day Franciscans and Dominicans were oftentimes bitter rivals, the praise of Francis of Assisi, founder of the Franciscan order, that is offered by St. Thomas Aquinas, a Dominican, inspires St. Bonaventure, a Franciscan, to praise the founder of the Dominican order. There is no rivalry in heaven because there is no pride or ego; all are united in worship of the Creator.

because he understood how his language lost its intensity of voice — and with that its power of inspiration — when locked in type.[40]

And, finally, it is important to note that Traherne saw the Psalms as so exclusively the province of praise that he ignored those portions of the Psalter that appealed to most other devotional writers in the seventeenth century, such as the

---

Significantly, Dante understands participation in a circle of praise to be the condition of the blessed in heaven; such purity can exist only in Paradise, which offers a transcendent model to which those on earth can aspire. Traherne, conversely, was determined teach his reader, as Martz has shown, that Paradise can be found on earth, can be found within the person.

[40] Print tradition's inability to sustain oral and manuscript tradition's epic authority is clear when one contrasts Dante's description of the blessed souls in heaven singing eternal praise with Abraham Cowley's description of Samuel's College at Rama in Book 1 of his *Davideis*. Earlier in the poem, Cowley had occasion to digress on the power of music to harmonize a discordant world when he reported on the effects of David's harp-playing and singing upon troubled Saul. In disciplining "ungovern'd Parts" by "Numbers and fixt Rules," the poet imitates "the Eternal Mind's Poetick Thought" by which the world was originally created:

> Water and Air he for the Tenor chose,
> Earth made the Base, the treble Flame arose;
> To th'active Moon a quick brisk Stroke he gave,
> To Saturn's String a Touch more soft and grave.
> The Motions strait, and round, and swift, and slow,
> And short, and long, were mix'd and woven so,
> Did in such artful Figures smoothly fall,
> And made this decent measur'd Dance of All.

(*The Complete Works in Verse and Prose of Abraham Cowley*, ed. Alexander B. Grosart, 2 vols., repr. ed. [New York: AMS Press, 1967], 1: 441–82.) Music harmonizes the microcosm (Saul's troubled mind) as well as the macrocosm (the sin-jarred universe), expressing the poetry that is within the body by striking the sounds that are without: a doctrine of sympathetic response similar to the ideal of *koinonia* realized by responsorial psalm-singing in the medieval church.

At Samuel's College, priests and prophets sing the Lord's praise thrice daily, making "their whole Life" into "their dear Maker's Praise" (854; see esp. 773–782). The College is a world of such peace and harmony that when Saul arrives, bent on wreaking vengeance upon David, he finds his angry thoughts immediately dispelled; instead of curses, he speaks blessings. Ideologically, the world depicted in Cowley's poem is perfectly in keeping with that of Dante's *Paradiso* or Traherne's *Centuries*.

The artificiality of Cowley's verse, however, suggests how difficult it was to imagine in Civil War England a world where men are at peace and praise God continuously. Locked in print, Cowley's description of Samuel's College sounds, not an idealized extension of the reader's or auditor's world, but an impossible utopia. Whereas the manuscript epic still depended to some extent upon the spontaneity of the spoken voice, the print epic is simply too self-conscious in this regard to stimulate praise.

penitential psalms, and those written *de profundis*, from out of the depths of an agonized speaker's soul.[41] It is as though his felicitous eye edited out any portion of the Psalter not given to celebration of the Creator and His creation. Traherne's attraction to the ecstatic portion of the Psalms explains why his text initially failed to secure an extended audience, circulating as it did in the aftermath of the Civil War when religious enthusiasm had become deeply suspect. For the Restoration period marked a turn against the very kind of ecstatic religion that Traherne inscribes in *Centuries*, as becomes clear when one contrasts *Centuries* with subsequent uses of the David figure. Dryden's use of the David story in *Absalom and Achitophel* (1681), for example, not only exploits for satiric purpose the biblical figure's sexual profligacy (an aspect of the David story to which Traherne seemed oblivious), but ignores centuries of tradition that holds David to be the primary model for the devotional poet. One has to look almost another century for a similar appreciation of David as a model of praise. In *A Song to David* (1763) Christopher Smart addresses David, whom he calls "minister of praise at large" (1.14), asking him to accept "this wreath" that the poet Smart weaves. But no reader is inscribed within the poem, whether in the poem proper or at its margins, upon whom Smart depends to extend the circle of praise, as Traherne inscribes and depends upon Mrs. Hopton.

The joy that infuses every page of *Centuries* derives both from Traherne's consciousness of breaking the boundaries of the self and joining a larger devotional and poetic community given to praise both of the Creator and His creation, and from Traherne's appreciation of biblical David for showing other people how to praise God. *Centuries* is among the last great works of the Reformation ideologically as well as chronologically, the seventeenth-century wars of religion making increasingly impossible the idealized psalm-singing community envisioned by Jerome, Erasmus, and Traherne. *A Song to David*, Smart's extraordinary reworking of the Psalms, was popularly believed by his contemporaries to have been written on the walls of a madhouse, as though Smart's inability to find others with whom to share the ecstatic praise of David and God circumscribed him

---

[41] Mary Ann Radzinowicz, for example, analyzes Donne's reliance upon the *anima mea* psalms in his devotional poetry, particularly in terms of the model that they provide a sinner for self-scrutiny. In terms of the tack taken in this essay, it is worth noting that she emphasizes how the psalms model a stance that is "both univocal and congregational" insofar as they "exemplify the combination of personal and congregational lyric voice," the achievement of which Radzinowicz sees as being central to Donne's career ("'Anima Mea' Psalms and John Donne's Religious Poetry," in *"Bright Shootes of Everlastingnesse": The Seventeenth-Century Religious Lyric*, ed. Claude J. Summers and Ted-Larry Pebworth [Columbia: University of Missouri Press, 1987], 40–58, here 41).

rather than placed him in an expanding circle.[42] "*For I blessed God in St. James's Park till I routed all the company*," Smart himself exclaims in *Jubilate Agno*, indicating the extent to which praise alienates others who are made uncomfortable by the psalmist's enthusiasm in the modern world.[43] Little wonder that Smart's *A Song* sees David as the representative of — as the poem itself voices — the Romantic egotistical sublime, marking Smart as the victim of his age's solipsism rather than, as Traherne would have such imitation of David, the initiator of an expanding circle of praise.

---

[42] Reviewing *A Song to David*'s first appearance in print in 1763, John Langhorne reported having been informed that the poem was written during the period of Smart's incarceration in a madhouse "when the Author was denied the use of pen, ink, and paper, and was obliged to indent his lines, with the need of a key, upon the wainscot" (quoted in *Eighteenth-Century Poetry: An Annotated Anthology*, ed. David Fairer and Christine Gerrard [Oxford: Blackwell, 1999], 389).

[43] Christopher Smart, *Complete Poetical Works*, ed. Karina Williamson, 6 vols. (Oxford: Clarendon Press, 1980–1996), 1:26 (B 89).

Motions of Writing in
The Commentaries of Heaven:
The "Volatilitie" of "Atoms" and "Ætyms"

Finn Fordham
University of Nottingham, UK[1]

Accurateness is either the adding of care to work or care to care. It signifies a Care upon Care, that the Work may be perfect wch is undertaken.

> *The Commentaries of Heaven*, "Accuratness,"
> British Library, MS. 63054, fol. 24r

Thomas Traherne ambitiously intended *The Commentaries of Heaven* to be a spiritual encyclopaedia whereby "The Mysteries of Felicitie are opened: and all things discovered to be Objects of Happiness. Evry Being created and Increated being alphabetically Represented (as it will appear) in the Light of GLORY" (British Library, MS. 63054, fol. 2r).[2] He wrote an estimated 350,000 words covering about four hundred pages, with a hundred or so "articles" that begin with "Abhorrence." He only got as far however as "Bastard."[3] Traherne represents that

---

[1] I would like to thank the Leverhulme Trust for a Special Research Fellowship which made possible the pleasurable but painstaking work of reading Traherne's *Commentaries of Heaven* and writing this article. It is written in memory of Jeremy Maule.

[2] References to *The Commentaries* will appear in brackets in the text. They will take the form "folio number" followed by "r" or "v" to indicate "recto" or "verso." The article title and its subcompartment will be given where it is felt to be relevant.

[3] The manuscript was brought to public attention by Elliot Rose's article in the *Times Literary Supplement* in 1982. Allan Pritchard then described it more fully, transcribing a few sections for the *University of Toronto Quarterly* 53 (1983): 1–35. D. D. C. Chambers produced facsimiles of all the poems in 1989. Denise Inge, with Calum MacFarlane, "'Seeds of Eternity': A New Traherne Manuscript (Lambeth Palace Manuscript 1360)," *Times Literary Supplement* (2 June 2000): 14, included excerpts from two unpublished articles. Only a few allusions have been made to the work in scholarly criticism since. See Stephen

individual in English culture who became rare — a priest as spiritual master who
hopes to instruct people to realize their mystical powers of perception. In the fact
that his writings made no impact at the time can be traced the demise of an English spiritualism, a transcendental metaphysical thought, even a theory of devotional meditation, around the time of the appearance of Lockean empiricism, and
the methodology behind Newtonian mechanics. Taking this view, it is hard to
agree with Richard Jordan's comment that he was "a man of the Enlightenment."[4]
Nor would we wish to suggest that Traherne's rediscovery might provide a sense
of hidden continuity that has been waiting to surface, as some have seen by noting
similarities with Blake and Wordsworth. Indeed this fails to do justice to Traherne's originality. Instead the fact that Traherne's writings are often unfinished,
that they frequently show a weak absorption of scientific discoveries, that they are
prone to hyperbole, and the fact, finally, that they're largely unpublished, should
be read historically as all symptoms of shifts in the history and philosophy of
knowledge. These shifts can be traced in the most minute struggles that Traherne
had with his own expression — as evidenced in his manuscripts. And it is with
such tracing that this chapter will, in part, be dealing by observing Traherne's revisions to the *Commentaries of Heaven* (British Library, MS. 63054). Its aim is to
relate the modes of Traherne's composition to some of the visionary substance of
his work: comparing the processes with the intentions and preoccupations. It will
concentrate in particular on his revisions, and as part of the conclusion we will
propose that for any future edition of the *Commentaries* . . . — something still
"much to be desired" as Allan Pritchard said twenty years ago — the possibility
of reproducing it in facsimile should strongly be considered.[5]

   My method aims to address the hypothesis that *formation determines content*;
to which we can add the possibility that the experience of writing affects what
the writing is trying to represent. This becomes all the more likely when the writing and content carry self-reflective material, as the *Commentaries* do. The work,
after all, is a mirror, as its title page says, exhibiting "Transcendent Verities [. . .]
and Objects [. . .] in a clear Mirror" (fol. 2r). As a reflected image is mediated by
glass, so eternal truths are mediated by what is written. Writing is therefore like
a mirror — reflecting truth, but at one remove from it. The making of that mirror
of the written is at one remove from the written, but dimly the making will itself

---

Clucas, "Poetic Atomism in Seventeenth-Century England: Henry More, Traherne and
'Scientific Imagination'," *Renaissance Studies* 5 (1991): 327–40; Nabil Matar, "The Political Views of Thomas Traherne," *The Huntington Library Quarterly* 57 (1994): 241–53.

   [4] Richard D. Jordan, "The New Traherne Manuscript: 'Commentaries of Heaven',"
Quadrant 27 (1983): 73–76, here 74.

   [5] Allan Pritchard, "Traherne's *Commentaries of Heaven* (With Selections from the
Manuscript)," *University of Toronto Quarterly* 53 (1983): 1–35, here 35 n. 29.

be reflected. As an example of how the formation of writing works its way meta-phorically into content, Traherne writes that God "is infinitely Accurat in com-posing the Manner and the Matter of our Happiness: making it perfect in extent and Excellency" (fol. 24v). "Accurate in composing" strongly implies the vision of God as a kind of author of texts. While this is just one metaphor amongst many, it indicates how the experience of writing provides a context for Traherne's theo-ries — especially theories of making and of perfection.

Traherne's Modes of Composition and his Preoccupations

While Traherne is discreet about the concreteness of writing, as he is discreet about concrete matters generally, we are still able to deduce some of Traherne's working practices in the *Commentaries'* composition by examining the appear-ance of the manuscript itself. One feature of his writing is its abundance and its facility; he composed serially with few cancellations. The writing generally moves forward with light, though often significant, revisions. This may be be-cause it was a fair copy prepared for printers as Pritchard believed: Traherne cop-ies material from other texts of his, with little reworking, but much of the ma-terial is nonetheless clearly being drafted for the first time. A work-in-progress, with apparent breaks in its composition, large sections were written swiftly, in an even hand, though with some variations in speed. It is organized into articles with compartments and subcompartments, but on occasions it overflows them as the work gets carried away with itself. Sometimes Traherne would complete an article or compartment, and write in the next section's heading. But before continuing, he would return to revise the previous article, and then over-run its original limit, so he had to cancel the heading drafted for the next article. In ad-dition, the project is unfinished, the writing ultimately interrupted — whether by death or something else, we can only hazard.

As well as these methods of composition, it is possible to abstract Traherne's preoccupations, his main themes, aims, and theories, then lay them beside each other. The titles of some articles correspond immediately to the modes already identified above. There are, for example, the topics "Abundance," "Ambition," "Amendment," "Alacritie," "Abridgement," "Alone," "Author," "Backsliding." There are other themes (familiar in Traherne generally) with a less direct relation to these practices: that God is perfect; that everything, potentially, is for the best; that Eternity is now; that making (and therefore writing) is an imperfect action, because "transeunt"; that ideas, however abstract, must have a source in "real-ity," or else they are illusions; that atoms are volatile and potentially in perpetual motion; that God has the power to still them. Though these can be seen as only tangential reflections on the production of texts, we shall nonetheless relate them to the writing processes.

Of all these, the central issue in the relation between content and formation is the following: the oscillation between the perfection of God's world and the imperfections in representing that world.

Writing Between Ambition and Over-ambition

Traherne's central intention is highly ambitious: not only that everything from heaven's perspective is an object of happiness, but also that man has potential to perceive and enjoy every object from precisely this perspective. After all, "we please God when we are most like Him."[6] Early on in the manuscript Traherne observes that anything, even a feeling, can ascend to God: "Speaking with reverence, it [Abhorrence] can Ascend up unto GOD, & in Heaven Examin His Nature" (fol. 3r). But a transcription should run: "~~Speaking with reverence, it can Ascend up unto GOD, & in Heaven Examin His Nature~~." For, crucially, he cancelled it as insufficiently reverent, and too easy, perhaps, to be mistaken as arrogant. So how can Traherne's general ambition be communicated without it appearing to be hubristic? The problem appears again on the very title page. Traherne's first version said "EVRY BEING Created & Increated being Alphabetically represented in the Light of GLORY" (fol. 2r). In the second he added a parenthesis: "EVRY BEING Created & Increated being Alphabetically represented **(as it appeareth)** in the Light of GLORY." In the third version the parenthesis was revised to read: "(as it **will** appeareth)." (bold print indicates revision material.) Initially the representation of every being happens directly and unproblematically "In the Light of Glory" and appearance is not, at first, an issue. This is qualified, however, by the interlineation, with the appearance of "appeareth," so that *seeming* is stressed above *being*. The next qualification codes further worlds of difference, not just of temporalities, but of points of view: "every being appears," describes Traherne's vision *now*; but "every being **will** appear" implies readers' visions in the future, visions that will have been sharpened from absorbing and enjoying Traherne's work once it has been completed. One is a declaration, the other a promise. The initial present tense declares how "EVRY BEING" unfolds with the writing; the future tense implies that the state is yet to be achieved, invites the possibility of its becoming. The qualification softens the hyperbole of the original. Needing qualification, the writing was initially overstating its case.

In another illustration of this, Traherne qualifies a central issue of his intention when dealing with "Human Abilitie." Traherne originally wrote:

---

[6] *Century* 1.13, in Thomas Traherne, *Centuries of Meditation*, ed. Bertram Dobell (London: Dobell, 1908), 9.

> The Ey faileth at any Distance, ye Ear heareth not too remote a sound: but it is a Great Question whether all Objects to ye Soul are not ever present. ("Human Abilitie," fol. 5v)

But in revision it became:

> The Ey faileth at any Distance, ye Ear heareth not too remote a sound: but ~~it is a Great Question whether~~ all Objects to ye Soul are ~~not ever~~ present.

The revision moves us from a questionable hypothesis — "it is a great question whether [. . .]" — to an affirming statement: "all Objects to ye Soul are present." Needing less qualification, the writing was initially *understating* its case.

Writing Between Imperfection and Perfection

Writing and representation then are imperfect — which is hardly a surprising outcome. But its imperfection becomes significant when the aim of the soul is to become perfect. Traherne says, modestly, his design is:

> only to introduce Light into the understanding and make the Apprehension ~~of men of all men~~ more perfect

He believes perfection is both possible and desirable. The illogicality, in a strict sense, within the notion of making something "*more* perfect," expresses the dilemma: can something be made so much more perfect that it becomes *absolutely* perfect, akin to the perfection of God? Yes: men are part of a perfectly made universe, and should emulate it by yearning to make things perfectly too:

> Ought not we to be Accurat too? [. . .] O y^t Men would consider this; & Remember how Great Workmen they are made; y^t they also might be Perfect in Working! ("Accuratness: Superadded engagements," fol. 24r)

Ambition desires and fuels such perfection:

> Ambition desireth to appear in perfect Beauty, & cannot digest ye least Spot of Error, ye least Defect, or ye least Deformitie.
> Natural Ambition is infinitly pure: for it hateth evry Stain & Blemish: It cannot endure ye least Obliquity. ("Amendm^t," fol. 91v)

The bodily metaphor of "beauty" and "deformity" doesn't exclude the possibility of textual "beauty" and "form" as an aim. Natural Ambition will also desire the stainless and unblemished appearance of a printed work and therefore of completion — but in the meantime it will have to make do with the imperfections of manuscripts, the imperfect acts of human making. We find this thread of anxiety about the work not being completed — since what remains unfinished is a fundamental sign of imperfection (the un-made-through) — working its way through the book: "A book is in making, but not made, till it is ended. The Letters Lines & Leavs are Minutes Howrs & Days, ye Paragraphs & Chapters are Months & Years." ("Ages," fol. 59v).

Writing as "transeunt": Affection as "imanent."

In hoping to become perfect, imperfect actions, however perfectible, will pose a problem. Despite being the means and the medium for "representing" everything "as it will appear[eth]" in the "Light of GLORY," writing is imperfect. It is a kind of making, and, in the established philosophical terms of the day, which Traherne uses, all making is "transeunt Action," opposed to "imanent Action." The binary here transfers, roughly (according to the OED), to "outward" and "inward," and more roughly still to "passing" and "permanent." Traherne's hierarchy finds that anything inward and permanent is better than outward and impermanent: "affections" ("feelings") are better, because they are inward expressions of the permanent soul. Thus:

> To see, to Love, to prize, to rejoyce ar the sovereign Actions in GOD & Man. To enjoy is infinitly more y^n to make. Yet y^t is an Imanent, this a Transeunt Action. To enjoy is more necessary, ~~more noble~~, more Blessed, & more Divine, to Create being Servile in Comparison, & ~~worthless as~~ unprofitable ~~without it~~. It is impossible to open ye Beauty ~~& Excellency~~ of Immanent Actions, for lack of words. ("Action," fol. 33r)

Being transient actions, to make and to Create are external, temporary, always provisional, liable to be changed and revised, always imperfect. Words fail us, are inadequate and lacking, Traherne says just at the moment he has employed an excess of them and has had to emend his excesses. The imperfection of writing can be seen in each revisionary act of return, correction, supplement, and also in those moments when the writing overflows the extent originally set out for it. "To Create," moreover, is "servile," the servant of those "sovereign actions", the feelings which, in themselves, perform their tasks more perfectly and never need revision. Traherne goes so far as to say here that creation is "unprofitable" — though he originally wrote that it is "unprofitable without" the presence of enjoyment. So Traherne originally implied the possibility of a special case of creation which *is* enjoyable. But this would necessarily combine a transient with an immanent action, and in so doing Traherne might be collapsing the distinction between them: hence the revision. For the distinctions and hierarchies maintained between transience and immanence, externality and interiority, are crucial for Traherne. For it is by the way of the interior, of immanence, that the permanent truths of God will be apprehended.

This is remarkable given Traherne's prolixity. He seems to have devoted himself to textual production, as if duty-bound. But behind the production there was clearly a set of emotional experiences so intense that they triggered a need for them to be communicated; writing therefore became the servant of such a group of master emotions. In the case of the *Commentaries*, those emotions are presented generously as felicity, happiness, love and joy at having a heavenly perspective: "I have found man to be a Centre in Worlds of felicitie, & myself a Sphere of infinit Centres" ("Ages: Their Commonness," fol. 63v). The ambition to communicate this will be carried out by writing, but this involves the translation of an interior into an external state. If "All objects to the Soul are present," then communicating their "infinit Centres," "innumerable and endless" (63v) into textual form will involve an ambitious coverage of actual space, on a vast and unfulfillable scale. Book production tantalizes with the actual encircling embodiment of such an abstract idea, with the physical encyclopaedic emergence of such an intangible state of Grace, and the materialization and translation of such an emotional discovery. To do justice to these, the book will have to be vast, somehow coding "infinitie" in its own abundance and growth, and coding also the collapse of time with its own swiftness and motion.

In its attempt to do so, the writing creates an abundance of deferrals, where neither the writing nor the scheme kept pace with the thought, or delivered Traherne's original discovery. A sense of the inter-relatedness of all the *Commentaries'* articles is also ultimately hollow, because so few, relatively, managed to get written. Traherne wrote instructions to his reader "to see," that is, to perceive the reticular structure of the whole:

> vid. Image, Love, End. &c.
> ("Astronomie," fol. 161v)

> vid. Swiftnesse, Motion, Light.
> ("Atom," fol. 172r)

> vid. Act, Eternity, Contradiction, Beginning, etc. And to prevent Mistakes
> See Choice, Liberty, Freedom, Chance, Time, etc. ("Atom: Whether an
> Atom is Eternal," fol. 166r)

But they lead nowhere, except to a sense of the inter-connectedness of Traherne's thoughts. They are proleptic notes, reminders of what Traherne might one day get to. Nonetheless Traherne's very facility in writing, the easy flow of textual production, seems to make a description of "all things" a possible as well as a desirable goal. The facility may also have determined the grasp his soul had on infinity, recalling my introductory hypothesis that formation determines content. The prolixity of Traherne's prose appears to be driven then by a desire to fulfill his grand scheme *perfectly,* or else the facility Traherne experienced in writing drives the desire to believe in the possibility of grand perfection. The desire is so great that it can overwhelm him, as we see in the following where Traherne continues to meditate on "Accuratness," and "its Effects":

> By Accuratness ye Work may be made Perfect & the End attained which we Design. **Wth** Honor, Prais, Esteem & Glory. But loosness scattereth all those, Removing Worth ~~& Honor~~ from ye Workman, Spoyling His Work, Bereaving him of his End, at last Distasting him, & displeasing all. Now how much is it to be Desired y^t Worth should be in our selves, y^t our Works should be perfect, y^t our Design attained, others pleased, our Work admired, & our persons Crowned wth Glory & Honor. It would make a Man even Desperat to consider the Weightiness of these Effects, and even to faint wth longing to secure their Attainm^t. ("Accuratness: its Effects," fol. 24r)

It is as if the longing to see perfection encodes but barely conceals the possibility of failure. The longing is even a hope to overcome that fear of failure. That which proffers the possibility of expression also proffers the possibility of failing.

Writing and Theories of Imperfection

That writing is self-evidently imperfect and acknowledged as such requires Traherne to develop a position towards imperfection. So again, the experience of writing as imperfect determines Traherne's theories concerning imperfection. Like everything else — whether negative or positive — imperfection must be an "Object of Happiness": it can be so only insofar as it can be perfected. It is not an object of happiness, but only something with the potential for being so. We see a struggle with this idea when he writes about "Abstinence":

> It is a seeming Paradox, but certain truth, GOD had not made all Things Perfect, if he had made y^m perfect. For by ye Rules & Measures of Felicitie [. . .] we clearly find, y^t out of Imperfection far Greater Perfection doth arise, And y^t all our Joys ~~flow~~ Eternally flow from a Regulated Abstinence. W^{ch} if it be not understood at present by any other means y^n this, it is sufficient. ("Abstinence: its Necessitie," fol. 9v)

This use of "Paradox," and the worry of its not being understood, is sending Traherne towards the "obliquity" which, as we know, he couldn't endure ("Natural Ambition cannot endure ye least Obliquity"), priding himself on clarity.[7] Traherne

---

[7] As he makes clear: "our design in these present volumes under our Hand accounting clear & perfect Apprehensions of all Objects, in their several Classes, in all their Circumstances" ("Aristotle's Philosophy," fol. 129r). See also his views in the article "Authority."

cancels this entire passage. But he returns to the idea later, writing in an interlinear addition squeezed in to "Accuratness" (Traherne uses the sign # to indicate an addition):

> # GOD is Accurat in other mens Defects; & bringeth y^m to an Excellent Workmanship. ("Accuratness: Observations," fol. 24v)

So it's possible to see how Traherne has own perfected his aesthetic and ethic of perfectible imperfection.

Writing and Idealism

Writing is also imperfect in a quite other sense, in its dangerous relation to fantasy, or a corrupted Idealism. Traherne discusses the importance of being accurate in initial definitions:

> as a little crup in the mothers womb is of Great Consequence afterwards; or a little Alteration in an Acorn produceth strange Effects in an Oak, and sometimes destructive: so here a slight mistake in the signification of words may be of pernicious Importance in their continual use; and a little Accuratnes in the Beginning produces ~~an Exact and [?]~~ a mature & perfect understanding in the later End. ("Accuratness," fol. 25v)

Writing must be tightly signifying because it has the potential to signify inexactly, referring inaccurately to some non-existent or inappropriate idea. Words can therefore be like those dangerous Ideas that become viewed as superior to the reality to which they are supposed to refer and from which they are supposed to stem:

> Melancholy men & Mad-men know ye Force & Importance of such ~~Fancies~~ ideas, ye Beauty & ye Terror, ye Greatness & Power & Realitie of y^m to speak nothing of the Pleasure and Torm^t. It would seem a bold word to say that an Idea is neerer to ye Soul & more Excell^t y^n ye Object it representeth. ("Ages," fol. 60r)

Traherne's Platonism led him to believe in Ideas whose Objects it is difficult to prove definitely exist, so an Idea may come to seem "neerer to ye Soul [. . .] y^n ye Object it representeth." Perhaps from this difficulty, a rawness of feeling can be found accompanying some of his writings, especially concerning the "Ideas" of "Ages" which he promotes most insistently and defensively. "Ages" are historical periods of a hundred years in length, each with a specific character, and he wants to believe that they have an actual existence "outside" the mind, a Reality from which the Ideas get their "Truth." Communicating the reality of "Ages" is crucial for Traherne, as a way of arguing that the "eternitie" in which they exist can in fact be grasped now. Understanding the "Idea" of "Ages" is one means of accessing "all time" in the present instant.[8] Any such visionary apprehension must be more than just fanciful. It would be a bold madness to feel that representations and ideas — worse still "Fancies" — are superior to "the Objects" they represent: truth, the real, actuality, being. Traherne, then, has to guard against finding in his own "work," as expression of his own ideas, something superior to reality. This would be to fall away from "truth" into the superstitious illusions of "apparitions." Language that describes Ideas (being the representation of representation) must not simply be describing illusions: the Ideas must be produced by the Real, however abstract that Reality may be.

What is at stake can be seen in Traherne's revisions to a section titled "Whether Ages are within us, or without us?" (60r) in which Traherne vigorously revised passages where problems with Idealism crop up. But the revisions also reveal problems with a theory of the structure of language which is conducive to the production of Idealism. This structure involves the transcendental signified, which we just saw Traherne promoting, and which defines linguistic signs as part of a system which must involve reliable linkings to stable referents. For Traherne's notion of a language which is structured in such a way that it ensures safe arrivals at accurate and fixed definitions for abstractions comes, I propose, from a certain need for order. If this is the case it provides some further ground for the hypothesis that formation determines content. The need for order in language could arise in those modes of composition and of thinking whose "volatilitie" and speed ("alacritie") of production and of association threaten the composition with disorder. The fixity of referents that arise when defining abstractions is a correlative for Idealism, where our ideas of objects (say, the abstract noun itself and its meaning) are themselves produced by "Real" objects (the definition) but which we can know only through the ideas they produce. Writing is imperfect in this context because, with the occasional speed of its emergence "upon the Wing" as in Traherne, its capacity for precise signification may get lost, so requiring caution and revision. Idealism and transcendent signifiers are produced in reaction to the emergence of an uncontrolled and unconscious flow of language in writing produced at speed. Speed, then, threatens to destabilize the celebration of God's perfection. But, in introducing speed right at this moment, I am getting ahead of myself.

In order to present Traherne's revisions to this passage about "Ideas" and to make comparing the versions easier, I am arranging the "before" and "after" texts

---

[8] Another reading of Traherne's emphasis on "Ages" is that he is advocating the development of a historical consciousness, something arguably emerging in European thought at this time.

in parallel in the table below. A word should be said about the editorial choices I have made. The left side shows the first draft, prior to any of Traherne's revisions. The right side shows a kind of "last intentions" text, an edited version which incorporates all the revisions and eliminates the cancellations. In both I am indicating, in bold, points of revision: on the left, words in bold are those destined to be cancelled or replaced, while the star indicates where there is to be an addition; on the right words in bold are replacements or additions to the previous text, while stars indicate cancellations (invisible holes, if you like, left by them). The overall idea is to give a dynamic sense of the *fault-lines* of a text — either going to happen or having already happened.

They [Ages] affect ye Soul by y^{ir} Ideas of y^m, & y^{ir} Ideas **of them pleas** us more, bec. they are no fals witnesses; **but** * realy Representatives of w^t is. **Our Ideas affect us by y^m as well as they by our Ideas. They** are in us, ye Ages in Eternitie. **Did we say y^t** ye Ages (**w^n seen**) are in us by Ideas, by y^{m}selves in Eternitie, **it were not much amiss. Tho perhaps** they are in us more perfectly **too** y^n by Ideas only. But admit they were **enjoyed** by Ideas only, w^t would follow? Not y^t they are absent, or not existent, or Weakly enjoyed. They are **enjoyed** as ye Sun is, as y^e **Brightness of** Heaven is, as ye Earth is, & all the Glory of ye univers. They are all present **by their ideas only** to ye sence & fancy, * however they are in ye Understanding. (60r)	They [Ages] affect ye Soul by y^{ir} Ideas of ym, & y^{ir} Ideas **affect** us more, bec. they are no fals witnesses; **they pleas us bec. they are** realy Representatives of w^t is. **Ideas** are in us, ye Ages in Eternitie, * ye Ages * are in us by Ideas, by ymselves in Eternitie. * they are in us more perfectly y^n by Ideas only. But admit they were **in us** by Ideas only, w^t would follow? Not y^t they are absent, or not existent, or Weakly enjoyed. They are **as much before us** as ye Sun is, as Heaven is, as ye Earth is, & all the Glory of ye univers. They are all present * to ye sence & fancy, **only by Ideas,** however they are in ye Understanding. (60r)

We can identify three kinds of revision here: 1) eliminating doubt, 2) eliminating confusion about "*our* ideas" and "*their* ideas," 3) eliminating the "affections" of "pleasure" and "enjoyment."

1. Eliminating Doubt

Both the defensive construction, "Did we say [x], it were not much amiss" and the unsure "Tho perhaps" are eliminated. The particularizing qualifier "wn seen" implies too strongly that Ages are at times "not seen" — a distinction Traherne doesn't want to deal with. Traherne hopes to leave a more confident prose; but it is not yet necessarily clearer nor more convincing.

> ideas are in us, ye Ages in Eternitie, ye Ages are in us by Ideas, by y^mselves in Eternitie, they are in us more perfectly y^n by Ideas only.

Taking out doubt has not made the argument tighter: Traherne is wrestling precisely with questions about the source of our Ideas and about what guarantees the existence of their source if it is not guaranteed by experience through the senses.[9] Only some five or six years later Locke would be working out, in drafts that eventually became the "Essay concerning Human Understanding," a radical alternative to the kind of vision Traherne has.[10] And Traherne registers these questions as contemporary problems, when he begins this section with the following dismissal: "There is one thing more wch I do not very well like in Philosophers. Being generally Heathens, & not understanding ye Excellency of Souls, they had but sleight Thoughts of Ideas" ("Ages," fol. 60r). Even such abstract concepts as "Ages" are as real as the most empirically "present" objects of the sun, the sky, and the earth. In the first version Traherne says the Ideas are enjoyed just like the "Brightness of Heaven." But this appeals to those sensations in people that are brought about by physical objects. Traherne wants precisely to appeal to people's faith in abstract "Objects," so he cancels the "brightness" of Heaven and produces the simpler but ambivalent "Heavens," meaning both "skies" and God's domain. The argument is being forced to run: "how do we know these Ideas have a source in reality? Because they are like those things we know to be real, like the Heavens, which are abstract to boot." And this is false reasoning: ("how do we know that door is green? Because it is like those things — leaves, grass — which we know to be green"). But Traherne challenges his reader: if you can believe only in empirically sensed truths, do you then not believe in Heaven? Writing is suspect then, as we shall see, because as a kind of "making" it can contribute to the "making *up*" of Fancies, or even, rather, Ideas without a source in reality.

2. Eliminating Confusion

As long as "we" have Ideas they are "our Ideas." But if Ideas are produced by something else, they belong to them and are therefore more properly "their Ideas." Traherne needs the Ideas of Ages to be produced by some reality other than our-

---

[9] In "Human Abilitie: its Obscurity" Traherne is happy to give way to the "mysterie" of the origin of thought ("Abilitie," fol. 5v).

[10] Peter Nidditch, ed., *Draft A of Locke's Essay Concerning Human Understanding* (Sheffield: Sheffield University Press, 1980).

selves, that is by Ages themselves; he needs "our ideas" to be "their ideas." Hence the following confusing sentence is entirely crossed through: "Our Ideas affect us by y^m as well as they by our Ideas." The first clause is a strange construction that contains a doubling of agency: "Our Ideas affect us by [them]." This might be aiming at such syntactic forms as: "Dogs affect us by their smell" or "Our Ideas affect us insofar as they are formed by their Object," but it doesn't reach either. The syntactical compression seems rather to indicate confusion. Traherne initially balanced it with the idea that reality, the reality of Ages, is affected by "our Ideas." But in suggesting this, he seems to be stumbling across the notion that Reality is an imagined construct. This inverts the proper relationships for Traherne and is utterly anathema to his theme. Ideas mustn't have so much autonomy in relation to the source that produces them. Otherwise you might say that God, then, is only what we say he is; or furthermore that he provides none of his meanings and is on the contrary an invention of our imaginations.

Writing has led Traherne towards these heterodox "constructivist" views, for writing may construct truths as the writing emerges. Writing "upon the wing," as we'll see Traherne calling it, has produced a disordering of the proper hierarchy of signification, illustrating again my idea that the mode of the formation of writing may construct meaning just as much as forms of writing reflect the ideas which the writing represents. Traherne's careful reading (which means that the mode of composition has slowed down) enables amendment of this imperfection. Reading and rewriting enables a restitution of the hierarchy, a reinvocation of Idealism.

3. Eliminating "affections"

The third set of revision concerns "enjoyment." Over three revisions Traherne bleaches the text of feeling, neutralizes it. "Ideas of them **pleas** us more" becomes "Ideas of them **affect** us more"; a "species" is replaced with a "genus," and we move up a level of generality. "Admit they were **enjoyed**" becomes "admit they were **in us**," so the cancellation is not even a synonym. The same is true of the replacement "**enjoyed** as much as the sun is" which becomes "**present before us** as much as the sun is." The fact of the Idea being enjoyed is inadequate proof: they have to be "present" instead. All of this is curious given Traherne's powerful emphasis elsewhere on happiness and felicity. It is as though when the philosophy gets tough, the recourse to feelings might compromise the presence of an already weak logical link in the argument. Arguing from the standpoint of "affection" threatens whatever logic there is supposed to be for the argument. Though the "Action" of "to enjoy" was previously rated as superior to the Action of making, Traherne is having to jettison emotion as a rhetorical strategy, for the sake of a cooler art of persuasion (moving unwittingly away from a Lockean perspective).

In revising this passage on Ideas, Traherne has hardened (made less doubtful), disciplined, and cooled his text. His writing must be pulled back from the accusations of simply making a world of fancy. Cautious rewriting is encountering and qualifying earlier modes of writing that embrace flow, release, movement. These may originally in fact approximate the feelings — of joy, happiness, felicity, and enthusiasm (as possessing God, rather than being possessed by God) — which the writing is supposed to represent.

This brings us to another imperfection of writing (and our last), which is in its excess of motion and of speed. We said earlier that writing is imperfect because it tempts a writer. Like thought, it can move over a wide range of ideas; but it has the advantage over thought of materializing, spreading and growing over a blank space that becomes textualized. Writing invites its practitioners to entertain the Babelian possibility of thinking of a structure beyond their abilities. Then writing falls short of the dreams it tempts the writer with. But writing is imperfect for the opposite reason too: because it overflows the limits it sets itself.

Writing Between Flow and Overflow

Traherne's writing is sometimes carried away with its own speed, taking off, as it were. As Chambers noticed, this can bring Traherne to a stop so he can comment upon this very process:[11]

> [W]hen a mans Soul is upon ye Wing; and clear Notions offer y^m selves [. . .] they ought not to be restrained, for a Ceremonious Respect to the meer Rules of Art [. . .] for Clear Notions, Supprest for a Time, are often extinguished. ("Article," fol. 137r)

Traherne's rate and care of composition clearly varied, as the hand varies considerably in size. The first pages, for instance, have a fairly consistent average of ten words per line and 75 lines per column (making 1500 words per page). Towards the end of "A," there are pages with six words per line and 45 lines per column (making just 600 words per page). A denser hand emerges when Traherne begins "B," indicating some sort of break or breather after the dramatic climax of "Awake" which completes the "A" articles. This illustrates something self-evident: that Traherne experienced different rates of composition, from steady and care-

---

[11] Thomas Traherne, *The Commentaries of Heaven: The Poems*, ed. D. D. C. Chambers, Salzburg Studies in English Literature, Elizabethan & Renaissance Studies, 92.22 (Salzburg: Universität Salzburg, 1989), v.

ful to fast and flowing. Since there is no major revisionary overhaul that would indicate any tortured experience of the text as an obstacle, and since what we see instead is a steady drip of revision (as we mentioned earlier), it is possible to argue that Traherne's experience of writing did not, it would appear, extend to writer's block.[12] Traherne, as we are becoming increasingly aware from the wealth of work that has been emerging in recent discoveries, must have found writing easy. The many appearances of imagery of flow and fountains will reflect this ("so are we made indeed fountains of our own Actions that by things so Beautifull, we might appear before Him in Glory"). So too will the meditations on speed.

Speed — in writing and in thought, and speed as a virtue in itself — is a distinguishing feature of Traherne. Dobell thought Traherne felt compelled to "write down as rapidly as might be the thoughts that surged through the author's brain."[13] Speed is celebrated in his brief article "Alacritie" (which was itself written quickly, since it needed revision of quotations he did not at first complete):

> Alacritie is ye Activitie of ye Soul exorted with pleasure [. . .] Alacrity was given & is enjoynd for ye Greater Beauty of ye Work we perform, & as a Sacred Oyl to make ye Wheels of our Charet move more delightfully. ("Alacritie," fol. 68v)

It is celebrated because it reflects the ability of the Soul and of thought, able to cross vast distances in an instant:

> The remotest Thing in rerum natura is immediately neer, becaus they are present [. . .] by an Act of understanding ("Affections: their Extent," fol. 52r)

As the soul collapses time and space, so thoughts move through the body. But this can be somewhat destabilizing:

> A Thought can dart through every membre, & while it is enthroned in ye Brain, hold ye Reins of ye Body, & affect it strangely. ("Of Affections in Men," fol. 51v)

This codes an admission of a vague danger in over-excitement. It also correlates with both Traherne's sense of the motion of atoms and the way his articles interrelate, calling each other up across the whole scheme, just as the thoughts do that "dart through every member." Stephen Clucas, who provides fine contexts for

---

[12] Perhaps the work is unfinished because of writer's block — but we prefer to think the work was carried on up to his death, since it postdates earlier works, elements of which it contains.

[13] Traherne, *Centuries*, xxviii.

the discourse of 'atomism' in seventeenth-century poetry, proposed that "a history of the atom in literature is a history of anxieties and unspoken fears."[14] But it might reflect pleasures too. I would suggest that many expressions in his article "Atoms," especially concerning their "volatilitie," are produced by the pleasures and the anxieties within the experience of writing. So, again, formation determines content.

Traherne's description is scientifically inaccurate, focusing on issues that Newton is far more successfully about to investigate, as if Traherne's more worn-out ideas are being extended beyond their natural life. But this is all the more significant in that it suggests the ideas arise not from empirical observation but as translations of the experiences of both writing and thinking: "A single Atom being loos & free, is infinitly prone to Motion, upon ye least Occasion" (fol. 168r/r[15]). From this Traherne poses a problem: "how its volatilitie doth conduce to y^e (~~Swiftness, &~~) perpetuitie of Motion in ye World" (fol. 168v/r) and comes up with the following:

> So y^t it is a Wonder how an Atom once in Motion, shld ever be appeased. It is easier to move quiet things, y^n to quiet moving ones: [. . .] An Atom hitting one Atom may put it in Motion, & continue in Motion, y^t may mov another, & y^t another, till all be in motion. Thus is it possible y^t innumerable Atoms by Degrees may be moved by one, & all w^{th}out ceasing be Eternaly moved. ("Atom," fol. 169r)

From this Lucretian vision of the universal motion of atoms there follows an illustration and proof of God's restraining power: "thus it would be, did not ye Wisdom of GOD prevent it" (fol. 169r). Just as moving atoms produce motion in other atoms, and just as darting thoughts produce chains of other thoughts, so articles, in the frequent and volatile proleptic allusions to other articles, generate other articles. The "volatilitie" of writing — and the need to control its primary meanings (its "aetyms") — I suggest lies behind the "volatilitie" of atoms, and the need to control them.

With speed and this sense of inter-relation comes a sense of momentum, as the work gathers itself to be a spinning and many-centred, interlinking and abundant whole. Abundance contributes to this momentum and is a consequence of it. In the article "Abundance" Traherne's praise reflects his own abundant writings, something that in his longer lists seems almost self-parodic. Traherne catalogues "several kinds" of "Abilitie" in Creatures, listing forty-seven of them

---

[14] Clucas, "Poetic Atomism," 338.

[15] The second "r" here and in the following reference represents the right column of the page.

before stopping to add "with innumerable others wch time will not permit me to name." Another list appears in the "Attributes" of God, but it is a list Traherne makes too quickly and has to revise. Here are both the first and the expanded/amended versions (following the earlier procedure):

fol. 181v (cleaned up)	fol. 181v ("final intentions")
We **shall** treat of y^m [. . .] in y^e **following Order:** Allmighty, Allsufficient, Blessed, Bountifull, Compassionate, Divine, Dreadfull, Eternal, Fatherly, Gracious, Heavenly, Holy, Jealous Immutable, Indivisible, Infinite, Just, Kingly, longsuffereing, Loving, Mercifull, Near, Omnipresent, Omniscient, Provident, Righteous, Saving, Simple, Strong, True, Understanding, Wise, Wrathful, Zealous.	We treat of y^m in **yeir proper places** Allmighty, Allsufficient, **Beautiful**, Blessed, Bountifull, Compassionate, Divine, Dreadfull, Eternal Fatherly, **Friendly**, **Furious**, Good, Gracious, **Great Glorious** Heavenly, Holy, Jealous, Immutable, **Inaccessible**, **Incommunicable**, **Incomprehensible**, Indivisible, Infinite, Just, **Kind** Kingly, **Living** longsuffereing, Loving, **Meek**, **Majestick**, Mercifull, Near, Omnipresent, Omniscient, **Perfect**, Provident, **Pure**, Righteous, Saving, Simple, Strong, True, Understanding, Wise, Wrathful, Zealous.

This is an odd mix of ambition and deferral: he extends the list, but says he'll deal with them "in their proper places." That is he will no longer deal with them directly in this article, but as they arise in articles designed specifically for them.

Such listing can be frequently seen as a stylistic mode elsewhere. And, after all, the *Commentaries* are an alphabetical arrangement intended to list "All things." The sense of abundance that comes from these lists correlates to Traherne's vision of the "wonderfully" innumerable atoms and the "innumerable" nature of all. The tendency to list is a means of accruing textual matter without having to reason any relation between the elements. This is what distinguishes most encyclopaedias from traditional philosophical investigations, in that they do not allow arguments to develop in an open-ended if linear fashion, arranged in continuously adjoining stages. The relation of adjacent parts will be limited by what the alphabetic arrangement offers. Like many encyclopaedists, Traherne tries to overcome this, or make a virtue of it, but his options are limited. An article has clear boundaries and sets of limits, but Traherne often overflows the limits he sets himself, as though the potential volatile motion that is found in Atoms has been released. The counter principle for this is found in Traherne's "Abridgement," which begins with a rare moment of witty self-allusion: "Concerning Abridgem^t I shall speak but little."

That the Soul can extend yᵉ Rays of its understanding to all Objects in Heaven & Earth is as Spacious a Wonder, as infinit. But yᵗ it can draw all these into a little Abstract, & lodg yᵐ in fit & convenient Repositories, even in a Centre, containing in it Self Rooms enough wherin to Dispose yᵐ, in clear Light, in fair Treasuries, in Distinct Accessible Orders, so yᵗ it can Approach & make a familiar use of yᵐ, intimats to us a far more Glorious Art than his was, yᵗ Enclosed Homers Iliads in a nut-shell.[16] ("Abridgement," fol. 7v)

The Soul can "draw all objects into a little Abstract," and "Dispose yᵐ [. . .] in distinct" and "accessible order" clearly continues the self-reference that the article began with. For the "abstracts" are the "articles," and their "Accessible Orders" is the alphabetical arrangement of the whole. So, as clearly as anywhere in the project, the mode of composition and the very construction of the Soul's capabilities reflect each other. The Soul is moreover an Artist "more Glorious" than the literary artist (or scholar-critic) who gives a version of the *Iliad*. The Soul is the artist, the workman, greater than the abridger, translator, or engraver of Homer.

Traherne, according to Allan Pritchard, "does not provide much discussion of his literary principles."[17] But if we read the Soul as an artist — as Traherne suggests here — then we can see that every description of the Soul is a description of the artist, and as such embodies literary principles. While there may indeed not be much explicit discussion of his literary principles, the pervasive discussions of the finer qualities of the Soul can be read implicitly as reflections — portraits even — of the artist.

These literary principles can be inferred, not only from the myriad values that Traherne opens up in the text, but also from the writing processes themselves: the revisions, the overflows, the second thoughts, and the corrections, just a fraction of which I have discussed here. In describing these processes it is possible to present these principles being developed, underlined, or qualified.

Unfinished Business

That partly explains why, as I mentioned in my introduction, it is particularly desirable that any edition of *The Commentaries of Heaven* should consist, prior to the consideration of any transcription, of a simple facsimile of the whole manuscript. Transcriptions have been made of selected prose excerpts, and all of the poetry, but they comprise only a fraction of the whole.[18] It is more practicable now to act on

---

[16] Traherne's source is Cicero, *Academics* 2.81, later repeated by Pliny, *Natural History* 7.85.

[17] Pritchard, "Traherne's *Commentaries*," 14.

[18] See n. 3 above.

Bertram Dobell's early sense (though writing of a different manuscript) that "there is a picaresqueness, a beauty, and a life about the manuscripts which is lost in the cold regularity of type."[19] Aside from this aesthetic of nostalgia, a facsimile would place the drama of the writing centre stage. For this and other revisionary doubles provide a dynamism and drama for a text which might otherwise be thought of as lacking narrative or that concreteness endowed by characterization in realism; too abstract in its reiteration of Absolutes, too static and repetitive.[20] The dramatic dynamism is encoded in the acts of writing which are visible in the manuscript itself, and which would be visible in a facsimile. The drama partly codes Traherne's aesthetic values; as Pritchard says, "many revisions appear that have been made for the sake of sound and artistry."[21] But we can also place an intellectual motivation. A facsimile edition allows us to read the variety of textual markings and re-markings as *intrinsic* to the thought and meaning of the *Commentaries*, and as central contexts for placing Traherne's theories. Several revisions, as we have seen, are made as Traherne wrestles with philosophical problems, especially concerning action, creating, and making. From a historical perspective, moreover, textual production should be considered in ways where aesthetic concerns about choosing between the "better" of two versions need not apply. The moments of difficulty that Traherne had with expression can be read as reflecting points where Traherne's culture is facing certain challenges to its thinking.

Cancellations have provided some significant readings in work on Traherne,[22] but the revisions themselves appear in marginal positions that have been hard to

---

[19] Dobell, ed., *Thomas Traherne: The Poetical Works*, lxxiii–lxxiv.

[20] As Pritchard wrote: "In some articles there are long arid passages of Aristotelian and Scholastic definition and classification" ("Traherne's *Commentaries*," 14) and Chambers, in order to justify publishing almost nothing but the verse, writes inaccurately that "Most of the prose [. . .] has little either of the imaginative force of the essays of Bacon and Cowley [. . .] most of it is frankly downright dull" (Chambers, ed., *Poems*, iii).

[21] Pritchard, "Traherne's *Commentaries*," 15.

[22] Bertram Dobell for example emphasized the following: "Socrates, ~~the glorious philosopher~~ was wont to say "They were most happy,'" ("Traherne, *Centuries*," 331). Pritchard noted the following important line about inspiration in *Commentaries*: "And beginning to consider which they were ~~I thus concluded (I think by Inspiration)~~ I remembered, yᵗ Gods goodness was infinit" [("Ages: Their Commonness," fol. 63v)] (Pritchard, "Traherne's *Commentaries*," 35). He also noted that Traherne revised the following under "Astronomie": "the first thing considered in Astronomie is the number of the Spheres." Crossing out "is" and substituting "of old, was" "so that we catch him in the very moment of his belated acceptance of the new astronomy" (11). It is this notion of "catching [someone] at the very moment of" many different kinds of thinking that a facsimile edition makes possible. For comparanda from different periods, see Bernard Cerquiglini, *In Praise of the Variant: A Critical History of Philology*, trans. B. Wing (Baltimore: Johns Hopkins University Press, 1999).

access, taken out as though they're obstacles to the smoothness of reading. To engage with Traherne, especially at his most philosophical, needn't be a smooth experience: how better to see the activity of thought than in the processes of re-thinking some earlier record of thought in writing? The cancellations, and all the revisions, should be placed in the foreground, then, not set aside or marginalized as foot- or endnotes.

The cult of perfection that is part of chirographic book culture need not be embarrassed by those imperfections of process, of that *thinking* and rethinking in single authors, the direct evidence of which most published texts conceal through the acts of polishing and preparing for publication. For, in our age, as Traherne would say, we now live, as Traherne would not say, in an imperfect world, a world whose imperfections we can at best represent as perfectly as we can — without imagining that we can actually perfect them. Such a practice is really always be-yond us, just as the Faith in its possibility now lies behind us.

Masquing/Un-masquing: Lambeth MS. 1360 and a Reconsideration of Traherne's "Curious" Visual Language

Carol Ann Johnston
Dickinson College

It was your friends Delight to Meditat the Principles of Upright Nature: and to see how things stood in Paradice before they were Muddied and Blended and Confounded. for now they are lost and buried in Ruines. Nothing appearing but fragments, that are worthless shreds and Parcels of them. To see the Intire Piece ravisheth the Angels. It was his Desire to recover them and to Exhibit them again to the Eys of Men.
— Thomas Traherne to Susanna Hopton,
Centuries of Meditation (4.54)

In the one hundred years since the first publication of Traherne's poetry, discoveries of new Traherne manuscripts have reached the status of scholarly folk legend: pulled from fires; bargain-hunted from bookstalls; sleuthed out of piles of uncatalogued library materials. Even so, the late Jeremy Maule's remarkable detective work in identifying Lambeth Palace MS. 1360 as a new, substantial Traherne discovery places him in the pantheon of "scholar detectives." Though the manuscript actually contains five separate volumes, the catalogue of the manuscripts in the Lambeth Palace Library describes it as "Three Theological Treatises" (two of the works are untitled).[1] This description, along with the initial title (though not the first work) in the manuscript, beginning *A sober view of Dr. Twisse's his Considerations* [. . .], suggests why the manuscript had gone unidentified for hundreds

---

[1] See E. G. W. Bill, *A Catalogue of Manuscripts in Lambeth Palace Library: Mss. 1222–1860* (Oxford: Oxford University Press, 1972), 78–79. In his unpublished notes describing the manuscript, Jeremy Maule assigns titles to the two untitled works: he entitles the first work in the manuscript "Inducements to Retiredness," and the third "Love."

of years, and attests to Maule's patience and perseverance. Its language is far from that typifying Traherne's clean visual diction in *Poems of Felicity* and *Centuries of Meditation*. However, the titles and descriptions of two subsequent works — *Seeds of Eternity or the Nature of the Soul in which Everlasting Powers are Prepared* and *The Kingdom of God* — are rendered in language familiar to readers of Traherne. Once Maule evaluated the manuscript, in other words, the identity of the author was unquestionable.[2] Indeed, in these works Traherne combines poetry with prose, as he does in *Christian Ethicks* and elsewhere,[3] and in all five works Traherne both characterizes as well as advances topics he addresses in his well-known poems and *Centuries:* Felicity, "Heavenly perspective," the goodness of the world, and eternity. In addition to embellishing Traherne's signature styles and subjects, these five volumes also help to unravel several inter-related questions hovering over every reading of Traherne: why do we know so little about his life, and why does Traherne affect a style that renounces the particular? By drawing comparisons between Traherne's visual theory in the new work to that in his work that we know well, I will show that Traherne's engagement with the visual culture that defines the seventeenth-century Jacobean and Caroline courts forms a central structural element of his ideal Christian world. Not only does his language combine several theories of perspectival vision, but, as I will show here, it also draws specifically upon the court masque, the most public embodiment of perspectival theory in seventeenth-century England, and the least likely of visual genres for Traherne to embrace.

Several aspects of the Lambeth manuscript have seemed anomalous to first readers. Because the second work in the manuscript, *A Sober view of Dr. Twisse,* presents a polemical theological argument that shows Traherne firmly caught up in the Calvinist-Arminian debate concerning the nature of grace, Denise Inge and Calum MacFarlane suggest that this new manuscript "may radically change the way we read Traherne in the new century." This manuscript does give us the first overtly systematic treatise in the Traherne *oeuvre*, and much of the last piece in the manuscript, *The Kingdom of God*, exhibits complex periodic sentences often couching contemporary issues. Yet while these characteristics may seem to be anomalous, they are, rather, explicit examples of what has been implicit in Traherne's work all along: the manuscript answers questions about the Traherne we already

---

[2] For a full description of the manuscript see Denise Inge and Calum MacFarlane, "'Seeds of Eternity': A New Traherne Manuscript (Lambeth Palace Library Manuscript 1360)," *Times Literary Supplement* (2 June 2000): 14. Other kinds of evidence, such as similarities in the various hands in the work to other Traherne autographs, also ensure its authenticity.

[3] One of the poems in *Christian Ethicks*, "For Man to Act," appears also in *The Kingdom of God*.

know, a Traherne who at his core is systematic and complex, though quietly so. Throughout his work, including MS. 1360, Traherne shows himself to be complicated and paradoxical, his gravity often couched in simple and pure language.

"The Soul of Man. . . . composed for Divine Enjoyments"

As I have argued elsewhere, though the received view of Traherne's visual language strips it of sophistication, the complexity at the crux of his work lies precisely in that language. Traherne's language is visual, though neither metaphoric nor descriptive in the ways we have traditionally discussed visual language in seventeenth-century lyrical works. Traherne realigns limiting human vision that sees with false objectivity — as if it saw *all* — toward the kind of vision he believes God possesses on His heavenly throne, that is, concurrent vision; he sees individual objects both in their three-dimensional entirety, and atomistically, as a child might. For Traherne God sees the general and the particular simultaneously.[4] Traherne couches the dual perspectival nature of human vision and the divine vision that synthesizes it in the emerging technical terminology of linear perspective.

Traherne understands the false objectivity inherent in this theory of perspectival vision. Single-point perspectival vision emphasizes a single viewer's focus upon a central point in a "big picture." By focusing on a central "vanishing point," linear perspective convinces viewers that they see "real," three-dimensional objects in paintings and in scenic designs for masques and plays, even though this coherent vision is two-dimensional and can be viewed correctly only from a privileged, centrist position. Before the invention of single-point perspective in the Florentine Renaissance, vision and visual representation were focused upon individual objects. Aligning objects within perspectival scenes, with an organizing centrist point, draws attention from individual objects themselves to the relationship of objects around that central point.[5] Perspectival paintings and

---

[4] For a detailed account of this argument, see Carol Ann Johnston, "Heavenly Perspective; Mirrors of Eternity: Thomas Traherne's Yearning Subject," *Criticism* 43 (2001): 377–406.

[5] Martin Kemp, *The Science of Art* (New Haven: Yale University Press, 1990) details the history of Brunelleschi and Alberti's discovery of perspective. Kemp also summarizes various critics on this controversial subject to give an overview of the issues surrounding the discovery of perspective: Samuel Y. Edgerton, *The Renaissance Rediscovery of Linear Perspective* (New York: Basic Books, 1975); Ernest B. Gilman, *The Curious Perspective* (New Haven: Yale University Press, 1978); William Ivins, *Art and Geometry* (Cambridge, MA: Harvard University Press, 1946); Michael Kubovy, *The Psychology of Perspective and Renaissance Art* (Cambridge: Cambridge University Press, 1986); and John White, *The Birth and Rebirth of Pictorial Space*, 3rd ed. (Cambridge, MA: Harvard University Press, 1987).

scenes were controversial for English painters such as Nicholas Hilliard, who understood them to represent copies of nature as if they were real.[6] Traherne shapes his work around this controversy, understanding the seductive and false nature of perspectival vision, but also using single-point perspective for his own ends.

Traherne constructs vision and perception as a three-part process, a process that unfolds both in historic time and during the period of the individual's life. Pre-perspectival anamorphic vision also is analogous to the decentered and fractured vision of a child. Without learning the single-point perspectival system around which adults in western culture arrange both time (narrative) and visual perception, children have no central point of emphasis that makes sense of experience. For Traherne, this is both the good and the tragic news. Without structure, individuals cannot process experience with clarity or understanding. With the hierarchical order provided by linear perspective, however, experience and perception become falsely organized around earthly objects and individuals, aggrandizing some things at the cost of all other worthy aspects of God's creation. Traherne emphasizes that all earthly things contain beauty and sanctity, because God is in them. A child gives the deserved attention to individual objects in the world, but cannot put the pieces together to understand the story of its creation, or the creator himself. Combining these two forms of vision, anamorphic and linear, Traherne invents a system for the ideal relationship between the faithful Christian and God.

Viewers of perspectival scenes are analogous to the faithless in Traherne's schematic: non-Christians believe that their single-point vision is totalizing and objective, rather than impossibly subjective and limited by the frame that linear perspective imposes upon observers. The faithless can believe their vision is objective only because they neither move their centrist viewing position nor step out of the perspectival frame. Traherne argues that faith in God can transform human understanding of vision, since God's position in Heaven gives him truly objective and infinite vision. "Heavenly perspective," as Traherne names it in the *Church's Year Book*, is both pre- and post-perspectival. God sees particular, individual objects in their entirety, as pre-perspectival vision emphasizes, and he sees objects relationally, organized around a central point in the visual field, as perspectival vision emphasizes. The faithful, contemplative Christian can visualize the world as God sees it, though he can realize that world only in Heaven.

Continuing Traherne's perspectival work, the first of the five works in Lambeth MS. 1360 opens with an epigraph describing the work in perspectival terms:

---

[6] Hilliard in *The Arte of Limning* (Manchester: Carcanet Press, 1981) argues that perspective is actually an "effect or judgment of the eye" which has the purpose of "deceiv[ing] both the understanding and the eye" (71).

"For Everything Rests most Composedly in its proper place, & the Soul of Man is not in its Proper place till it be sweetly disposed and composed for Divine Enjoyments" (fol. 1r).[7] The concepts in this epigraph are consistent with those elsewhere in Traherne: God sits on a throne in Heaven and views the world as if he were viewing a perspectival scene. Further, the epigraph uses variants of "compose" twice in this one sentence, emphasizing the technique unique to linear perspective of grouping objects around the centrist point. While it may seem to replicate adult single point-vision, God's perspective does not lose sight of those objects absent from the centrist point. His vision simultaneously is centered and decentered. Every object in God's purview may be central. As Traherne explains in an expanded version of this idea in *Christian Ethicks,* human souls must desire to be seen in proper relationship to other objects in the world in order for God to view them properly. While God has both an infinitely shifting frame and an infinitely shifting centrist point, he allows individuals to ignore his viewing them. His is the true perspective, but we must shift to be seen by him:

> IT is a natural Effect of infinite Wisdom to make every of its Treasures suitable to its own excellence. And that the Wisdom of GOD has done, by making even the smallest Thing in his Kingdome infinitely serviceable in its Place, and station, for the manifesting of his Wisdom, Goodness, and Glory to the Eye of a clear Beholder. And this he hath done by making all his Kingdome one Intire Object, and every Thing in it a Part of that Whole, Relating to all the innumerable Parts, receiving a Beauty from all, & communicating a Beauty to all, even to all objects throughout all Eternity. While every one among Millions of Spectators, is endued with an Endless Understanding to see all, and enjoy all in its Relations, Beauties, and Services.[8] (*CE*, 69)

Here Traherne emphasizes that "the smallest thing" has its central place; God's visual field is ordered and centered around each "thing," forming a dazzling combination of multiple centers and a totalizing whole. Important to Traherne's ideal of vision, all objects and persons draw the kind of focus that linear perspective offers the object at the center of the representational frame. Neither pre- nor post-perspectival vision represents ideal vision. On the one hand, pre-perspectival vision fails because individual objects receive concentrated attention without the order that single-point perspective gives to a whole. On the other hand,

---

[7] All quotations from MS. 1360 are from my transcription and are used by permission of the Lambeth Palace Library.

[8] All quotations from *Christian Ethicks* are from Carol Marks' [Sicherman] and George Guffy's edition, *Christian Ethicks* (Ithaca: Cornell University Press, 1968) and will be noted by page number in the text.

perspectival vision distorts "reality" by placing too much emphasis on the single center of a restrictive whole. God's vision combines the two into ideal vision of multiple centers, all within a single orderly scene. In addition, as Traherne stresses throughout his work, this diverse, yet whole, vision is one available to all: "every one among millions of spectators."

The lengthy discussion following the epigraph for the initial, "Retirement," section in Lambeth MS. 1360 follows Traherne's design for God's vision in *Christian Ethicks*. For all faithful Christians the way to enter Heaven is through perfect vision, simultaneously centered and multiple, which Traherne describes in perspectival language. His emphasis in the first section of the new manuscript, however, falls upon how and where we may achieve this heavenly vision. For Traherne the external visual field that one sees as an adult is fraught with evil and temptation, as he makes explicit in such poems as "Wonder," in the Dobell sequence. The Christian's preferred method of encountering that world outlined in this new "Retirement" section is to withdraw from it into the reflective soul — which in "Retirement" he names "the Inward EY" — the soul that both sees and reflects the world as God sees it:[9]

> In retirement we see the Grandure & Glory of our True Estate. . . . evry man is Heir of all His Works, & . . . the Best Way wherin they can be Enjoyed is the Divine Image . . . we are all Kings, because we are all pleased in all the places of Gods Dominion. . . . one Soul is a Greater Treasure than the Whole frame of the Visible World,[10] that all Things considerd the World is a place of Eternal Joys, a Region of Heavenly Light, a paradice of Glory, & all Kingdoms evry mans Possessions. That to retire to them is to enter into Heaven, & that the way is so perfect wherby all things are ours, that we are to rest satisfied in God with infinit Joy, & to Glorifie his Name for evermore. (Lambeth MS. 1360, fol. 9v)

---

[9] The soul/eye/mirror trope is familiar from the poems and the *Centuries*, as in this representative stanza of "The Preparative":

> Then was my Soul my only All to me,
>   A Living Endless Ey,
>   Far wider than the Skie,
> Whose Power, whose Act, whose Essence was to see.
>   I was an Inward *Sphere of Light,*
> Or an Interminable Orb of *Sight,*
>   An Endless and a Living Day,
> *A vital Sun* that round about did *ray*
>   All Life, all Sence,
> A Naked Simple Pure *Intelligence.* ("The Preparative," 11–20)

[10] "Whole frame of the" has been struck through in the manuscript.

"Retirement," Traherne suggests, is literally introspective: "But it is impossible to see unless only within; Souls, Angels, Time, Eternitie, wisdom holiness, Glory, Blessedness. GOD is an Object only of the Inward EY" (fol. 1v). In visual terms, the only response that a Christian can make to the corrupt world he sees around him is to withdraw — or "retire" — within to "the Inward Ey." There, the Christian may see reflected through God's perspectival frame his "True Estate" which is without the artifice either of "the Whole frame" or of the center imposed by corrupt human perspectival vision. In retirement the soul becomes the "Sphere of Treasures, the point of Concurrence, wherein all the Influences of Heaven meet, the pupil of vision out of which all the Rays & Beams of Sight disperse themselves & so like God, an Invisible Sphere of all his Kingdom" (fol. 10v). Much of this language — "pupil of vision," "Rays & Beams of Sight" — echoes one of the many manuals of painting and perspective available to English readers.[11] Yet Traherne carefully draws this perspectival language out of its concrete context and argues for its transformation through the mirroring eye of the soul. There God's multiple frames and centers offer emphasis and focus on all, and to all.

The terminology and philosophical underpinnings for painting in single-point perspective found in English translations of painters' manuals were first detailed by the Florentine humanist Leon Baptista Alberti. Linear perspective depends upon two central points: one at the center of the painting, to which all of the rays and angles of the work direct the eye, and the other, corresponding position which mirrors this so-called "vanishing point," where the viewer places his viewing eye. As in this passage from his epideictic cycle, the *Thanksgivings*, Traherne discusses image formation on the soul in terms of rays, points, light, and frame, all pictorial terms from Alberti's formulation:

He that could bring the Heavens *thro the Eye*,
And make the World within the Fancy lie,
By beams of Light that closing meet in one,
From all the Parts of His celestial Throne,
Far more than this in *framing Bliss* can do,
Inflame the Body and the Spirit too:
Can make the Soul by Sense to feel and see,
And with her Joy the Senses wrap'd to be.
(emphasis added; "Thanksgivings for the Body II," 15–22)[12]

---

[11] Theoretical texts describing perspective began appearing in English in 1598 with Richard Haydocke's translation and adaptation of *A Tracte Containing the Artes of Curious Paintings, Carving, and Building* (Oxford, 1598), Lomazzo's treatise on painting and carving. This text, as well as others, had previously been available in Latin.

[12] All references to the *Thanksgivings* are from H. M. Margoliouth's edition, *Centuries, Poems, and Thanksgivings*, 2 vols. (Oxford: Oxford University Press, 1958). I note line numbers parenthetically in the text.

Here the "Body and the Spirit" "fram[e]" sensory impressions of "the world" which are transmitted "thro the Eye" by "beams of Light that closing meet in one." The properly circumscribed soul contains the spiritual "centric ray." These sensory impressions originate from the "celestial Throne" of the creator, at the center of the universe. The relationship of the Christian soul to the creator in his universe has its basis in the relationship between the viewer of a painting and the painting itself. As in a painting, the rays and centric point work reflexively; the Christian soul also sends out rays to the creator just as the creator sends rays from his throne. Throughout his *Commentaries of Heaven*, a manuscript in which Traherne offers imagined "Heavenly perspectives," he uses perspectival terminology to express this reflexivity: "He [the Christian] darts invisible and precious Rayes / Out of his Soul ten thousand other Ways" ("Ages II," 9–10). In "Atom" he speaks of the spiritual universe as if all spiritual eyes were reflecting the rays of the sun (God) back to him:

> From *evry single Point* with in the Sun
> A shatterd Sea of Mites dispersed com,
> That, loosened by interior flames, doth flie
> From thence, and cover all the Spacious Skie.
> Som, *from each Centre of it,* to a Star;
> Som to the Earth. Som to a Coast more far;
> *Divaricating, breaking all the Way,*
> *In Motes that seem an Universal Ray.*
> *Which makes that Centre whence it came, appear*
> *In evry Place, as if alone twere there.*
> The very Means which brings its Parts together,
> Its Parts (even Contradictions working) sever.
> *Because a Ray from evry Point doth flie,*
> *And Spread to all the Parts of all the Skie,*
> *From all the Parts of all the Shining sun*
> *Rayes crossing Rayes to evry Point do com.*
> So shadowing forth the Way most fair and sweet,
> How Contradictions in the Soul may meet:
> How it alone may be confined here,
> And yet even then be wholy evry where. (emphasis added; "Atom," 101–120)[13]

Every faithful Christian's point of view has the idealistic perspectival view of objects: multiple perfect viewing points, multiple focal points, a frame that shifts infinitely with these moving central and focal points. Because of these multiple,

---

[13] All quotations from the *Commentaries* are from D. D. C. Chambers' edition, *Commentaries of Heaven: The Poems* (Salzburg: University of Salzburg, 1989). I note line numbers in the text.

yet central, points of view, the soul of each Christian has "an universal way," and "a ray from every point doth flie." Traherne paints a picture of a cosmos criss-crossed with centric rays, emanating from the creator, and from every single object, because God is the focus of a Christian's vision, and he exists in each object. Christian souls reflect their multiple frames and centrist points back to God, thus providing him multiple views of himself, organizing the disparate parts of the universe. God's multiple vision of himself within individuals depends upon the individual Christian's aligning himself with God's centrist points. In other words, God's vision depends upon human agency.

This principle of the centric ray issuing from the Christian's soul leads to the Christian's ability to perceive even the most "obscure" objects in the center of a balanced perspectival frame, as Traherne writes in "Hosanna," from *The Poems of Felicity*:

> *Transcendent Objects* doth my God provide,
> In such convenient *Order all contriv'd,*
> *That All things in their proper place*
> My soul doth best embrace,
> Extends its Arms beyond the Seas,
> *Abov the Hevens its self can pleas,*
> *With God enthron'd may reign:*
> Like sprightly Streams
> My Thoughts on Things remain;
> *Ev'n as som vital Beams*
> *They reach to, shine on, quicken Things, and make*
> *Them truly Usefull; while I All partake.*
> (emphasis added; "Hosanna," 48–52)[14]

The idea of the soul grasping the balanced proportions of objects in space is central to Traherne's work. The "Order" of Traherne's "Transcendent Objects" is such "That All things in their proper place / My Soul doth best embrace." His work here also follows Alberti's in interlocking perspectival harmony with spiritual harmony. Neo-Platonic texts borrow this trope from Alberti as well. The marked difference from these precursors lies in the scale and fluidity Traherne gives his framing vision. God and the faithful Christian see every object at once in the mirroring soul as if every object were the central focus of the visual field.

In addition to typifying Traherne's perspectival language, these passages depend upon our understanding the issue of "circulation" of images between God and the human soul, a subject that is unique to Traherne. He modifies the mirroring

---

[14] All quotations from the *Poems of Felicity* are from Margoliouth's edition. I note line numbers in the text.

relationship that Alberti describes between the vanishing point of the painting and the centrist point of the viewer, and creates an actual set of mirrors. The human soul and God's soul are two mirrors held up to one another, each reflecting the person of the other. "For till the Symmetrie & Proportion of the Soul is seen," Traherne explains in *Seeds of Eternity*, "as it is subject to God & Superior to all other Things till all its powers can be drawn from Eternity to Eternitie [sic], & its Inclinations infinitely brought from GOD to GOD, till he appeareth in the Soul, as the Exemplar of it . . . it cannot appear to the object of his love. . . . It being represented like a broken monument whose fragments are seen but lying in their rubbish" (137 fol. v).[15] God sees himself seated in the throne in the reflective eye/mirror of the human soul, and because God is enthroned there, the human soul itself is the seat of correct human vision. From that soul where one reigns on the throne with God, one also can see oneself and one's world in the reflection of God's soul as God sees.[16] Withdrawal into the reflecting soul puts the Christian's soul in the proper frame and proportion for God's viewing. With his emphasis on the pieces of a broken monument, Traherne here stresses that an alternative and parallel sense of vision exists alongside of "heavenly" vision. That vision is "broken," without either the frames or the focal points of "Heavenly perspective." Earthly vision sees objects in the world nihilistically or, as he discusses elsewhere, with a false frame and hierarchy. Throughout Lambeth MS. 1360 Traherne's perspectival language is as pointed as in any of his other work.

The issues in Traherne's "simple" visual language, then, are culturally complex. He makes reference to a visual and perceptual culture at the heart of modern ways of thinking about the physical world, as well as about perception of that world. MS. 1360 sharpens our perception of visual culture as the underlying concern of Traherne's work. Throughout the manuscript, as elsewhere, his writing lacks the texture of the specific. He names few particular objects in the external world, arguing that one should "retire from External Things to Things Internal" (fol. 1v), and stressing that ideas — "Things Internal" — have the properties that we mistakenly give to objects in the external world: "things we see without are the remote, & last objects we discerne, but the Ideas, are the nearest, & most Immediate" (fol. 351r). Traherne's claim that ideas have more material substance than external objects aims at dissolving human notions about subject and object relationships. The invention of linear perspective both engenders and exposes this problem at the center of modern concerns. Stress on the position of the viewing subject in relationship to external objects of central focus exposes the separation

---

[15] This passage is heavily rewritten in the manuscript.

[16] Faith allows one this divine vision, though Traherne also is careful to insist that while the Christian sees in his soul accurate images of the "real," he must not confuse the felicity of those visions with eternity; only then will he realize this vision.

among these subjects and objects. Traherne's project is retrospective in terms of this set of issues: the introspective Christian will see that the ideas within his soul are "true" and "real" objects, and thus will experience no separation between subject and object. Objects are within the subject, and thus in Traherne's design, subject and object are conjoined. Traherne bases this discussion upon his foundational theory of how human vision may be corrected through Christian faith: because these "objects within" are reflections of God in heaven that allow us to see "aright," they hold authority over the man-made objects that might catch one's eye in the external world.

Traherne at Court

While these five new volumes in the Traherne canon help to redirect discussion of Traherne's visual language in terms of linear perspective, they also bluntly and negatively fix upon issues familiar to Traherne through his exposure to the court, a subject often neglected by Traherne's readers. Yet his criticism of the court is explicit in Lambeth MS. 1360 and beyond, and that criticism leads him to an unusual place. Commensurate with his attention to linear perspective, Traherne takes the court masque, the emblem of court arrogance and power in the Jacobean and Caroline courts, and reshapes it. In his hands, the masque becomes a powerful tool to criticize the court. The language in MS. 1360, especially in *The Kingdom of God*, amplifies Traherne's use of references to the court throughout his oeuvre. These references are particularly difficult to isolate; references to "kings, thrones, and diadems" indicate for the Christian the language of the Old Testament prophets (e.g. Isaiah 62:3) whose discussion of kings and kingdoms is used to signify the coming of Christ. In Traherne, however, these allusions to God's kingdom often occur in contrast to earthly kingdoms, which of course fall witheringly short of the heavenly court. Moreover, in Traherne's comparisons, earthly kingdoms suffer particularly sharp attacks, and those comparisons in MS. 1360 that slip into the particular suggest the discomfort he must have suffered in his direct contact with Charles II's court as chaplain to Sir Orlando Bridgeman, the Lord Keeper of the Seal. The third chapter of *The Kingdom of God*, with the verbose title "The Glory of Gods Kingdom being seen Inspireth Courage & Virtue in the Soul. The Variety of Lives & Treasures in the World. The combat between the flesh & Spirit. All Christians are in the Kingdom of GOD allready," offers as pointed a criticism of the court as we see anywhere in Traherne:

> For as much as God is greater than man, so much in proportion is his Kingdom more Excellent: And it is far better to be the meanest Servant there, than the Greatest Monarch here. The Death is Eternal the Life Eternal, the Happiness Eternal: All is Immeasurable true & Endless; nothing transitory

or Counterfeit in the Kingdom. The Rewards of Virtue in the Kingdom are not an Olive Branch, or a Crown of Bayes; a Medal, or a Statue Erected in its Memory; a Masque or a feast in the King's Banquetting house; an Aerie Title, or an Earthly possession: nothing is there so frivolous & vain: but a Life that shall never End: power to become the Sons of God; the Lov of Angels & ArchAngels, an Eternal Inheritance of his Master's Joys, Communion with the most high in all his Delights, and Intire friendship with the King of Kings, & Lord of Lords,[17] & the fruition of his essence for Evermore. For our Warfare is not with flesh & Blood, but against Principalities & powers, against the Rulers of the Darkness of this World, against Spiritual Wickedness in high places: yea fleshly Lust which War against the soul. (Lambeth MS. 1360, fol. 153rv)

"Frivolous and vain" are Traherne's words for the earthly court, though the rhetorical shape of this argument buffers the impact of the statement by burying it at the end of a list of courtly rewards. Traherne's harsh criticism here is informed by experience in the court;[18] he shows knowledge and mastery of the court's self-aggrandizement in the form of statuary, medallions, titles, flashy possessions, and most specifically the "Masque or . . . feast in the King's Banquetting house."[19]

---

[17] "Lord of Lords" has been struck through.

[18] Inge and MacFarlane note that *The Kingdom of God* can be dated "no earlier than 1670" ("'Seeds of Eternity'," 14).

[19] This comparison of earthly and heavenly courts in "The World," from *The Poems of Felicity*, mirrors closely that in the "Retirement" section of MS. 1360:

And great King's Thrones,
    Compared with such Benefits,
      [are] But empty Chairs; a Crown, a Toy
        Scarce apt to pleas a Boy,
All others are but petty trifling Shews,
      To that which God bestows.

A Royal Crown, inlaid with precious Stones,
      Did less surprize
      The Infant Eys
Of many other little Ones,
    Than the great Beauties of this Frame,
      Made for my sake,
      Mine Eys did take,
    Which I divine, and Mine, do name.
Surprizing joys beyond all Price
      Compos'd a Paradise,
Which did my Soul to lov my God enflame,
    And ever doth the same. ("The World," 91–108)

Traherne's specific scorn for the court masque here is hardly surprising. Stephen Orgel and Roy Strong's now classic works on the court masque and power have shown that the masque form began as lavish pageants celebrating and reinforcing James I's power in Inigo Jones' Banqueting House, the structure to which Traherne here specifically refers. The outrageous expenditures on the masques especially rankled during the budgetary crises of Charles I's government. Traherne's familiarity with the form, however, may seem unusual. In spite of much scholarship to the contrary, the received view of the court masque persists: the masque disappeared at the onset of the Civil War and the closing of the theatres in the 1640s, at least twenty years prior to Traherne's experience in government. Traherne's obvious familiarity with the genre and its primary royal venue, however, suggests otherwise.

As Pepys and Evelyn report, Traherne's employer, Sir Orlando Bridgeman, frequented social occasions, including pageants and plays, as a member of the King's entourage. Traherne no doubt accompanied him.[20] Abundant evidence shows that the masque and masque-like pageants survived in performance inside

---

The court takes a distant second place compared to the natural world, "that which God bestows." Traherne ends the poem with the speaker remembering his infant perception of the world, a perception beside which "A Royal Crown, inlaid with precious Stones," is less tantalizing than the beauties of the world framed as the speaker has framed them in the poem, all "pleasant Prospects" in place, with the enthroned sun providing "his nimble Rays" which illuminate and inscribe the scene. "Surprizing Joys beyond all Price," the speaker concludes, "Compos'd a Paradise" (105–106).

[20] Whether or not Traherne actually viewed a masque during the forties, he could have read the texts available; Jonson's *Opera* containing his masques was published much earlier, in 1616. In addition to documented publication and performance of masques after 1640, dramatic metaphors exist in sources other than in dramatic works or performance. Dramatic elements pervade the work of Milton. As his contemporary, Traherne could have read Milton's *A Masque at Ludlow (Comus)*, published in revised form in 1637, a masque in which Milton adapted various Jones-Jonsonian forms, such as the antimasque-main masque structure in *Hymenaei* (1606), as well as in *The Haddington Masque* (1608), and detailed in Jonson's preface to *The Masque of Queenes* (1609). Masque convention and structure pervade all of Milton's work; John J. Demaray argues that Milton adapts this form for *Paradise Lost*, which relies on many gestures and conventions borrowed from masque and Italian *Intermezzi* traditions. "Ode: On the Morning of Christ's Nativity" represents the figure of Peace, who comes through "amorous clouds dividing" (l. 50), a move indebted to the elaborate flight machines developed for the *Intermezzi* and used in the masque. Although Milton actually wrote a masque early in his career, various elements of the masque appear in Milton's oeuvre to a degree that indicates that these elements are more than simply vestiges of a once-practiced genre. See Demaray's *Milton's Theatrical Epic: The Invention and Design of Paradise Lost* (Cambridge, MA: Harvard University Press, 1980), for discussion of dramatic elements in Milton's work.

and outside of London during the Interregnum and on into the eighteenth century.[21] James Shirley wrote his *Cupid and Death* for private performance between 1651 and 1653, probably for the sixth-formers he was then teaching. In 1653, during Cromwell's protectorate, it was performed for the visit of the Portuguese Ambassador.[22] In 1654, a masque written by Thomas Jordan was performed on several occasions. Davenant's *The Siege of Rhodes* was performed publicly at Rutland House in 1656. Subtitled *Made a Representation by the Art of Perspective in Scenes, and the Story sung in Recitative Musick,* the work shows its former incarnation as the final court masque presented for Charles I, especially in its use of perspectival scene.[23] Dryden could write his *Secular Masque* (almost sixty years after the execution of Charles I) to celebrate the close of the seventeenth century, confident in his audience's familiarity with the genre. While Traherne clearly apprised himself of the performative masque, the masque also enjoyed a rich afterlife in apocalyptic

---

[21] Joanne Altieri, *The Theatre of Praise: The Panegyric Tradition in Seventeenth-Century English Drama* (Newark, DE: University of Delaware Press, 1986), argues that the masque tradition, far from disappearing, spans the Interregnum and passes on certain conventions to the developing genres of opera and musical theater. Like masques performed privately during the Interregnum, public pageants also exemplified certain of the masque stage conventions. Though the change in government stopped masques in Whitehall in the 1640s, "there was no inherent incompatibility between Puritan sympathies and interest in masques. By the 1650s, Cromwell created a *de facto* court and staged a masque for the wedding of one of his daughters" (106). For further discussion of the survival and performance of masque-like forms during the Interregnum see James R. Jacob and Timothy Raylor, "Opera and Obedience: Thomas Hobbes and *A Proposition for Advancement of Moralitie* by Sir William Davenant," *The Seventeenth Century* 6 (1991): 205–50; and Susan J. Wiseman, "History Digested: Opera and Colonialism in the 1650's," in *Literature and the English Civil War*, ed. Thomas Healy and Jonathan Sawday (Cambridge: Cambridge University Press, 1990), 189–204.

[22] Notes in the first edition of the masque reveal that the "Scenes wanted no elegance, or curiosity for the delight of the spectator," that "the musical compositions had in them a great soul of harmony," and that the "gentlemen that performed the dances . . . shewed themselves masters of their quality." In other words, this was not a scaled-down, bare-bones performance that stereotyped views of Puritan rule might lead us to expect, but a masque presented in the tradition of the full court masque.

[23] The closing of the theaters after the Civil War forced many performances of plays and masques into private Inns and homes and into countryside venues, such as the Inn at Hereford where Traherne lived with his uncle; see John Webb, *Memorials of the Civil War in Herefordshire*, 2 vols. (London: Longmans, Green and Company, 1879). Records of such provincial performances are sparse, as are many records of events and publications outside of London during Puritan rule, and we are fortunate to have accounts of Davenant's effort. Though musical recitative replace the masque dances, the scenes are "framed" in scenic perspective so familiar to the masque. Like the masques performed in private theaters during the Interregnum, Davenant's play had changeable scenery and machines for flying characters, giving it a heroic grandeur in scene and in sound, which dwarfed the plot and the acting.

literature after the death of James's eldest son, Henry. As I will discuss, this apocalyptic masque also finds representation in Traherne's work.

Traherne had many opportunities, as his pointed reference in *The Kingdom of God* confirms, to become intimately familiar with the masque in performance. This confirmation of what had heretofore been substantial, though subtle, evidence in Traherne's creative work of his direct understanding of the masque invites examination of how the masque figures into Traherne's work at large. Given his pointed criticism of the genre, his use of the masque as the fundamental structure in his imaginative spiritual configuration of interior space seems at best contradictory. However, several aspects of the masque form appeal to Traherne. Lambeth MS. 1360 underscores emphatically that Traherne's visual language is indexed to the language and practice of linear perspective. Linear perspective initially received widespread exposure in England after 1605 through the form of the court masque; Inigo Jones's visits to Italy, where he observed Italian *Intermezzi*, convinced him to offer perspectival stage design in the Banqueting House where he and Ben Jonson put up the majority of the court entertainments for James I.[24] As critics in the Warburg school — D. J. Gordon, Stephen Orgel, and Roy Strong — have shown, the function of centrist perspective in the masque was not merely to give masque scenes the illusion of reality. The centrist point for viewing these scenes became both the ideal place for viewing the stage and the symbol of James's power. Jones designed the perspectival lines so that they would meet in James's eye, giving him a perfect three-dimensional view of the "scene." Only the king seated on a raised platform could view the scene correctly. Other viewers were seated around James in hierarchical order, the favorites closest to his central and elevated position. Thus his central position invited onlookers to marvel at James as much as or more than at the stage itself. In this manner, Jones used perspective both to symbolize and to empower the royal position.[25]

---

[24] The first perspectival scenery to appear on an English stage was constructed for Jonson and Jones's *Masque of Blacknesse* (1605). Jones's introduction of perspective scenery, with its inherent centrism, followed the Italian Serlio's design for the theater. The profile and ground-plan from Serlio's *Architettura* shows from the side and from above a detailed perspective drawing of the ideal perspective stage, with a point specified from which the nobility would achieve a perfect view; see Lily B. Campbell, *Scenes and Machines on the English Stage During the Renaissance* (Cambridge: Cambridge University Press, 1923), 32–42, which remains the best introduction to the staging of the masque.

[25] As Helen Cooper summarizes, "The action [of the masque] emanates from the chair of state — it begins when the King takes his place, and describes the condition brought about by his presence, and it is also presented to him, in terms of dramatic focus and as a kind of homage": see "Location and Meaning in Masque, Morality, and Royal Entertainment," in *The Court Masque*, ed. David Lindley (Manchester: Manchester University Press, 1984), 135–48, here 137.

The passage I quoted earlier from "Retirement" shows a striking and almost verbatim repetition of how the court masque worked in James's rule. The soul replaces the king in Traherne's visual world and becomes the "Sphere of Treasures, the point of Concurrence, wherein all the Influences of Heaven meet, the pupil of vision out of which all the Rays & Beams of Sight disperse themselves & so like God, an Invisible Sphere of all his Kingdom" (fol. 10v). The difference here is the availability of this privileged position to all believers. Traherne summarizes his use of the masque in "Eas":

4
That all the Earth is one continued Globe,
And that all men theron are Living Treasures,
That fields and Meadows are a Glorious Robe,
Adorning it with Sweet and Heavenly Pleasures;

5
That all we see is ours, and evry One
Possessor of the Whole; that evry Man
Is like a God Incarnat on the Throne,
Even like the first for whom the World began;

...

8
This shows a Wise Contrivance, and discovers
Som Great Creator Sitting on the Throne,
That so disposeth things for all his Lovers,
That evry one might reign like GOD alone. ("Eas," 13–20; 29–32)

As he describes it in "Eas," Traherne's project of creating an enclosed visual world shared between the reflecting soul of the faithful Christian and God finds its perfect expression in the image of the court masque as Jones designed it. While the *Poems of Felicity* read as a sequence present a spiritual autobiography figured around the notion of faith and redemption as processes of re-visioning — seeing again as a child sees — Traherne's technical description of this visual process is anything but childlike. His language, as many readers have noted, is non-metaphoric or "transparent," stripped of the particular.[26] This language is visual, as I

---

[26] For pioneering discussions of Traherne's language and metaphor, see Barbara K. Lewalski, *Protestant Poetics and the Seventeenth-Century Religious Lyric* (Princeton: Princeton University Press, 1979), 352–87; and Stanley N. Stewart, *The Expanded Voice: The Art of Thomas Traherne* (San Marino: Huntington Library, 1970).

have argued, though not mimetic. He alludes to objects in the concrete world, relying upon the particular of "things" being ensconced already in the mind's eye. In refusing to name, he silently removes emphasis from the external world. Instead, the technical vocabulary of linear perspective functions in Traherne's work as an overarching structuring device, one he employs to convey his conception of spiritual vision. That conception is technical and unique, and based principally upon Jones's conception of the court masque. As Traherne's world is not a veil through which individuals may see God, neither is his language.

Lambeth MS. 1360 particularizes Traherne's contact with the court masque. Further, his clear knowledge of the form, though expressed in the negative, supports his almost introverted use of the form as a substructure in his creative work. Traherne's poetry in the Lambeth manuscript further adds to the catalogue of instances in which he employs the masque form as a substructure in his unique version of religious faith. His poem beginning "A Wise Man will apply his mind" sets out to list characteristics of several virtuous types. "A Wise Man," "A Good Man," "A Holy Man," "A Righteous Man," "A Man that hath a tender sence," "A Greatfull Person," "A Heavenly Person," and "An Activ Man": these are the subjects of the first six stanzas of the poem, the first three discussed in stanza one, and each of the next five having its own stanza. In stanza seven, individual characters he discusses in the previous stanzas collapse into one astonishingly powerful person:

7
A Wise, a Good, a Holy Man,
To End where we began;
A lively Righteous Gratefull Soul,
A pious Learned Wight
A Blessed Man that doth Controul
The Powers of the night,
An Active Heavenly Glorious Person is
Employd, & Busy, in the Work of Bliss.

(Lambeth MS. 1360, fols. 274v–275r)

Traherne's method here of isolating characteristics into individual persons and then collapsing them into one individual stylistically reenacts his use of perspective, with the many limiting and limited individual points of view merging into his expanded and ideal one. This individual, further, develops his visual sense to be the way God's is from his heavenly throne, paradoxically both bound and unbound:

8
He feels, he sees, he tastes, he knows,
He like his Maker Grows.
He loves, & prizes all his Works

Even as his God doth doe,
And ponders oft what Glory lurks
In all things he doth view.
While evry thing enflames his Soul with Love;
And evry thing his Joy, his Bliss, doth prove.
(Lambeth MS. 1360, fol. 275r)

As with the collapsing of all virtuous traits into a single representative person,
Traherne here shows a progressive development of that person's senses — "he
like his Maker Grows" — and continues to describe that sensual growth towards
sharing the heavenly throne throughout the poem. In the following stanza, "His
Noble sence exalteth all / That is before his Ey," and he begins to name things
on earth by "their Heavenly Names"; this naming ability shows a new capacity
to see everything as God sees it. As he gains this facility, he also moves toward
divinity, with the stanza ending "for he / Is Holiness & all felicitie." Indeed, as
Traherne asserts in stanza 10, looking and seeing *are* becoming: "His God in
Evry thing / All Heaven descends, environs, enters him; / He is transfigurd to a
Seraphim." "A sight of happiness is happiness," Traherne writes in the *Centuries*,
and "The Contemplation of Eternity maketh the Soul Immortal. Whose Glory
it is, that it can see before and after its Existence into Endless Spaces. *Its Sight is
its Presence*" (*CM*, 1.55; emphasis added). In these quotations from the *Centuries*
Traherne emphasizes that the ideal visual world he sets up is a world where objects — things — are abstractions and emotions, and where seeing one of these
internalized objects leads to instantaneous feeling. In this Lambeth MS. poem,
he describes the process of reaching that idealized state of "beatifick vision," as
he names it in the final stanza of this poem: "Being transformed," he describes in
stanza 11, "himself he is / A very Spring of Bliss. / And evry thing he sees, his ey
/ Doth Bless & Magnifie." Moreover, as in the *Centuries*, the transformed viewer
brings his new state to "The objects he doth see," and these objects transform into
objects as God in his heavenly masque sees them. Because the transformation is
complete in the poem, Traherne now gives us heavenly names of objects on earth,
and these names are coeval with the abstract objects that Traherne tells us elsewhere (in the series of "Thoughts" poems, for example) exist in the "beatifick"
person's mirroring soul: what the viewer sees is "burnt, & turnt to fire; / Love,
Pleasure, & Desire / Joy, Praise, Peace, Gratitude, & Bliss, / When well Digested evry creature is."

In his signature language of simple phrase upon phrase, Traherne manages
to offer in the final stanzas of this Lambeth MS. poem a complex sense of the
world as the newly beatified Christian may see it. Here Traherne circumscribes
most comparisons of that new world, creating a clever verbal shorthand parallel to the circumscribed space imposed by linear perspective: "sphere," "mine,"
"map," "womb," "ocean," "World." The notable exception, "Abyss," the Vulgate

word for "the deep" in Genesis and Revelation, is immediately qualified with "Of Joys"; typically Traherne tucks an odd duck into a group of likes, in order to impose the characteristics of the likes onto the dislike, and in order to suggest a metaphor without using one in the traditional way. "Map," juxtaposed with "Abyss," is paradoxical, though not in the traditional sense of "my love is like a lawnmower," where simile or metaphor offers the paradox. As with a traditional paradox, Traherne attempts to create an entity that does not exist in language, in this case an infinite space with the characteristics of a carefully contained and ordered finite space, a space organized around *both* linear perspective *and* decentered perspective. I quote the final three stanzas of this poem in their totality.

13
A Glorious Region of Delights,
A Blessed Sphere of Sights
A fair transparent Mine of Treasures
A Real Map of Bliss
A fertile Womb of Heavenly Pleasures,
An Ocean, or Abyss
Of Joys; a World of Glory is the place,
Wherin in Evry thing he sees his face.

14
The Common, Constant, freely given,
The neer, tho daily seen,
The necessary, nay & even
Eternal, Lov, (the Queen
of Bliss,) doth for these Causes more
Esteem them, & adore
The Doner more: He takes far more Delight
That sees them with a Beatifick Sight.

15
Natures Corruption he doth hate
Seeking his former State;
Or rather that Exalted one,
Which truly is Divine,
To be Enjoyd, when on the Throne
Of Glory he doth Shine.
Where all his Body shall be purified
Flesh turnd to sense, & sense be DEIFIED.
(Lambeth MS. 1360, fols. 275v–276r)

The end of the poem rests where Traherne philosophically and technically rests many of his poems and arguments: the beatified Christian may finally reach a deified, as well as beatific state, where he sits on the throne with God and sees as God sees. Traherne's language moves here and elsewhere from the merely perspectival to the particular visual language of the masque, the king on a throne viewing an all-encompassing scene.

Lambeth MS. 1360 shows Traherne's metaphor of the court masque as deifying vision, and its strong emphasis sends us back to Traherne's other work to mine for similar language. "The World," from *The Poems of Felicity,* epitomizes perspectival linguistic movement in "A Wise Man will apply his mind." The poem depicts a turning point in the speaker's spiritual autobiography in which he remembers the pure vision he had as a child. Typically, Traherne renders this return to a childhood perception in a clean language evocative of childhood, thus bringing into sharp relief language that does not pertain to a child's experience. In "The World," that language is the language of vision, the court, and the theater. In the context of Lambeth MS. 1360, we understand that this visual, courtly language constructs Traherne's ideal world as the masque. Before using masquing language, Traherne lays out the three-part progression of a Christian's vision. As I have noted, childhood vision for Traherne is analogous to anamorphic vision, and Traherne emphasizes here a return to that pre-perspectival vision:

> What shal I render unto thee, my God,
>> For teaching me
>> The Wealth to see
> Which doth enrich thy Great Abode?
> My virgin-thoughts in Childhood were
>> Full of Content,
>> And innocent,
> Without disturbance, free and clear,
> Ev'n like the Streams of Crystal Springs,
>> Where all the curious things
> Do from the bottom of the Well appear
> When no filth or mud is there. ("The World," 25–36)

The speaker's envisioning the world again from his pre-perspectival point of view as a child leads to his "Felicity," a state of being in which the speaker finds himself back "in frame" with his world. The "curious things" at the bottom of the well are at once clear, but also have their own perspective: "curious" in the sense it often appears in this period, referring to anamorphic perspective, perspective literally "without center," the corollary to vision trained to see by linear perspective. Traherne consistently uses this term for non-linear perspective in association with a child's vision, a kind of perspective that God gives to a child in order that he may see purely. For example, Traherne explains God's educational method in "The Approach":

> Those Thoughts his Goodness long before
> Prepard as Precious and Celestial Store;
> With curious Art in me inlaid,
> That Childhood might it self alone be said,
> My Tutor, Teacher, Guid to be;
> Instructed then even by the Deitie. ("The Approach," 37–42)

As in this final stanza of "The Approach," the pure, decentered perspective of this child's vision — "with curious Art in me inlaid" — Traherne emphasizes is quite apart from the centered and false vision of an adult's world. "[I]n-laid" refers also to the use of marquetry — wooden inlays — in "curious" cabinetry and boxes, a sophisticated combination of perspectival trickery and craft that offers multiple perspective within a circumscribed space. God in this instance becomes the perspectival craftsman, inlaying alternative views in the child's soul. The adult must adjust his viewing position to see again the alternative view that he saw as a child. As I have argued, Traherne understands the visual field as spiritual recovery in three stages: the anamorphic stage of a child's vision, untrained and uncorrupted by totalizing perspectival vision; an adult's vision given over to the false objective vision of the perspectival system; and the Christian vision, a rediscovery of decentered perspective through the visual field of linear perspective, offering the Christian the best of both visual systems. This is God's visual field. Since he now sees in proper perspective, the speaker's description of his rediscovery of felicitous space is markedly different from his descriptions of his visual and mental frustration in lyrics such as "Solitude" and "Felicity." In these earlier poems, Traherne as speaker is in a disengaged, disjointed condition. However, this memory of childhood vision initiates the speaker's achievement of heavenly vision, which incorporates both decentered and perspectival vision into "Heavenly perspective." In the last stanzas of "The World," the language echoes the speaker's new sense of visual balance and proportion, with all things in their proper places, and he in the best place to see them. Here the language moves into the masquing metaphor prominent in the Lambeth MS. I underline that emerging theatrical language in these stanzas:

> The Skies abov so sweetly then did smile,
> > *Their Curtains spread*
> > Above my Head
> And with its hight mine Ey beguile;
> So lovly did the distant Green
> > That fring'd the field
> > Appear, and yield
> *Such pleasant Prospects to be seen*
> From neighb'ring Hills; no precious Stone,
> > Or Crown, or Royal Throne,

Which do bedeck the Richest Indian Lord,
    Could such Delight aford.

The Sun, that gilded all the bordering Woods,
    Shone from the Sky
    To beautify
My Earthly and my Hevenly Goods;
    Exalted in his Throne on High,
    He shed his Beams
    In golden Streams
That did illustrat all the Sky;
    Those Floods of Light, his nimble Rays,
    Did fill the glittr'ing Ways,
While that unsufferable piercing Ey
    The Ground did glorify.

The choicest Colors, Yellow, Green, and Blew
    Did all this Court
    In comly sort
A mixt variety bestrew;
Like Gold with Emeralds between;
    As if my God
    From his Abode
By these intended to be seen.
And so He was: I him descry'd
    In's Works, the surest Guide
Dame Nature yields; His Lov, His Life doth there
    For evermore appear. ("The World," 49–84; emphasis added)

Early in the poem, Traherne establishes the kind of perspective that he gains by returning to and then transcending childlike vision. Once his vision is re-formed in these stanzas the speaker describes his visual experience in the more specific language of the court as an extended metaphor. The speaker of "The World" understands that "the great Beauties of this Frame" are revealed when the skies sweetly "Their Curtains spread," revealing "pleasant Prospects" (perspective views) illuminated by God as the sun and king "Exalted in his Throne on high." The speaker details the space that he encloses in the poem as a work of art, but more specifically as a work within the court: "The choicest Colors, Yellow, Green, and Blew / Did all this Court / In comly sort / A mixt variety bestrew" (73–76). As with the passages I quote from "Retirement," Traherne uses the trappings of the earthly court to place the heavenly view into relief: this scene contains no earthly "precious Stone, / Or Crown, or Royal Throne" (though here he covers himself in Shakespearean fashion, dislocating this inferior court to India). Traherne's language so closely parallels certain aspects of court performances that he could easily have a script in hand as he designs the poem. His language, understated and distilled throughout his work, here represents the speaker's recovery of a pure relationship with God in terms specific to court entertainment.[27] As important, Traherne describes God as desiring to be seen within this perspectival world, and he is seen, both as he sits on the throne and in a decentered fashion, within every object in the scene, replicating the child's innocent vision. Traherne stresses that, unlike the court masque, God's vision for its part goes beyond the perspectival, and may see individual objects within the scene, as one could see before the invention of perspectival vision. This perfect amalgam of kinds of vision is God's ability, and his gift, to those who wish to see as God sees.

"The World" singularly describes the movement from a child's decentered vision, to spiritual tunnel vision, to heavenly, masque-like vision that is the model for salvation in all of Traherne's work. Comparing "The World" with a specific masque, Ben Jonson's *Masque of Beauty*, confirms the newly invigorated understanding of Traherne's visual language that the Lambeth MS. provides. While *Masque of Beauty* may not be the specific context for Traherne's poem, the striking resemblances make it an instructive comparative tool. The masque emphasizes the role of the sun as a model for perfect, kingly perspectival vision. As in the passages from "Atom" and "Hosanna" I quote above, Traherne's sun in "The World" finds its metaphoric antecedent in Jonson's invention. The black Æthiopian women in Jonson's masque suffer from Petrarchists' elevation of their pale English counterparts to the highest standard of beauty. Their blackness caused, the masque argues, by overcooking by the sun can be repaired only by the sun, and the King of course plays the role of restoring their porcelain skin, and their beauty. Thus, the panegyric gesture suggests, the king is more powerful than the

---

[27] The concept of private space was emerging in the Renaissance, and Traherne's perspectivism reflects that development to some extent. See *History of Private Life* 3, *Passions of the Renaissance*, ed. Roger Chartier, trans. Arthur Goldhammer (Cambridge, MA: Harvard University Press, 1989). In addition to his poems that use the image of the masque as the organizing principle for the discovery of true spiritual vision, the *Centuries of Meditations* also make reference to theatrical space: Earth is the "theatre of God's righteous Kingdom" (*CM*, 2.97), the "theatre of virtues" (*CM*, 4.39); infinity is the theater for God's "Almighty Power" (*CM*, 5.4), while God's omnipresence is "a theatre of infinite excellency" (*CM*, 5.9). Throughout his work, in other words, the poems, the *Centuries, Christian Ethicks*, up to the latest discovery, MS. 1360, Traherne expresses an understanding of space by analogy to the theater, imposing the circumscribing description of a "theater" upon the boundless concepts of spatial infinity and temporal eternity.

sun. Like James in the masque, Traherne's king can transform human beings from the darkness of the fallen sinner to the beauty of the faithful Christian.[28]

In a fashion parallel to that of Jonson's masque, Traherne casts God as king, and then God as king playing the sun, "Exalted in his Throne on High." As sun, God sends out his rays like perspectival orthogonal lines. As D. J. Gordon observes in his discussion of the masque, the social analogy between the king and the sun's place in the solar system was a commonplace. But Jonson also draws upon the Neo-Platonic concept of the sun as the central star that in sending out its rays gives proportion and balance to the universe.[29] This theory of beauty for Neo-Platonists such as Ficino and Pico (adapted from Alberti's treatises on perspective) stresses that perfection depends upon a single object, which synthesizes several different elements harmoniously and in proper proportion. Harmony — the proper relation of all created objects to one another — is essential to beauty, and harmony of diverse aspects of single objects is most essential to beauty. The prevalent Neo-Platonism of the court masque echoes the strong Neo-Platonic elements that readers have long identified in other aspects of Traherne's work.[30] In its Neo-Platonism, the masque both complements and shapes Traherne's Neo-Platonism.[31]

---

[28] Traherne elaborates in *Christian Ethicks,* as well:

THE sun is a glorious Creature, and its Beams extend to the utmost Stars, by shining on them it cloaths them with light, and by its Rayes exciteth all their influences. It enlightens the Eyes of all the Creatures: It shineth on forty King-domes at the same time, on Seas and Continents in a general manner; yet so particularly regardeth all, that every Mote in the Air, every Grain of Dust, every Sand, every Spire of Grass is wholly illuminated thereby, as if it did entirely shine upon that alone. Nor does it onely illuminate all these Objects in an idle manner, its Beams are Operative, enter in, fill the Pores of Things with Spirits, and impregnate them with Powers, cause all their Emanations, Odors, Vertues and Operations; Springs, Rivers, Minerals and Vegetables are all perfected by the Sun, all the Motion, Life and sense of Birds, Beasts and Fishes dependeth on the same. (*CE*, 39–40)

[29] D. J. Gordon, *The Renaissance Imagination* (Berkeley: University of California Press, 1975), 143.

[30] Roy Strong further discusses the masques' Neo-Platonism in *Art and Power: Renaissance Festivals, 1450–1650* (London: Boydell and Brewer Press, 1984), 156–57.

[31] Humanists in general, and especially Neo-Platonists such as Marsilio Ficino and Pico della Mirandola, knew Alberti's *De pictura*, the first work to discuss the philosophical underpinnings of the invention of linear perspective. These two readers function as both Alberti's audience and his context; they emphasize the fundamental ideas of this treatise: its associations of whole vision with perspectival drawing and of proportional balance with human well-being. The central term that conveys the relationship between complete and

I use "The World" to illustrate Traherne's masquing because the poem compactly epitomizes the outline of the spiritual journey that Traherne narrates in visual terms throughout his work. Individual poems and prose passages throughout Traherne's oeuvre contain synecdoches of the masquing structure that emphasize a further important characteristic of the genre which gives it such currency for Traherne. As I have pointed out, God's place on his throne is analogous to the king's view of the masque, down to the smallest detail of where the orthogonal lines meet to ensure the perfect perspectival view. In such poems as "The Improvment," Traherne assumes that we as readers hold this knowledge always in reserve, and so gives us merely fragments of information. "To make the Product of far distant Seas / Meet in a point, be present to mine EY / In Virtu, not in Bulk . . . / Is far more Great than to create them where / They now do stand. . . ." (31–33; 38–39) Besides retooling the visual aspects of the masque, Traherne also machines their more broadly representative and metaphoric aspects in relation to kingship, a part of the Neo-Platonic constellation of ideas associated with the masque.

The masque, besides offering a symbolic parable of kingly power, also showed the attending audience a model of the king's mind. The ordering that occurred on stage in Jonson's masque when blackness became beauty represents the essential

---

balanced perspective and rational balance is Alberti's concept, *istoria,* an idea that has no English approximation, but can mean variously "story" or "history." *Istoria* is also the term for the first level of medieval textual exegesis. Though it appears rather late in Alberti's work (in the middle of the second book), *istoria* as Alberti reconfigures it becomes one of the controlling principles in the treatise, one that Alberti places at the apex of his theory:

> Composition is the procedure in painting by which the parts are composed together in the painting. The great work of the painter is not a colossus but an *istoria* for there is far more merit in an *istoria* than a colossus. Parts of the *istoria* are the bodies, part of the body is a member, and part of the member is the surface. The principal parts of the work are the surfaces, because from these come the members, from the members the bodies, from the bodies the *istoria,* and finally the finished work of the painter. From the composition of surfaces arises that elegant harmony and grace in bodies, which they call beauty. (Alberti, *On Painting,* trans. C. Grayson [New York: Penguin, 1991], 73)

By *istoria,* Alberti does not mean simply "story" or "history," but rather an ordering of objects in the space of the painting so that the order will inspire emotional response from the observer. The Neo-Platonic aspects of the masque draw upon this idea of the ordering of the minds of viewers of the masque with the ordering of the space, representing the king's mind. I am grateful to Melinda Schlitt for discussions of Alberti's *istoria.* See Mark Jarzombek, *On Leon Baptista Alberti: His Literary and Aesthetic Theories* (Cambridge, MA: MIT Press, 1989) for a comprehensive discussion of his aesthetics and their relationship to rhetoric.

blueprint for every masque, and the ethos that the masque represents; the king's mind may suffer onslaught from forces attempting to derail his power, but in the end the power of his person, and his mind, overcome all. This feature of the masque perfectly suits Traherne's creation of the delimited visual world that circulates between the faithful Christian's soul and God: God's being infuses itself into the universe and gives it order. Like the king viewing the masque, he enjoys seeing himself displayed in such a way. And the best way for him to see this essential self is in the perspectival soul of the believer. The first two stanzas of "Felicity" from the *Poems of Felicity* make Traherne's use of this aspect of the masque explicit:

> Prompted to seek my Bliss abov the Skies,
>   How often did I lift mine Eys
>   Beyond the Spheres!
> Dame Nature told me there was endless Space
> Within my Soul; I spy'd its very face:
>   Sure it not for nought appears.
>   What is there which a Man may see
>   Beyond the Spheres?
>   FELICITY.
>
> There in the Mind of God, the Sphere of Lov,
>   (In nature, hight, extent, abov
>   All others Spheres,)
> A Man may see Himself, the World, the Bride
> Of God *His Church*, which as they there are ey'd
>   Strangely exalted each appears:
>   His Mind is higher than the Space
>   Above the Spheres,
>   Surmounts all Place. ("Felicity," 1–18)

The poem itself is well ordered with three stanzas of nine lines each, each stanza mirroring the others (the number nine perhaps reflecting the number of the spheres). The likewise well-ordered "Mind of God," like the king's mind in the masque, contains all, and shows all in the universe. Moreover, the particular space of the soul becomes the miraculously contained, but infinitely expanding, Banqueting House. If the believer shifts his perspective to God's point of view, which his faith makes available, he, too, can see this model of God on display, and may see there "Himself, the World" and "*His Church*." Admittedly, the things that comprise God's mind have little resemblance to the collection of faeries, demons, animals, and exotics populating the Jonsonian masques. Yet the masque is what Traherne bases this poem and his entire program for redemption upon: the end of the poem notes that this experience is "A Scene abov / All Interludes," employing both of the well-known synonyms for the masque, "Scene" and "interlude." For Traherne, then, the unlikely genre of the court masque provides the model of God's vision, and a pattern for the faithful Christian. Traherne is undeterred by what he sees as the corrupt use of perspectival vision by the court. God offers the form for all things, and the clever propagandist James with his doctrine of divine right would of course appropriate God's visual field for his own uses. But without the sensibility of a child's decentered vision, the masque as the court uses it is a corrupt misappropriation of heavenly forms.

Apocalyptic Masquing

This unifying principle of the court masque — that a single mind can be simultaneously on display, interior, and containing all visible persons and things — also found a sympathetic cause in the English apocalyptic movement. The Cambridge Neo-Platonist John Smith, whom Traherne had read, incorporates the masque into his prose in a discussion of the book of Revelation, the apocalyptic section of the New Testament. Smith's use of the masque in his *Select Discourses* (1660) resembles Traherne's; both writers draw upon the masque as a visualization of the interior person.[32] Smith writes,

> We must remember what hath been often suggested, *That the Prophetical scene or Stage upon which all apparitions were made to the Prophet*, was his imagination; and that there all those things which God would have revealed unto him were acted over Symbolicallie, as in a Masque, in which divers persons are brought in, amongst which the Prophet himself bears a part: And therefore he, according to the exigencie of this Dramatical apparatus, must, as the other Actors, perform his part, sometimes by speaking and reciting things done, propounding questions, sometimes by acting that part which in the Drama he was appointed to act by some others; and so not only Speaking, but by Gestures and Actions come in his due place among the rest.[33]

[32] Traherne's reading of and debt to the Cambridge Neo-Platonists has been well rehearsed. See T. O. Beachcroft, "Traherne and the Cambridge Platonists," *Dublin Review* 186 (1930): 278–90; Gerard R. Cox, "Traherne's *Centuries*: A Platonic Devotion of 'Divine' Philosophy," *Modern Philology* 69 (1971): 10–24; Itrat Husain, *The Mystical Element in the Metaphysical Poets of the Seventeenth Century* (Edinburgh: Oliver and Boyd, 1948), 264–300; J. B. Leishman, *The Metaphysical Poets* (Oxford: Clarendon Press, 1934), 188–224; Carol L. Marks [Sicherman], "Thomas Traherne and Cambridge Platonism," *Publications of the Modern Language Association* 81 (1966): 521–34; and Elbert N. S. Thompson, "The Philosophy of Thomas Traherne," *Philological Quarterly* 8 (1928): 97–112.

[33] Quoted in Demaray, *Milton's Theatrical Epic*, 23.

Smith's "Prophet" is John on Patmos, who related his visions of "last things" in the book of Revelation. The masque attracted comparison with the book of Revelation, since both the masque and the apocalypse were composites of word and image.[34] In *Centuries* Traherne, like Smith, explicitly connects the idea of the king on his throne and the apocalypse: "To sit in the Throne of GOD is the most supreme Estate that can befall a Creature. It is Promised in the Revelations. But few understand what is promised there, and but few believ it" (*CM*, 71). These connections between the masque and the apocalyptic movement had their origins in the masque form in the court. Through a series of cues and miscues in the Stuart court, the masque became the literary tool of the radical Protestant movement and its attempt to bring about the apocalypse by Protestantizing the world.

James's eldest son Henry, a vehement champion of the arts and a student of the perspectivist Salomon de Caus, encouraged perspectival experimentation in masques written for his festivals. Since Henry disagreed with his father about the necessity of the radical Protestant cause, the public genre symbolizing royal power was a natural place for Henry to test his abilities and his power. Indeed, Roy Strong argues that frictions between James and Henry over the Protestant cause and the role of England in Continental politics were aired publicly and perspectivally in several of Jonson and Jones's masques written for Henry. *Oberon* (first performed in 1611) shifts perspectival focus from James to Henry.[35] The content of the masque mirrors the perspectival shift from king to prince; the action concerns elevating Oberon (Henry) to "Arthur's chair": "Melt earth to sea / . . .

---

[34] For a discussion of this aspect of the masque, see Joseph Wittreich, *The Apocalypse in English Renaissance Thought and Literature* (Ithaca: Cornell University Press, 1984), 19ff.

[35] In addition to *Oberon*, in which Henry danced the part of Oberon, Jonson dedicated *The Masque of Queens* (1609) to Henry and also wrote the speeches at Prince Henry's *Barriers* (1610) and *Love Restored* (1612) for Henry. Roy Strong elaborates in *Henry, Prince of Wales and England's Lost Renaissance* (London: Thames and Hudson, 1986):

> The *Barriers* and *Oberon* are the earliest examples of perspective being used to focus the eye on the central masquer, the Prince. There is no evidence in any of the earlier masques that perspective had ever been used in this way. Instead, the perspective element was more concerned with the King, from whose onlooking eyes the visual triangle radiated. The extension of this to arrangements on stage was logical. It reinforces the view that the initial use of perspective was always in symbolic terms rather than as a fundamental premise for the total reordering of pictorial space, and that these new moves concerning perspective must have stemmed from the Prince himself. Henry, in fact, worked from knowledge, for . . . he had been taught perspective by Salomon de Caus, who was to dedicate to him in 1612 his *La perspective avec la raison des ombres et miroirs*. (169–70)

Whilst we, in tunes, to Arthur's chair / Bear Oberon's desire."[36] (243–246). We can only imagine James's discomfort as he heard of "Oberon's desire" borne to "Arthur's chair," that is, of Henry's desire to assume the Arthurian heritage of the English monarchy. *The Barriers,* performed on Twelfth Night 1610, shows, Strong argues, "the young Prince present[ing] the new court of St. James's as the thinly veiled focus for a revival of the Elizabethan war party, fiercely Protestant and anti-Hapsburg. James I, the British Solomon, must have viewed his son's début as a man-at-arms with very mixed feelings."[37] Henry's death at nineteen, however, arrested the apocalyptic development in the masque. Strong asserts that if Henry had lived, "the art of festival in Stuart England would have taken a very different course from that which ended in the sterility of the self-adulatory masques of the Caroline age."[38] The Caroline masque would not have become the locus for the withdrawal of Charles I into a hermetic, private world, but would have, under Henry, served as a public announcement of Henry's apocalyptic vision for England.[39]

David Norbrook further argues that Prince Henry, and the group surrounding him, planned for the court masque to become an apocalyptic genre, representing the impending day when Henry would take the throne and lead England, the supreme Protestant nation, to victories over the papist antichrist.[40] At this juncture, Henry's champions believed, a time of peace would descend upon the earth, extending to the millennium.[41] These masques in the "reformed" tradition would

---

[36] In *Ben Jonson: Works*, ed. C.H. Herford, Percy Simpson, and Evelyn Simpson, 11 vols. (Oxford: Clarendon Press, 1925–1953), 7:243–46.

[37] Strong, *Henry*, 141.

[38] Strong, *Henry*, 139.

[39] Drawing on the work of Roy Strong and Stephen Orgel, Jennifer Chibnall sees a progression mirrored in court pageantry from Elizabeth's rule through James's and Charles's courts. That continuum is represented by the way each court dealt with its pageants. The less assured the monarch and court became, Chibnall argues, the more the court entertainments controlled certain elements that threatened that security. See "'To That Secure Fix'd State': The Function of the Caroline Masque Form," in *The Court Masque*, ed. Lindley, 73–93, here 80–81, for a detailed argument.

[40] David Norbrook, "The Reformation of the Masque," in *The Court Masque*, ed. Lindley, 94–110.

[41] These apocalyptic predictions concerning Henry's kingship are reflected in Donne's elegy for the Prince:

Was it not well beleev'd that hee would make
This generall peace, th'Eternall overtake,
And that his times might have stretch'd out so farre,
As to touch those, of which they emblems are?

prefigure and represent the apocalypse, when the material world would become fully spiritual again, with England as the paradise of the reconstituted Eden.[42] Thus the literary counter-tradition of the masque began as a groundswell of support for Prince Henry's vision of an imperialistic (and apocalyptic) England, and continued after his death, chiefly in commentaries on the Apocalypse. As Christopher Hill notes, these commentaries represented a popular vision: "Many in the seventeenth century believed the end of the world was imminent . . . Milton was . . . in good company when he wrote of Christ as 'shortly expected King.' . . . In the sixteen-fifties the doctrine had become almost a commonplace."[43] Because the court masque (especially under James with his doctrine of Divine Right) had represented the court as an ideal merger of heaven and earth, the use of the masque as a representation of apocalypse (which believers thought would foreshadow the time when heaven and earth would combine under the reign of Christ) was both an easy transition to and a pointed commentary on the use of the masque by the court. In an effectively neutered form, the masque continued to be performed during the Civil War, but became more powerful during the 1650s in a strict literary mode as a legacy of Henry's politics, ironically the same politics that undermined the form.

Traherne's stripped world, the world relieved of its manufactured beauty, is strikingly evocative of the 1613 "reformed" masque championed by the radical Protestant movement. The Inns of Court planned to present this elaborate masque for the marriage of Elizabeth to Frederick V of the Palatinate (Henry's death preempted the performance).[44] In the masque the world was split open to

---

> For to confirm this just beleefe, that now
> The last dayes came, wee saw heav'n did allow,
> That, but from his aspect and exercise,
> In peacefull times, Rumors of war did rise.
> But now this faith is heresie: we must
> Still stay, and vexe our great-grand-mother, Dust.
> (35–44; in *The Poems of John Donne*, ed. Herbert Grierson, 2 vols. [Oxford: Oxford University Press, 1912], 1:268)

The language of this passage mirrors that associated with the coming reign of Henry and the Protestant millennium that Donne, among others, predicted for that reign.

[42] Joanne Altieri, "Carew's *Momus*: A Caroline Response to Platonic Politics," *Journal of English and Germanic Philology* 88 (1989): 332–43, takes up Norbrook's argument and applies it to Carew's masques.

[43] Christopher Hill, *Puritanism and Revolution* (London: Mercury Books, 1958; repr. 1967), 325.

[44] Parts of this discussion of the 1613 apocalyptic masque rely upon Norbrook, "The Reformation of the Masque." Norbrook provides a broader context for his argument in idem, *Poetry and Politics in the English Renaissance* (London: Routledge and Kegan Paul, 1984).

reveal paradise. This anonymous masque mixes apocalyptic language with Jonesian and Jonsonian classicism and ritualism to present the invisible Protestant church in the form of Aletheia: Truth. This figure representing Truth was one parallel with the woman of Revelation 12, wandering in the wilderness, who had been the model for Una in Book I of Spenser's *Faerie Queene* and for the heroines of several sixteenth-century "reformations" of medieval mystery plays by Protestant playwrights. As David Norbrook argues, this 1613 masque meant to lend explicit apocalyptic imagery to the court. James would be lauded for seeking the Truth and allowing it to be preached. The union afforded by the marriage between Britain and the Palatinate would inspire preaching the Protestant word not only in Britain, but throughout the world:

> [W]hen the process [of preaching] had been completed, the apocalypse would be near. The Muses were to call on the different nations to abandon their quarrels and recognise the pure Truth preached in Britain. At this point the globe was to split in two and reveal a vision of Paradise, guarded by an angel with a flaming sword. The Muses would lead the repentant nations into Paradise to the sound of heavenly music, and the gates would shut behind them.[45]

The 1613 masque had as its center the revelation of paradise, with the globe split open to reveal the "Truth."

Traherne's description of "Heavenly perspective," as I have shown, follows the masque in its manifestation as a court entertainment. Traherne's project also is apocalyptic in its imagery, and further draws upon the masque's incarnation as a literary form. Though in principle Traherne's use of the masque parallels the ethos of the 1613 masque, Traherne's world doesn't quite split apart to reveal paradise and truth, as did the masque. Rather, Traherne reasserts anamorphic vision as a crucial ingredient of "Heavenly perspective" and argues for an anamorphic paradise, one existing concurrently with the perspectival world. "What Structures here among God's works appear?" ("The City," 1.1) Traherne asks in one of the final poems of *The Poems of Felicity.* "Such wonders *Adam* ne'r did see / In Paradise among the Trees, / No Works of Art like these," he continues, describing an alternative reality available to a child's anamorphic vision that supersedes even Paradise. Once the Christian "retires" to the mirroring eye of his soul, he may return to an enhanced version of his childhood vision, one that shows the alternative world created by the powerful ordering tool of linear perspective.

---

[45] Norbrook, "The Reformation of the Masque," 99.

"With curious Art in me inlaid":
Traherne's anamorphic "Christendom"

With this idea of unmasking paradise through perspectival sophistication, Traherne demonstrates a deep engagement with his visual culture. Although Leonardo was the first to experiment with anamorphosis, the technique enters England through Holbein's famous painting, "The Ambassadors" (1533),[46] which now hangs in the National Gallery in London. Much has been written about the painting, which shows two ambassadors standing in their finery surrounded with various texts and tools, designed to show their arrogance. The elongated disk floating over the floor tiles at their feet is an anamorphic skull; one must step away from the centrist viewing position and move to the side of the painting in order to see this *memento mori* in linear perspective.[47] While Holbein's use of anamorphosis is nihilistic — no matter how you look at things, you will die — anamorphic work did have a rich life in religious symbolism on the Continent. In the seventeenth century mirrors became widely used in anamorphic art. Held up to the seeming confusion of an anamorphic representation, refracting mirrors pulled the image together to reflect a recognizable and "realistic" representation. Often the effects of this kind of recovery of a single-point perspectival image were thought to imitate divine miracles, particularly in seventeenth-century France. The French perspectivist Jean-Francois Niceron, in his *Perspective Curieuse* (Paris, 1638; Latin version, *Thaumaturgus opticus*, 1646) emphasizes the relationship of anamorphic perspective and miraculous ability:

> If, I say, these authors ascribe these miraculous productions — [the automata] and an infinity of others which we read about in books — to the power operations of artificial Magic, we can certainly claim the same thing about the effects of perspective which are no less to be prized and admired. Philo the Jew in his book *De specialibus legibus* states expressly in these terms that true magic or the perfection of sciences consists in Perspective, which enables us to know and discern more perfectly the beautiful works of Nature and Art and which has been at all times in high esteem not only among the common people but among the most powerful monarchs of the world.[48]

Niceron here emphasizes the ability of perspective to show the hidden aspects of nature to all viewers. If linear perspective can achieve this feat, he argues,

---

[46] We know from Leonardo's notebooks that he was the first to experiment with anamorphic perspective within a linear perspectival system.

[47] My understanding of the painting is indebted to Jurgis Baltrusaitis: see *Anamorphic Art*, trans. W. J. Shachan (Cambridge: Chadwyck-Healey, 1977).

[48] Niceron, quoted in Baltrusaitis, *Anamorphic Art*, 39.

anamorphic perspective (manifest in automata, or machine-induced perspectival exhibits) shows even more clearly the ineffable aspects of the creator. God places the potential for miraculous acts in the world, but only the spiritually gifted, such as the saints, may lead others toward a point of view where these miracles can be seen. Anamorphic perspective thus serves Niceron as a kind of allegory for corrected spiritual vision. Niceron belonged to the Order of Minims, a group of monks who occupied themselves with making anamorphic murals that revealed the miracles of Christ, or portraits of various saints, bishops, and popes. Examples of these kinds of compositions appear in the enlarged edition of Niceron's *Thaumaturgus opticus:* one represents St. John the Apostle writing the Apocalypse, and the other St Francis of Paola, founder of the order of Minims. Emmanuel Maignan, like Niceron also a Minim, designed and painted the anamorphic mural *St Francis of Paola,* at the SS. Trinità dei Monti monastery in Rome, the only remaining example of an anamorphic mural from either the sixteenth or the seventeenth centuries.[49] Jurgis Baltrusaitis argues that, for these devoted members, the use of anamorphic principles must have involved something more than the simple manipulation of geometric postulates to create a clever *trompe l'oeil*. Rather, anamorphosis was used in religious works to represent a miraculous revelation. Johann Heinrich Glaser, in his 1638 engraving, hides a Christ head between scenes of the Fall and the expulsion from Paradise, thus emphasizing the redemptive design of God. Niceron and Maignan, Baltrusaitis contends, use rules provided by God's natural law to create their own miracles.

Understanding Traherne's vision of childlike vision in anamorphic terms explains the comparison in his poem "The City" of "The Hevens" with a "richly studded Case / Which did my richer Wealth inclose" (41–42); a part of anamorphic perspectival play included extravagant cases and cabinets revealing multiple views of various tableaux that required movement on the part of the viewer. As Traherne continues to describe his ideal city in terms of the anamorphic cabinet, he stresses its difference from perspective trickery as well: "No little privat Cabinet / In which my Gems to set / Did I contrive: I thought the whol Earth's face / At my Dispose" (43–46). Anamorphic games in England had been the purview of the privileged rich, but here, in a move similar to Niceron's, Traherne stresses the general availability of the richness of God's anamorphic world. Parallel to the circumscribed space of Jones's Banqueting House that contained the masques, these cabinets lock in the perspective entertainment, and block out all but the privileged few. One of Traherne's strongest impulses in his adaptation of perspectival entertainments entails opening the space for all; exclusivity for Traherne is that of

---

[49] See the foreword to Michael Schuyt and Joost Elffers, *Fantastic Architecture: Personal and Eccentric Visions,* text by George R. Collins (New York: Harry N. Abrams, 1980).

the faithful, not of the rich or pedigreed. Further, God's art is not confined, but has endless application and prospect, and as such forces the artists' anamorphoses to pale in comparison: "Such Treasures as are to be valu'd more / Than those shut up in Chests and Tills, / Which are by Citizens esteem'd" (71–73). Traherne takes perspectival art in general to task in the poem:

> 'Tis Art that hath the late Invention found
>   Of shutting up in little Room
>   Ones Endless Expectations: Men
>   Have in a narrow Penn
> Confin'd themselves: Free Souls can know no Bound;
>   But still presume
>   That Treasures evry where
> From Everlasting Hills must still appear,
>   And be to them
>   Joys in the New *Jerusalem*.[50] ("The City," 51–60)

The perspectival subject of the poem draws parallels between anamorphic cabinets and that "late Invention" shut up in a little room, the court masque. Once free of the limited uses by the wealthy and the royal, Traherne argues, perspective in its several earthly manifestations can reveal to Christians the city within the city, the New Jerusalem promised in the book of Revelation: "And I saw a new heaven and a new earth. . . . And I John saw the holy city, new Jerusalem, coming down from God out of heaven" (Revelation 21:1–2, Authorized Version). Any Christian may likewise see this vision, anamorphically inlaid in his soul. Traherne describes his view of New Jerusalem in "Christendom"; occurring just prior to "On Christmas Day" in the center of the *Poems of Felicity*, the poem explicitly discusses new vision in terms of the visual aspects of his culture Traherne works to revise:

>   Among ten thousand things,
>   Gold, Silver, Cherub's Wings,
> Pearls, Rubies, Diamonds, a Church with Spires,
>   Masks, Stages, Games and Plays,
>   That then might suit my yong Desires,
>   Fine Feathers, Farthings, Holidays,
>   Cards, Musick, Dice,
>   So much in price;
> A *City* did before mine eys present
> Its self, wherin there reigned sweet Content.

---

[50] Traherne is alluding here to Genesis 49:26.

> A Town beyond the Seas,
>   Whose Prospect much did pleas,
> And to my Soul so sweetly raise Delight
>   As if a long expected Joy,
>   Shut up in that transforming Sight,
>   Would into me its Self convey;
>   And Blessedness
>   I there possess,
> As if that City stood on reall Ground,
> And all the Profit mine which there was found. ("Christendom," 31–40)

His description of this "New Jerusalem" resembles the one he describes later in the sequence in "The City"; the town exists as an alternative to sight that had been "Shut up," and had seen only man-made — and strikingly courtly — aspects of his environs, especially "Masks, Stages, Games and Plays." Intriguingly, after asserting that a shift in position from which to view the world will reveal "reall" "prospects," and authentic "Masks, Stages, Games and Plays," Traherne follows this poem with one describing a Christmas play, or masque, in which the members of the Parish church — "the Plow-man" in "His gayer Weeds and Finer Band, / New Suit and Hat," — play the roles of the Christmas story. In their costumes, they sing praise to Christ "Who puchas'd their Repose: / Whereby their inward Joy they do disclose; / Their Dress alludes to better Works than those." These better works, of course, are those Traherne also alludes to in the previous poem, and embraces at the end of the *Poems of Felicity*, the apocalyptic return of Christ to unite heaven and earth into the New Jerusalem. The celebration of a church holy day, in this case Christmas, following a poem outlining how the Christian must change his visual stance in order to see the apocalyptic city, fits perfectly with Traherne's understanding both of the nature of God's vision and of the purpose of holy days. Holy days are means by which Christians may achieve shifts in perspectival vision; they are "Heavenly perspectives wherin we behold the Mystery of Ages, Mirrors of Eternity wherin we feed upon Revelations and Miracles" (*Church's Year Book*).[51]

---

[51] The passage, which recalls Revelation 1:6, is one of the more beautiful meditations in all of Traherne's work:

Why should we not spend som time upon Holy Days in Contemplating
the Beauty of Holy Dais them selves?
They are the Ornaments of Time, and the Beauty of the World.
The Days of Heaven seen upon Earth. . . .
The Lucid Intervals and lights of the Year. . . .
Wherin we might all be like Evangelists [Apostles and Angels].

Vision in Lambeth MS. 1360

Similar to Traherne's mirroring soul, Lambeth MS. 1360 gives us a mirror to
hold up to the corpus of Traherne's work, work that has been understood only
in terms of beatific happiness, infinity, erased boundaries, and mystical union.
Yet, as with Traherne's mirror, when we peer into the Lambeth manuscript we
see an alternative view of Traherne, one that has coexisted with these traditional
views of his work. Traherne does extol simplicity, childhood, and paradisal bliss
throughout his poetry and prose; there is little questioning that. But to draw
conclusions as we have done from these ecstatic celebrations about Traherne's
life and politics, we now see in the mirror of the Lambeth manuscript, has been
premature.[52]

Traherne's knowledge of the court and commitment to theological debate
suggest a powerful engagement with politics. Given the dearth of information
about his life, however, we may never know the depth of that engagement. The
very nature of his work argues against his acknowledging the facts surrounding
his life. Should he detail particulars about his life and work, he would then give
credibility to the world outside the closed synchronic visual system he constructs.
Traherne's lengthy advocacy of retirement in the first volume of the Lambeth
manuscript shows an anxiety about the world external to the self, and that anxiety informs both his erasing the notion of objective human vision and his eschewing the particular. Traherne's position is ironic. Damaged by politics, he

---

[Wherein we] are restored to the Joys of Heaven.
And Liv like Kings and Priests unto God.

Wherin we Antedate the Resurrection of the Dead.
And com from our Shops to our Saviors Throne.
From plowing our fields to manna in the Wilderness.
From Dressing our vineyards to the Wine of Angels.
From Caring for our Children, to be the Sons of God.
They are Heavenly perspectives wherin we behold the Mystery of Ages
[Mirrors of Eternity wherin we feed upon Revelations and Miracles]
Spiritual Regions, wherin we walk in the Paths of GOD.
(Bodleian MS. Eng. th. e. 51, fol. 101v)

[52] Both Nabil I. Matar, "The Political Views of Thomas Traherne," *Huntington Library Quarterly* 57 (1994): 241–53, and Julia Smith, "Attitudes Toward Conformity and
Nonconformity in Thomas Traherne," *Bunyan Studies* 1 (1988): 26–35, have argued for
Traherne's political engagement, as does the discovery of a political poem in Traherne's
hand. See Julia Smith and Laetitia Yeandle, "Felicity Disguised in Fiery Words: Genesis
and Exodus in a Newly Discovered Poem by Thomas Traherne," *Times Literary Supplement* (7 Nov. 1997): 17.

nevertheless fashions his whole interior world after a quintessentially political form. Safe within the room of his soul in his alternative world, Traherne insulates himself from war, dispute, and any unsettling personal divisions. Both the title and these lines from the poem "Silence" instruct us in Traherne's engagement: "When in my Soul the King of Kings did sit, / The World was more in me, than I in it" (79–80).

Traherne is a happy man, but only in the room of his soul, driven to this place by the profound discomfort he finds in his political milieu. With its emphasis on repudiating human perspectival vision, Traherne's work suggests that an age focusing upon subject formation also stresses as the reverse of the coin, the falsely objective, a focus that is untenable for the believing Christian. Likewise, for Traherne, weight on the specific in language would suggest a separation of subject and object. Traherne insists that the closed, "circulating" world of reverberating images is his reality, and thus any particular details about his exterior world would repudiate that reality. Traherne's perspectival world is of course as totalizing and restrictive as the linear perspective he reconstructs; yet for him, this is the "view aright." He supersedes the flashy world of Charles II in which he moves as Thomas Traherne, chaplain and theologian, with the subtle inner universe of the soul, where he circulates with the "reall" King and his true subject.[53]

[53] I am grateful to Barbara Lewalski and Helen Vendler for reading versions of this essay in its infancy. Thanks to Robert Aguirre, Kseniya Thomas, and Wendy Moffat for careful readings of this version. Dickinson College funded my time at the Lambeth Palace Library, making it possible for me to read Traherne's manuscript there.

very selves. They that place their ease in such a carelessness are of all others the greatest enemies and disturbers of themselves.[7]

Using forms of negation that are more likely to be employed in an apophatic account of God (or conversely in a Baconian use of the "negative instance"), Traherne here conjures up an existential modality that can only be characterized as what is not: it is a modality that is neither angelic, animalistic, nor can it be said to be even demonic as such. The accumulation of such negatives indicates the extent to which this perverse state challenges the accommodating powers of language. It is a form of virtual existence which demands that the term "virtual" be understood in an entirely different sense from the way Hall uses it when he speaks of "virtual devotion." Hall evokes the term "virtual" in order to imply that all actions of an ideally spiritual person are metonymies of praise. The modality, or more precisely (a)modality, that Traherne invokes here, however, is virtual in the sense that it is characterized by a lack of being, an indifference and carelessness that is nonetheless an active comportment towards oneself and the world. Unlike a rock, which is a-priori indifferent to itself, the subject Traherne addresses in this key passage is *actively* indifferent. What should thus not be missed here is that this (non)subject is not the opposite of being or spirit, but rather it is being's double — its de-animated mirror image, as it were. This modality arises when spirit becomes de-animated of that which makes it spirit, namely awareness of itself as a conscious being. Consequently, the only positive thing that could possibly be said of such a modality is that it constitutes a negation of its essence: it is a mode of being that *is* only insofar it is not *present to itself*. It is in this precise sense that this existential modality is spectral rather than substantial, uncanny rather than spiritual. Such a state is, as Traherne puts it in *Select Meditations*, "worse then [sic] death," for such "Spiritual Idleness is an Alienation of the mind from its Proper Objects," a "Separation of man from His True Happieness."[8]

In order to represent a modality that is not only characterized by, but is the very condition of, being out of joint, Traherne evokes the language of the *psychomachia* — the war within one's soul between spiritual and demonic forces. Only here it is not a metaphysical battle between externalized powers of good and evil, it is an existential question of failing to recognize oneself as an image of God. Whenever this state of inward conflict gets articulated in Traherne's work, the specter of the Civil War tends to loom large, and vice versa. Indeed, it is around the figure of the subject turned against itself, along with the nation at war with itself, that Traherne presents some of his most uncanny and spectral of

---

[7] Traherne, *Christian Ethics*, 22.

[8] Thomas Traherne, *Select Meditations*, ed. Julia J. Smith (Manchester: Fyfield Books, 1997), 37.

figures — each of which works, on the surface of things, to clarify the nature of a properly self-conscious soul but which, on closer view, distorts the image of an ideally self-conscious being. For instance, in "A Thanksgiving and Prayer for the Nation" — a poem in which Traherne speaks in the voice of David, the penitent Psalmist calling his nation to repentance — the speaker experiences England's conflict as an inward division within the self: "Let Wisdom speak that respecteth me; / But Love cry out with groans unutterable; / For thy Mercy and Long suffering, / Unto this my people. / O Lord mine will be the loss, / I the sufferer; / My Bowels torn by those Wars, / My Bosom the Stage of those Calamities" (62–69).[9] National conflict is registered here as an inward division within the physical and spiritual elements of the self. The conventional Christian topos of the *psychomachia* is thus adapted here in order to express the effects of social strife upon the individual subject — the most basic effect being a loss in the self's sense of unity. The implication here is that the conditions of possibility for self-awareness, the climate in which the ethico-spiritual life can be lived, are being lost.[10] And thus what the poem as a whole seeks to recover is an ordered vision of the nation — one that provides the occasion for the production of subjects whose every action constitutes a virtual act of praise.[11]

Through his diagnosis of the religious causes and spiritual effects of social unrest, Traherne politicizes the act of devotion and the art of thanksgiving in the manner explicated by Hall in *The Devout Soul*:

> That in a time when we hear no noise but of Drums and Trumpets, and talk of nothing but Arms, and Sieges, and Battels, I should write of Devotion, may seem to some of you strange and unseasonable; to me, contrarily, it

---

[9] Unless otherwise noted, all references to Traherne's poetry are to *Centuries, Poems and Thanksgivings*, ed. H. M. Margoliouth (Oxford: Clarendon Press, 1958).

[10] Christopher Ricks, developing William Empson's work, refers to the representation of external conflict as an inward conflict within the self as "the self-inwoven simile": see "Its Own Resemblance," in *Approaches to Marvell: The York Tercentenary Lectures*, ed. C. A. Patrides (London: Routledge and Kegan Paul, 1978), 108–35. The "self-inwoven simile" is one of the figures that Marshall Grossman implicitly addresses when he describes how "the organizing tropes of 'Upon Appleton House' constitute a seventeenth-century effort to represent an inward division of the self as a discontinuity in the relationship of individual action to providential design, of choice to destiny": see *Story of All Things: Writing the Self in Renaissance Poetic Narrative* (Durham, NC: Duke University Press, 1998), 202. See also Jonathan Sawday, "'Mysteriously Divided': Civil War, Madness and the Divided Self," in *Literature and the English Civil War*, ed. Thomas Healy and idem (Cambridge: Cambridge University Press, 1990), 127–46.

[11] The specter of civil war appears most clearly in "Dumbness" when Traherne uses civil conflict as a trope for representing the fall out of infant bliss into the world of language (lines 53–78).

seventeenth-century England Freud presumes as the *condition* for the uncanny return of the sacred within the interpretive horizon of the modern world. My point here is that the difference which passes between Traherne and Freud — the difference signaled by the qualifier "early" in the phrase "early modern" — is already at work within the historically specific rhetorical economy of Traherne's thought itself. This work is most clearly legible in his figures of de-animation.

Traherne's figures of de-animation do not present a shocking return of the repressed in the manner of Victorian gothic, but neither do they constitute a premodern mode of the uncanny as the eruption of the numinous such as we see in Genesis 28:17 when Jacob declares, "How dreadful is this place! this is none other but the house of Elohim."[22] On the contrary, what Traherne represents is the very process of de-animation itself. By diagnosing the loss of a sacramental conception of the nation in the form of a puppet show, Traherne expresses concern about the kind of subject that is produced in the absence of a nation whose subjects are self-consciously turned to God. What he signals in the figure of the dumb show, in other words, is a community (although that is entirely the wrong word) of subjects whose being is characterized by the utter absence of self-consciousness and consequently the capacity to praise. Traherne outlines the living-dead quality of such a being in *Commentaries of Heaven* when he delineates the form of self-alienation attendant upon a being incapable of praise due to inattention to the powers of its soul:

> Is not the Greatest Death that ere can be,
> A Separation from Felicitie?
> And what is Absence, had we but the Sence
> To feel its Sad and Direfull Consequence?
> If GOD the Glory be of Souls, their Life
> And Lov: then Separation is the Knife
> That kills a Soul! And we the Pain of Sence
> Should feel, but that we're slain [. . .]
> He that is Dead alive, when He doth die,
> Shall Quickened be to feel his Miserie.[23] (2, 1–8, 13–14)

---

[22] Rudolf Otto cites this as one of the exemplary articulations of the irrational dimension of the numinous, a dimension both awesome and terrifying. In this pre-modern mode, the sense of dread associated with the uncanny is subsumed within the realm of the numinous, while the modern form analyzed by Freud presupposes the vacating of the numinous. See Rudolph Otto, *The Idea of the Holy* (1917), trans. John H. Harvey (Oxford: Oxford University Press, 1957). For a discussion of the numinous in the eighteenth century see R. D. Stock, *The Holy and the Daemonic From Sir Thomas Browne to William Blake* (Princeton: Princeton University Press, 1982).

[23] Thomas Traherne, *Commentaries of Heaven: The Poems*, ed. D.D.C. Chambers (Salzburg: Institüt für Anglistik und Amerikanistik, Universität Salzburg, 1989).

This figure of a being who is "dead alive" returns throughout Traherne's work. This figure constitutes a kind of *revenant*, an uncanny double to the self-conscious, felicitous being venerated and articulated throughout Traherne's work. In the context of "A Prayer and Thanksgivings for the Nation," this uncanny figure emerges as a symptom of a disordered nation — a player in a dumb show, while here in the *Commentaries* it appears as a living dead creature who is unprepared not only for prayer but for his or her own death. Elsewhere, it will appear as the double of spirit itself.

Dead Puppets

In order to delineate the contours of a properly self-conscious being, Traherne often juxtaposes the vitality of human being with the inanimate quality of things existing in isolation from thought. In the poem "The Inference I," this kind of juxtaposition occurs in order to perceive the ontological distinction between animate and inanimate modalities, which then serves to clarify a mode of being characterized by a complete focus on God. As we have already seen, Traherne defines such an ideal mode of being in terms of "thoughtfulness" — the complete focus of mental attention on God: "Let all my Thoughts be fixt upon His Throne" (53). This state of complete devotion in the form of pure reflection is initially approached through a distinction between "thoughts" and "things": "Well-guided *Thoughts* within possess / The Treasures of all Blessedness. / *Things* are indifferent; nor giv / Joy of themselvs, nor griev" (1–4). This ostensibly straightforward opposition between animate "thoughts" and inanimate "things" then gives way to the seemingly un-Trahernian, not to mention logically destabilizing, remark: "The very Deity of God torments / The male-contents / Of Hell; To th' Soul alone it provs / A welcom Object, that Him lovs" (5–8). These "malcontents of hell" are represented as synonymous with, even as they are distinguishable from, dead things. More precisely, they are made to appear identical with inanimate objects divorced from an animating consciousness, while still sustaining a difference from pure objects insofar as they are subjects of discontent rather than totally "dead things." This strange complicating of the ostensibly straightforward opposition between "thoughts" and "things" is further complicated in stanza five of "The Inference I" when the difference between dead things and human perception — or in this case inattentive perception — is again blurred:

> How many Thousands see the Sky,
> The Sun and Moon, as well as I?
> How many more that view the Seas,
> Feel neither Joy nor Eas?
> Those Things are dead and dry and banished.

> Their Life is led
> As if the World were yet unmade. (39–45)

The object of the speaker's address is ambiguous at this point: is he referring to those inattentive, unselfconscious perceivers he is criticizing or the dead things which they are failing to animate with their consciousness, or both? The ambiguity is productive insofar as it heightens the uncanny quality of the highly curious state being pictured in the idea of living as though the world were unmade. To live before the world was made is not to live at all, but to haunt and to be haunted; it could only mean to be spectral, half-dead, and ghostlike. Traherne may be referring here to the state that Augustine argues existed before God invested creation with his image. In Augustine's reading of Genesis 1:3 in Book XII of *The Confessions*, creation was formless before it became "light":

> In its formless state it would not have been pleasing to you [God] unless it became light. And it became light, not simply by existing, but by fixing its gaze upon you and clinging to you, the Light which shone upon it.[24]

For Augustine, it is at this point that creation becomes animate, taking on the structure of a signifying system. Traherne thus seems to be implying that to live without being fully conscious of how one's mind animates things is to live as though those things, and indeed one's own self, had never been "made" or "animated" by God in the form of light; it is to live in a radically de-animated mode, a half-life.

To get a more precise sense of the state to which Traherne is referring, a mode so spectral as to be like living before the act of creation, we might turn to the moment in John Donne's *Devotions Upon Emergent Occasions* when Donne describes his condition of being physically ill in similarly uncanny terms. Feeling himself languishing in fever, Donne meditates on the similarities between his sick-bed and the grave:

> In the *Grave* I may speak thorough the stones, in the voice of my friends, and in the Accents of those words, which their love may afford my memory; Here I am mine owne *Ghost*, and rather affright my beholders, then instruct them; they conceive the worst of me now, and yet feare worse; they give me for dead now, & yet wonder how I doe, when they wake at midnight, and ask how I do to morrow.[25]

---

[24] St. Augustine, *The Confessions*, trans. R. S. Pine-Coffin (London: Penguin, 1961), 313.

[25] John Donne, *Devotions Upon Emergent Occasions*, ed. Anthony Raspa (New York and Oxford: Oxford University Press, 1987), 16.

It is telling that Donne evokes this uncanny state between life and death vis-à-vis a physical disease, while Traherne evokes it in relation to modes of knowing the world and oneself.[26] Donne, who is here preoccupied with diagnosing his own specific psycho-spiritual state, marshals this horrifying vision in order to express his individual experience of feeling isolated from the world. Traherne, on the other hand, evokes this uncanny state of non-being in order to make a general point about the responsibility individuals have to know themselves by coming to know their world. Traherne's meditation on perception thus turns, as his meditations often do, to a reflection upon the human person in the abstract and the modes of thought and self-awareness that characterize such a universal being: "O! What are Men, who can such Things [thoughts] produce, / So excellent in Nature, Valu, Use?" ("The Inference II," 9-10). "Inference II" concludes by reaffirming the point that when thoughts are properly pursued they are themselves acts of praise: "All that He [God] can receiv is this bare Sum / Of God-like Holy Thoughts: These only He / Expects from Us, our Sacrifice to be" (42–44). What is at stake in "The Inference" is not only the ontological priority of thoughts over things, but also the way in which thoughts vitalize the world, thereby animating the human person — a theme that is dilated upon in the following poem, "The City," in which human thoughts are materialized through architecture and other forms of artifice. For Traherne, human consciousness comes to fruition in and through its and God's creations. This view is expressed in Meditation Eighty-Three of the *Third Century* in *Select Meditations* when Traherne reflects on the phenomenology involved in his encounter with "a Little church Environed with Trees."[27] Looking at the churchyard, Traherne sees not only stones and trees but also the "Labor of them which in Ancient Ages Builded it; the conversion of a Kingdom to God from Paganism, its Protection by Laws, its subjection to Kings, its Relation to Bishops, usefulness."[28] What fascinates Traherne is the way that human consciousness becomes aware of itself through the intersecting forces of world, desire, memory, and labor embodied in human artifice. The object of human creation — whether it be a city, a nation, or a churchyard — provides an occasion for reflection, thereby becoming animated as a vital part in the process whereby the human soul comes to know itself by extending its will into a welcoming world.

Given the dialectical interplay between thoughts and material objects organizing Traherne's philosophy of being, it should not be surprising that the modalities of insentience and indifference with which he is fundamentally concerned do not involve the absolute nonawareness of dead things as such. More

---

[26] According to Stephen Greenblatt, the spectrality produced by Donne's rhetoric is a function of the cultural afterlife of purgatory in Protestant England: see *Hamlet in Purgatory* (Princeton: Princeton University Press, 2001), 40.

[27] Traherne, *Select Meditations*, 100.

[28] Traherne, *Select Meditations*, 100.

precisely, Traherne is concerned with the inhuman dimension within human subjectivity itself — a dimension that becomes apparent when human artifice is viewed in radical isolation from human consciousness and will. Indeed, Traherne constantly turns his attention to the extension of human and divine consciousness into the world through artifacts and ideas (one need only think of the many lists of objects and actions that populate his work)[29] in order to humanize or animate the potentially inhuman quality of such things. Traherne, that is to say, is concerned with the phenomenon that L. O. Aranye Fradenburg addresses in her discussion of the relationship between language and sentience. In her discussion of sentience and language, Fradenburg speaks of "the opacity, to us, of the inhuman structures that structure the human, and emerge in our artifacts. Paradoxically, the very regimens and artifacts we create to reduce our helplessness (which means also our non- or irresponsibility) reflect back to us the uncanny autonomy of all our objects, including those inside us."[30] It is this more radical form of inhumanity — the inhumanity that haunts and conditions subjectivity — that Traherne evokes in his rarely discussed poem "Walking." Here again the figure of the puppet emerges as a negative exemplum, operating as a way to distinguish between a self-conscious being who is all praise and a (non)being who is "alienated from his proper objects." In this case, however, the human-puppet becomes confused with the artifacts that are extensions of his (in)sentience:

> To *walk* abroad is, not with Eys,
> But Thoughts, the Fields to see and prize;
>   Els may the silent Feet,
>   Like Logs of Wood,
> Mov up and down, and see no Good,
>   Nor Joy nor Glory meet.
>
>   Ev'n Carts and Wheels their place do change,
> But cannot see; tho very strange
>   The Glory that is by:
>   Dead puppets may
> Mov in the bright and glorious Day,
>   Yet not behold the Sky. (1–12)

---

[29] For discussions of Traherne's cataloguing techniques see Gary Kuchar, *Divine Subjection: The Rhetoric of Sacramental Devotion in Early Modern England* (Pittsburgh: Duquesne University Press, 2005), chap. 4; James J. Balakier, "Thomas Traherne's Dobell Series and the Baconian Model of Experience," *English Studies* 3 (1989): 233–47; and Jonathan Sawday, *The Body Emblazoned: Dissection and the Human Body in Renaissance Culture* (New York and London: Routledge, 1995), 230–60.

[30] L. O. Aranye Fradenburg, *Sacrifice Your Love: Psychoanalysis, Historicism, Chaucer* (Minneapolis: University of Minnesota Press, 2002), 13.

The logical redundancy of *dead* puppets calls attention to the radically unnatural, untimely, and un-homely status of (in)human creatures who experience the world thoughtlessly. Such creatures belie all conventional categories of being; they are neither dead nor alive, neither animate nor inanimate. They cannot be said to exist either within or without the dialectical oppositions that structure Traherne's thought and Christian Platonism more broadly. They are, by definition, without place. Whatever else it does, the qualifier "dead" — a word that appears with surprising frequency in Traherne's work — distinguishes the modality of the de-animate from the inanimate. The modality of the de-animate is spectral in the precise sense Derrida ascribes to it when he describes the specter as the double of spirit, the soul's uncanny other: "specter is *of the spirit*, it participates in the latter and stems from it even as it follows it as its ghostly double."[31] In Traherne's poem, the uncanny quality of the spectral manifests in its automated movements, in its inability for purposeful motion, as in the following figure from "Walking" in which Traherne figures these specters as "statues dead":

> And are not Men than they [carts and wheels] more blind,
> Who having Eys yet never find
>   The Bliss in which they mov:
>   Like Statues dead
>   They up and down are carried,
> Yet neither see nor love. (13–18)

The forced movements of these de-animated figures are juxtaposed against the free motions of those who move directly in thought and through spirit: "To *walk* is by a Thought to go; / To mov in Spirit to and fro'" (19–20). The fundamental theme voiced in this poem is not simply that the movement of thoughts is more real than the movement of bodies, but that the failure of mind to move into the world and back to itself can render a person more *inhuman* than his or her own creations. The figure of the dead puppet is made of its own unmaking; it is a concretization of self-negation. Indeed, one of the main themes of Traherne's thought is the dialectic between alienation and communion inherent in *work* and human artifice, between consciousness and world. The "dead puppets" of "Walking" — these strangely zombie-like beings who, on the surface of things one presumes, appear physically like everyone else — materialize the radical alienation that inheres *in* human activity and artifice.[32]

---

[31] Jacques Derrida, *Of Spirit: Heidegger and the Question*, trans. G. Bennington and Rachel Bowlby (Chicago: University of Chicago Press, 1987), 125.

[32] I am tempted to draw a comparison here between "Walking" and the science fiction movie "Invasion of the Body Snatchers." In this 1956 film, families begin worrying

To put this another way, Traherne's dead puppets concretize existential care-lessness and alienation — the affectual dimension of which is given expression in Meditations Twenty-Two and Twenty-Three of the *Third Century*. Indeed, the following two scenes from *The Third Century* delineate the experience of onto-logical anxiety in its affective dimension — an experience that Traherne is con-stantly addressing even though he rarely speaks of it so directly:

> I remember once, the first time I came into a Magnificent or Noble Dining Room, and was left there alone, I rejoyced to see the Gold and State and Carved Imagery. but when all was Dead, and there was no Motion, I was weary of it, and departed Dissatisfied.[33]

> Another time, in a Lowering and sad Evening, being alone in the field, when all things were dead and quiet, a certain Want and Horror fell upon me, beyond imagination. The unprofitableness and Silence of the Place dis-satisfied me, its Wideness terrified me, from the utmost Ends of the Earth fears surrounded me. How did I know but Dangers might arise from the East, and invade me from the unknown Regions beyond the Seas?[34]

The mode of death that Traherne is addressing is not biological death, but a state of living death — a weariness accompanied by anxiety and homelessness; it is a state in which the world (emblematized as an unused ornate dining room and as an expansive geographical locale) is neither prized nor used. What we see here is a diagnosis of the world objectified to the point where it is disconnected from the desires and powers of the human soul; it is another version of the dumb show. In the case of Meditation Twenty-Three, the occasion for ontological anxiety is not civil conflict, but the expansion of cartographic space — an expansion that is associated with things that are generally the source of anxiety for Traherne,

---

that their loved ones have become emotionless and distant. As it turns out, aliens have begun abducting the bodies of real people and they remain empirically indistinguishable from their victims save for the alien's unusual disposition. These minor empirical differ-ences nonetheless distinguish between human and inhuman — separating out those with a human conscience and those without. Traherne, it seems to me, is drawing a similar kind of distinction — pointing out the subtle empirical differences between radically distinct spiritual modes of being. Traherne also reflects on this theme in Meditation 84 of *Select Meditations,* but he remains here within a relatively stable binary opposition be-tween human and animal consciousness: "A Beast cannot see into those Ends for which Temples are Erected: and Therefore all churches appear unto them, but an heap of Stones. A carcase Seen whose Soul is a way. It is mans Soul and the Excellencies of it, that makes and apprehends all other Excell[e]ncies": *Select Meditations,* 100–1.

[33] Traherne, *Centuries*, 3.22.

[34] Traherne, *Centuries*, 3.23.

including "unprofitableness" and "silence" (of the non-spiritual kind). These images again express a world emptied of purpose, action, and vitality. Dead puppets are figures for human beings living without intentionality, and for Traherne the thought that such creatures can exist — and exist within each of us — is an uncanny one in the fullest sense of the word.

From the *Ungrund* to the *Real*

The disturbing question that is raised by these images of existential homelessness and the anxiety over de-animation they embody is this: what makes it possible for a human being and the world such a being inhabits to become radically inhuman, that is, de-animate? Traherne phrases the question this way: "Here is the wonder, that man being so Great and peculiar Should So little understand it [himself/his place in the world]: and accustom Himselfe to the feeling of vanities, Being a Dead Apostate to all his Glories."[35] DeNeef implicitly addresses this question in Chapter Four of *Traherne in Dialogue* when he explains the differential structure of Traherne's thought in relation to Derrida's account of the supplementary economy organizing the Western tradition of Platonic-based onto-theology. While DeNeef's analysis remains, for me, the most penetrating reading of Traherne's thought to date, it does not take full account of how the *originary* difference organizing the differential relations of Traherne's system is registered at the same time it is repressed. My aim now, then, is to clarify how the dialectical structure of Traherne's thought relies on and yet seeks to disavow the radical negativity embodied in his figures of de-animation.

In his analysis of Traherne's rhetorical economy vis-à-vis Derridean supplementation, DeNeef addresses the structural moment in Traherne's work when the production of value, meaning, and being is disrupted through the rupture of absolute negativity — through the uncanny emergence of what Shakespeare's Queen Isabel, in *Richard II*, gestures at in the phrase a "something-nothing" — that un-symbolizable grief or disturbance which remains immune to symbolization. It is this rupture and all that it entails which discloses the conditions by which spirit not only can but in a more radical sense *must* fail to realize itself as self-consciousness. Failure, as DeNeef's whole reading works to show, is not the opposite of but is rather the condition for the supplementary movement of language, which for Traherne is also the movement of spirit as self-consciousness. The essential point of DeNeef's structural analysis is that Traherne's representation of the soul and of the order of being more broadly is organized on a principle

---

[35] Traherne, *Select Meditations*, 53.

of differentiation where no single unit of signification possesses meaning or value in isolation from any other unit. Every individual unit thus supplements an originary lack. This means that virtue/spirit/devotion and ultimately self-consciousness is, by structural necessity, in danger of reverting into its uncanny double. DeNeef explains the phenomenon this way:

> when Traherne argues that love can be only insofar as it loves, acts by loving or by willing to love, the predicate operates as a necessary and secondary supplement, a 'superadded' substitution. The verb, in other words, supplements a difference already present within the noun. The economy of the supplement allows, however, that initial difference to be both displaced and deferred, *submerged*, in fact, under the value the verb appropriates as an essence put to worthwhile work.[36]

DeNeef isolates only one moment in Traherne's work where this submerging of *différance* — the process of infinite deferral and differing that organizes the field of verbal representation — becomes discernible as a thematic issue rather than as a structural effect. He cites the following passage from *Christian Ethicks* as exemplary of how Traherne theorizes the dangers inherent within an economy of supplementation and the excesses it puts into play:

> All kind of Vertues must concur to Compleat [man's] Perfection. The Want of any one Denominates a Vice, and makes him Vicious. Nay the Want of any one destroys the form and Essence of the rest. Vertue is not Vertue but in order to felicity [now *another* supplement to supply the want of all supplements]. If it hath lost its force, it hath lost its Nature. As a little Poyson turnes the best Meat from Nourishment into Poyson so doth one Vice cherished and allowed corrupt and viciate all the Vertues.[37]

DeNeef rightly asserts that this passage discloses how the "chain of supplementarity opens the abyss that threatens it from within, the indifference to supplementary relatedness which is death to think and the cessation of life altogether."[38] To put this in the terms I have been employing, the radical negativity embodied in "dead puppets" is not simply an external otherness that one might succumb to through "indifference" — though Traherne often talks as though this were the case — but rather it is the innermost possibility of spirit as self-consciousness.

---

[36] A. Leigh DeNeef, *Traherne in Dialogue: Heidegger, Lacan, Derrida* (Durham, NC: Duke University Press, 1988), 185 (emphasis added).

[37] DeNeef, *Traherne in Dialogue*, 197 (brackets in original).

[38] DeNeef, *Traherne in Dialogue*, 197.

As my example suggests, what DeNeef does not consider is that this point of rupture — this ceasing of all tropological movement within the order of language — is repeatedly registered at the level of the image through the figures we have been considering. The repetition of such figures suggests that the submergence of this originary lack requires greater poetic force than DeNeef's delimitation of supplementation to adjectives, predicates, and imagination would seem to indicate.[39] For the apparently superfluous nature of "dead puppets," and the language of redundancy upon which such uncanny figures are built, call attention to how these images embody the cessation of the productive movement between dialectical opposites — presence/absence, full/empty, being/non-being — that organizes Traherne's rhetorical economy, even while defending against the emergence of such cessation. These structurally key, if textually marginal, images materialize the stopping of movement that is "submerged" by the economy of differentiation through which Traherne's system operates. To put this in the structural terms DeNeef employs, the adjective "dead" is not a necessary supplement to the noun "puppet," nor does it appropriate a value where there would otherwise be a difference waiting for a name. On the contrary, its semantic redundancy calls attention to that difference itself, thereby opening a gap in the generative force of Traherne's system. Rather than participating within a differential economy where every term is related to and involved with every other term, the figure of the "dead puppets" signals that one point isolated from all other points. In this sense it is more properly characterized as indifferent in the sense that Traherne uses the word in the poem "Another" when he describes how "Tis Death, my Soul, to be Indifferent" (17). By materializing such indifference, giving it a mechanical body and a name, the image of the "dead puppet" figures nothing other then the cessation of figuration itself. Traherne's images of de-animation work to demarcate, delimit, and *contain* the inhuman potential within subjectivity, but in the very act of evoking such modalities Traherne draws attention to their inescapability. They can be displaced and repressed but never annihilated because such modalities are inherent in the structures of thought and communication through which subjectivity is constituted. We are now at the point where we can anticipate the fact that what is most uncanny about the radical alterity opened by the figure of the "dead puppet" is that it occupies the space within the order

---

[39] DeNeef accounts for three modes of supplementation at work in Traherne's system of thought: "the supplement of the predicate, which seeks to describe the differential logic of Traherne's various binary sets by means of the grammatical relations between nouns and verbs. . . . the supplement of the adjective, which tries to define the operation of appropriating or annexing terms of quality and value to ones of ostensibly neutral description," and imagination itself (*Traherne in Dialogue*, 184).Yet it is at the level of image that the rupture of *différance* becomes most concrete and therefore most legible.

calls it, within the divine Spirit itself. This *Ungrund* is the abyss within the Divine Person, the Thing out of which the Absolute Spirit estranges itself in order to create the order of being. The *Ungrund*, as John Stoudt summarizes, is Boehme's "word for the absolute devoid of determination."[49] Boehme describes it as a craving or desire prior to the generation of a divine will: "The *Ungrund* . . . makes an eternal beginning as a craving (*Sucht*). For the nothing is a craving after something. But as there is nothing that can give anything . . . the craving itself is the giving of it, which yet also is a nothing."[50] The *Ungrund* thus names that Thing which marks the point where God is radically opaque to himself — while nonetheless marking the space where self-estrangement occurs so that a higher, more complete form of self-consciousness can evolve. The *Ungrund* names the condition of possibility for Spirit's capacity to achieve self-consciousness, while delimiting the specific point or moment in which there is no consciousness of self as such. Insofar as the *Ungrund* names the difference at the origin of things, it is conceptually proximate to Derrida's notion of *différance* and is even more closely related to Lacan's notion of the *real* — the absolute otherness of the self to itself.[51] Whatever else Boehme's postulation of the *Ungrund* may indicate, it constitutes the fully articulated expression of the absolute negativity that returns throughout Traherne's treatment of the movements of spirit as self-consciousness. It demarcates the radical lack that makes the dialectical movement towards self-consciousness possible, while also constituting the point at which no dialectical movement is possible. In Derridean terms, then, the *Ungrund* is the condition of (im)possibility for self-consciousness. In this way, we might say that Boehme's *Ungrund* is the truth of Traherne's representation of spirit as self-consciousness; it provides the missing theoretical co-ordinate that would fill in what is readable but which is, strictly speaking, absent from Traherne's view of Being. For in Traherne, this radical lack appears at the level of image — in various figures of de-animation — and at the level of structure through the dialectical

---

[49] Stoudt, *Jacob Boehme*, 114.

[50] Stoudt, *Jacob Boehme*, 203.

[51] Boehme's *Ungrund* is more closely related to Lacan's category of the real than Derrida's notion of *différance* because Lacan is more directly indebted to Schelling and Hegel who explicitly take up Boehme's term and work more generally. For a discussion of Schelling's indebtedness to Boehme see Robert F. Brown, *The Later Philosophy of Schelling: The Influence of Boehme on the Works of 1809–1815* (Lewisburg, PA: Bucknell University Press, 1977). For an analysis of Schelling vis-à-vis Lacan see Slavoj Žižek, *Tarrying With the Negative: Kant, Hegel and the Critique of Ideology* (Durham, NC: Duke University Press, 1993). For a discussion of Boehme's relation to American Ego Psychology see Suzanne R. Kirschner, *The Religious and Romantic Origins of Psychoanalysis: Individuation and Integration in Post-Freudian Theory* (Cambridge: Cambridge University Press, 1996), 130–48.

interplay of the organizing ideas of Neoplatonic thought, but it is absent at the level of concept — that is, as a fully theorized, thematic idea. It is in this sense, among others, that Traherne both evokes and avoids the *Ungrund* — the absolute difference of Spirit to itself.

What is disclosed in Boehme's concept of the *Ungrund* and in the various effects this absolute difference has on Traherne's articulation of the self-conscious soul is the fact that it is of the nature of spirit to become destitute. In other words, what Traherne's work insistently says without actually saying it as such, is that there is something inhuman within subjectivity — and this *something* is unthinkable and yet at the same time unavoidable. The various figures and scenes of de-animation that circulate throughout Traherne's work evoke the insistence of a certain radical loss, one that is always-already operating within the very concept of Spirit as the possibility of *plentitude*. Indeed, Traherne's puppet-persons, dumb shows, dead statues, and dead apostates concretize the constant risk of slipping from full to ventriloquized speech, from animate being to de-animate spectrality that haunts the human person. What these figures display is that the fully praising subject whose every gesture is a virtual act of devotion bears with it an uncanny double whose every action is a symptom of self-negation.

The particular mode of uncanny spectrality that Traherne's figures evoke is distinct from the forms which populate the pages and stages of Elizabethan and Jacobean culture, just as it is distinct from, even as it must be understood alongside, Freud's post-enlightenment version. The emphasis on simulacra and mechanical virtuality in Traherne's puppet-figures constitutes a different, newer mode of spectrality than the ghostly kind which predominates throughout late medieval culture and which lingers, albeit in slightly different form, in the late Elizabethan age.[52] According to Stephen Greenblatt, the forms of spectrality that predominate in Elizabethan and Jacobean England derive a large part of their power of fascination from the literary and cultural afterlife of purgatory. In Shakespeare, for instance, the ghost appears as a figure of false surmise, as a figure of history's nightmare, and as a figure of deep psychic disturbance.[53] While Traherne's figure of the dumb show is certainly another expression of the nightmare of history, its orientation — like that of other key figures of de-animation — is more towards the future than the past. Figures of dead puppets and dumb shows demonstrate how the modality of the uncanny in Traherne's work

---

[52] For a discussion of the modes of spectrality that predominated in the Middle Ages see Jean-Claude Schmitt, *Ghosts in the Middle Ages: The Living and the Dead in Medieval Society* (Chicago: University of Chicago Press, 1998). For a discussion of the spectral and daemonic in Shakespeare see Ned Lukacher, "Anamorphic Stuff: Shakespeare, Catharsis, Lacan" *South Atlantic Quarterly* 88 (1989): 863–97.

[53] Greenblatt, *Hamlet in Purgatory*, 156.

is mediated by and is a consequence of the forms of automata taking shape in the work of Hobbes, Descartes, and late seventeenth-century Baconianism. It is helpful to bear in mind here that it would take only until 1740 for these imaginary automata (which were initially evoked in order to describe the workings of the human body, social relations, and other phenomena) to materialize into actual inventions — forever changing (Freud, Derrida, Castle, and others have argued) our experience of the relations between the human and the sacred.[54] Traherne's work offers a glimpse of these effects at an early stage in their history. For the purgatorial echoes heard in Shakespeare and even in Donne are no longer audible in Traherne's representation of the uncanny. With Traherne, we are at a different phase in the process of de-animation that Donne diagnoses in *The Anniversary Poems* (1611). What haunts Traherne, we might hazard, is not the lingering ghosts of a Catholic past as such, but an anxiety that there will be no future as such, only the continuation of a dumb show, a charade or spectacle in which human artifice, actions, and groups are not emanations of gratitude but are materializations of something radically inhuman and yet profoundly familiar.

Viewed this way, Traherne should continue to matter (even to those of us who wish to further rather than withdraw from secularization — whatever "further" might mean here) because he offers an early diagnosis of the paradoxical effects of modern disenchantment. To the extent that Traherne registers and seeks to mitigate the experience of disenchantment, he participates in, even as he must be distinguished from, the tradition of thought that Derrida continues when the French philosopher reasserts the historically particular dimension of Freud's thesis on the uncanny this way: "[despite] what is normally thought, technological modernity doesn't neutralize anything; it causes a certain form of the demonic to re-emerge. Of course, it does neutralize also, by encouraging indifference and boredom, but because of that — and to the same extent in fact — it allows the return of the demonic [. . .] The domain of technology encourages demonic irresponsibility."[55] I can think of no better reason for continuing to read Traherne than the fact that he diagnoses and seeks to mitigate a form of "demonic irresponsibility" that is historically discrete even as it is continuous with the legion of indifference confronting us now.

---

[54] For a discussion of this critical tradition see Castle, *The Female Thermometer,* 11.

[55] Jacques Derrida, *The Gift of Death,* trans. David Wills (Chicago: University of Chicago Press, 1995), 36–37.

Traherne, Husserl, and a Unitary Act of Consciousness

James J. Balakier
University of South Dakota

In "The Preparative," a poem that occurs early in the Dobell sequence, Thomas Traherne avows "Tis not the Object, but the Light / That maketh Heaven [. . .]" (57–58).[1] Happiness or heavenly "Felicity," the central theme of these poems, is not in other words ultimately dependent upon objects themselves. It is in actuality determined by the quality of the experiencer's consciousness and his or her whole perceptual apparatus. He similarly asserts in the poem accompanying the "All Things" entry of the unfinished, alphabetically formatted *Commentaries of Heaven* manuscript that "Heaven surely is a State and not a Place" (25).[2] What then does Traherne disclose about this state of consciousness, which he calls the estate of Glory?[3]

The goal of this essay is to apply a consciousness-based approach to Traherne and thereby offer a fresh perspective on his thought and art. As a critical context for this study, a connection is made between this Oxford-educated, seventeenth-century Anglican cleric and the noted twentieth-century phenomenologist Edmund

---

[1] Thomas Traherne, *Centuries, Poems, and Thanksgivings*, ed. H. M. Margoliouth, 2 vols. (Oxford: Oxford University Press, 1958). This edition has been used throughout for Traherne's verse (volume 1), other than poems found in *Commentaries of Heaven*, and also for passages from *Centuries of Meditations* (volume 2). Line numbers for poems and identification for the *Centuries* have been added in parentheses.

[2] *Commentaries of Heaven: The Poems*, ed. D. D. C. Chambers (Salzburg: Universität Salzburg, 1989).

[3] For Traherne's definition of the estate of Glory, along with the other estates, Innocence and Misery, see *Christian Ethicks: or Divine Morality, Opening the Way to Blessedness, by the Rules of Vertue and Reason* (1675), ed. Carol L. Marks and George Robert Guffey (Ithaca: Cornell University Press, 1968), 4, 30.

Husserl, placed by specialists among the great philosophers of the past.[4] Husserl's importance in the critical tradition is notable. He located consciousness and its contents as a field for philosophical and, by extension, literary study.[5] The question that underlies his science of phenomenology is "What can remain, if the whole world, including ourselves with all our *cogitare*, is excluded?"[6] Husserl applied an intellectual process of "phenomenological reduction" or "bracketing" which he believed would supply insights into this fundamental question. In so doing he collapsed all the grounds of inquiry down to "transcendentally pure consciousness" (85). He endeavored in this way to establish the common ground between mathematical/empirical and philosophical/cognitive reality in a unitary act of consciousness. He postulates that

> *consciousness has, in itself, a being of its own which in its own absolute essence, is not touched by phenomenological exclusion.*[7] It therefore remains as the '*phenomenological residuum*,' as a region of being which is of essential necessity quite unique and which can indeed become the field of a science of a novel kind: phenomenology. (66–67)

Defending this mode of investigation against the charge of solipsism, he assures the reader that we have not "Strictly speaking [. . .] lost anything but rather have gained the whole of absolute being which, rightly understood, contains within itself, 'constitutes' within itself, all worldly transcendencies" (84). He argues as follows:

> If anyone reading our statements objects that they mean changing all the world into a subjective illusion and committing oneself to a 'Berkeleyan idealism,' we can only answer that he has not seized upon the *sense* of those statements. They take nothing away from the fully valid being of the world as the all of realities, just as nothing is taken away from the fully valid geometrical being of the square by denying that the square is round. (84)

---

[4] Barry Smith and David Woodruff Smith, eds., *The Cambridge Companion to Husserl* (Cambridge: Cambridge University Press, 1995), 2.

[5] For as Raman Selden and Peter Widdowson note, "The act of interpretation is possible, because the texts allow the reader access to the author's consciousness [. . .]": *A Reader's Guide to Contemporary Criticism*, 3rd ed. (Lexington: University Press of Kentucky, 1993), 51.

[6] Edmund Husserl, *The Essential Husserl: Basic Writings in Transcendental Phenomenology*, ed. Donn Welton (Bloomington: Indiana University Press, 1999), 66. Hereafter cited in text. All Husserl quotes are from *The Essential Husserl* unless otherwise noted.

[7] The italics here and in other quotations from his texts are Husserl's.

Husserl never doubted the reality of the concrete world, or the independent existence of other human beings. The "phenomenological explication," he claimed,

> does nothing but *explicate the sense this world has for us all, prior to any philosophizing*, and obviously gets solely from our experience — *a sense which philosophy can uncover but never alter*, and which, because of an essential necessity, not because of our weakness, entails (in the case of any actual experience) horizons that need fundamental clarification. (160)

It is not "metaphysical construction," in other words, "but proceeds within the limits of pure 'intuition,' or rather pure sense-explication based on a fulfilling givenness of the sense itself" (159).

Husserl's influential situating of theoretical study in the consciousness "not touched by phenomenological exclusion" (66) supplies a modern critical platform for exploring the contents of Traherne's so-called rational mysticism. The Traherne canon offers a medium for testing Husserl's proposition that "each of us is able to discover his ultimate transcendental self by reflecting on his or her own consciousness and its relation to the world."[8] Traherne's reiterated assertion that his innermost mind was the "Temple of his [God's] Whole Infinitie" ("My Spirit," 109) — a discovery upon which he brilliantly elaborated in a variety of seventeenth-century literary genres — bears comparison with Husserl's conception of a unifying residuum or field of pure, transcendental consciousness. Husserl's formidable logic in delineating a field of phenomenology grounded in consciousness gives theoretical strength to this proposed area of Traherne studies.

This inquiry is furthered by recent psycho-physiological findings on a state of consciousness qualitatively different from waking, sleeping, and dreaming. This "fourth" state of consciousness has been the subject of over six hundred scientific studies conducted over the past several decades at over two hundred independent institutes in thirty countries.[9] It is characterized by a profound state of "restful alertness" in which the mind is at the same time more rested than in deep sleep and more alert than in ordinary activity.[10] This state of restful alertness is produced by means of an effortless mental technique, with roots in the

---

[8] Herman Philipse, "Transcendental Idealism," in *The Cambridge Companion to Husserl*, ed. Smith and Smith, 280.

[9] Robert K. Wallace, David Orme-Johnson, and Michael Dillbeck, eds., *Scientific Research on Maharishi's Transcendental Meditation and TM-Sidhi Program, Collected Papers*, vol. 1 (Fairfield, IA: Maharishi International University Press, 1990). (Volumes 2–5 by various editors. Volume 6 in press.)

[10] Robert Keith Wallace, *The Physiology of Consciousness* (Fairfield, IA: Maharishi International Press, 1993), 34.

ancient Vedic culture of India.[11] It corresponds in Vedic literature to *turīya chetna* ["fourth state of consciousness"], which is described in extensive detail to be a state of *samādhi*, self-awareness or transcendental consciousness.[12] Repeated experience of this state has been shown to result in a wide range of physical and mental benefits. These improvements include the indicators of decreased physiological stress, namely "decreased cortisol (the major stress hormone), decreased muscle tension, normalization of blood pressure, increased autonomic stability, increased EEG coherence."[13] The alleviation of psychological and sociological stress is validated by studies showing "decreased anxiety and depression, decreased post-traumatic stress syndrome, and increased self-actualization. [. . .] decreased hostility, increased family harmony, and reduced criminal behavior in incarcerated felons" (61). Moreover,

> Creativity increases, as measured by tests of both verbal and pictorial fluency, flexibility, and originality. Perception becomes more accurate and less driven by preconceptions and misconceptions. Basic memory processes improve. [. . .] A ten-year longitudinal study following meditating college students after they graduated found significant increases on holistic measures of self development (ego development) compared to data sets for graduates for three control universities matched for gender and age. The meditators reached higher levels of moral reasoning, autonomy and integration than has ever been seen before in any other group. (63)

These impressive findings have prompted researchers to conjecture that "The repeated process of *fully* transcending to the silent state of pure consciousness [. . .] [normalizes] the nervous system progressively, freeing it from deep-rooted stresses that block development," while simultaneously leading to "a major functional reorganization of brain processes" and thereby "['unfreezing'] psycho-physiological development, which otherwise typically becomes arrested in adolescence or early childhood."[14]

---

[11] This simple, natural meditation technique, Transcendental Meditation, according to the Vedic literature produces a lively state of profound evenness of mind.

[12] See for example *The Śrīmad Devī Bhāgawatam*, trans. Swami Vijnanananda (New Delhi: Munshiram Manoharlal Publishers, 2001), 1170. See also *On the Bhagavad-Gita: A New Translation and Commentary, chapters 1–6*, trans. Maharishi Mahesh Yogi (New York: Penguin, 1969), 144, 147.

[13] David Orme-Johnson, "Summary of Scientific Research on Maharishi's Transcendental Meditation and TM-Siddhi Program," *Modern Science and Vedic Science* 6 (1995): 60–155, here 61. Hereafter cited in text.

[14] Charles N. Alexander and Ellen J. Langer, *Higher Stages of Human Development* (New York: Oxford University Press, 1990), 22.

These findings add plausibility to Husserl's theory of a unified state of consciousness. They also lend credibility to Traherne's parallel claims for an "Indivisible" and "Pure" ("My Spirit," 56) quality of mind in the estate of Glory. Examination of seminal Traherne texts in the light of the scientific research strongly counters the view that his writings exhibit an immature, "facile [. . .] optimism," as Douglas Bush alleged in a major literary history.[15] A close reading of Traherne supports the hypothesis that his exposition of a "A Naked Simple Pure *Intelligence*" [Traherne's italics] ("The Preparative," 20) in his poetry and prose is consistent with experience of the unique fourth state of awareness in which the brain is fully awake and the physiology as a whole is in a more balanced, "normalized" condition.[16]

Traherne emphasizes the phenomenal character of Felicity throughout his works. Considering the prevalence of his interest in restoring childhood Felicity in adult life, it may be seen as the nexus of his canon, from his metaphysically inspired poetry to his most original "meditational" prose. A logical starting point, then, in a consciousness-based profile of Felicity is its experiential nature. T. O. Beachcroft noted in the early years of Traherne criticism his "unusually objective"[17] presentation of his experiences. This proclivity sets him apart from "the Cambridge Divines [who] take the ultimate mysticism of religious experience as their foundation, in an academic mood." Traherne, on the other hand, "has the experience itself; and this, attended by his sheer writing gift lives with brilliant, sometimes astonishing vitality, in his written words" ("Doctrine," 296). In the following excerpt from *Select Meditations*,[18] for example, he records and comments upon, with clarity and force, a breakthrough experience of Felicity:

> This Endless Comprehension of my Immortal Soul when I first saw it, so wholy Ravished and Transported my spirit, that for a fortnight after I could Scarsly Think or speak or write of any other Thing. But Like a man Doteing with Delight and Ecstasy, Talk of it Night and Day as if all the Joy of Heaven and Earth were Shut up in it. For in very deed I saw there the Divine Image Relucent and shining, There I saw the foundation of man[']s Excellency, and that which made Him a Son of God. Nor ever shall I be able to forget its Glory. (4.3)

---

[15] Douglas Bush, *English Literature in the Earlier Seventeenth Century: 1600–1660* (Oxford: Oxford University Press, 1962), 158.

[16] N. N. Lyubimov of the Russian Academy of Medical Sciences found that during this state the latent reserves of the brain are activated (Orme-Johnson, "Summary of Scientific Research," 143).

[17] T. O. Beachcroft, "Traherne and the Doctrine of Felicity," *Criterion* 9 (1930): 291–307, here 292. Hereafter cited in text.

[18] *Select Meditations,* ed. Julia Smith (Manchester: Carcanet Press, 1997).

This is perhaps the most openly biographical account Traherne offers of his first-hand "comprehension" of Felicity. The circumstances surrounding its experience, the time and place, are absent from the passage, no doubt because he considers them of no real consequence. They have faded, as it were, permanently into the background. And of course it is couched in familiar religious terms such as "Soul" and "Son of God." It is natural that he would express this threshold experience within the framework of Christian hermeneutics — that he would correlate, however broadly, this epiphany or "Ecstasy" with his religious training. From a phenomenological standpoint, however, what stands out is the thoroughly satisfying feeling that got hold of him — an essential joy not directly associated with reading scripture or participating in a religious ceremony, but simply present within his mind itself. It has the air of a "Eureka" about it, a groundbreaking discovery of the brain's latent potential.

In another critical passage in *Select Meditations* he evocatively describes the self as intrinsically a pure state of awareness or knowingness:

> Were nothing made but a Naked Soul, it would See nothing out of it Selfe. For Infinite Space would be seen within it. And being all sight it would feel it selfe as it were running Parrallel with it. And that truly in an Endless manner, becaus it could not be conscious of any Limits: nor feel it Selfe Present in one Centre more then another. This is an Infinite Sweet Mystery: to them that have Tasted it. (3.27)

Presented as a thought-experiment, which is signaled by the "Were Nothing made [. . .] then" formulation, Traherne articulates a new non-localized identity for the self. In its primal or "naked" state, it knows no boundaries, "No Brims nor Borders" as he writes in "My Spirit" (7). By nature it is full and free and conscious of its nature as such. The notion of infinite extension figures significantly in Traherne's depiction, a concept promulgated by the spatial sciences of the day, which were brought to a high point of development in subsequent years by Newton. The relation of God to a material infinity — the latter phenomenon taking on practical meaning in the context of seventeenth-century astronomy and mathematics — was much argued over, with Henry More acting as the dynamic locus of the debate in England.[19] Here Traherne simply compares the internalized infinite to the externalized one, without becoming entrenched in the highly subjective, semantically colored battle. Also connected with spatialism is his comparison of his "naked" or primal self to a circle or sphere without a fixed center-point, his favorite image. Yet the simple and compelling intimacy of the experience is conveyed by the fact that it overflows with sweet feeling, as those who have "Tasted it" realize.

---

[19] Alexandre Koyré, *From the Closed World to the Infinite Universe* (Baltimore: Johns Hopkins University Press, 1979), 117–23.

His apprehension of such an "Enriching Veritie" (*Centuries* 1.3) is also presented in the *Centuries of Meditations*, within a series of autobiographical entries on his developmental years. He recalls how "seated among silent Trees" back home in the country (apparently) from Oxford, he had "all my Time in mine own Hands" and "resolved to Spend it all, whatever it cost me, in Search of Happiness" (3.46). His quest was not in vain, for he came to see that his similitude to God engenders the "infinit felicity" of enjoying "the most perfect Treasures in the most Perfect Maner." Upon the dawning of this realization, a distinctive physiological response occurred:

> This Spectacle once seen, will never be forgotten. It is a Great Part of the Beatifick Vision. A Sight of Happiness is Happiness. It transforms the Soul and makes it Heavenly, it powerfully calls us to Communion with God, and weans us from the Customs of this World[.] It puts a Lustre upon GOD and all his Creatures and makes us to see them in a Divine and Eternal Light. I no sooner discerned this [truth] but I was (as Plato sayeth, In summa Rationis Arce Quies habitat) seated in a Throne of Repose and Perfect Rest. All Things were well in their Proper Places. [. . .] (3.60)

The "Perfect Rest" and orderliness he mentions, which accompanied his penetration of his "heavenly" nature, suggest the physiological correlates of transcendental consciousness.[20] In this most settled state, the mind is spontaneously coherent and wholly satisfied. His delineation of an unforced, natural state of restful alertness gives authenticity to his disclosure.

A leading idea of the thirty seven Dobell poems, Traherne's major poetry sequence,[21] is the re-awakening of a non-fragmented, pre-lapsarian sensibility, which parallels in detail the fourth state of consciousness. The disarmingly simple last line of "Innocence," which reads "I must becom a Child again" (1.60), epitomizes the series. Earlier in this poem he states that:

> A serious Meditation did employ
> My Soul within, which taken up with Joy
> Did seem no Outward thing to note, but flie
> All Objects that do feed the Eye. (13–16)

Childhood is associated with a purer state of consciousness not yet over-shaded by outer things: "all within was Pure and Bright" (6). But as should be evident to anyone who has carefully read these poems, Traherne is not a sentimentalist; his

---

[20] Orme-Johnson, "Summary of Scientific Research," 69–70; Wallace, *The Physiology of Consciousness*, 60.

[21] They were first attributed to Traherne and published by Bertram Dobell in 1903.

vision of getting in touch with "the inner child," however radically optimistic, is not blind to the dark corners of human psychology and the moral vagaries of social life. Evil is certainly de-emphasized in the poems, but not ignored. "The Instruction" illustrates the estate of "Miserie" (15), in fact, in rather ugly terms ("Spue out thy filth, thy flesh abjure" [1]). The defilement it declaims comes across as harshly real. Traherne is not some high-minded Pollyanna naively unaware of evil. He seems acutely mindful of the "sad Distemper" (15) which may afflict the mind, as he reveals also in "Mankind is sick," a poem appearing in *Christian Ethicks*.[22] His belief in natural goodness is particularly strong, especially for someone who must have seen something of the ravages of the Civil War in his home county, Herefordshire, and must have known something of the moral ambiguities of the Restoration court through his employment to the pious Keeper of the Seal, Sir Orlando Bridgeman, who fell from the randy King Charles II's good graces.[23] His conviction that happiness is within everyone's reach is, I believe, so absolute because of his direct knowledge of a transformed state of consciousness.

His most comprehensive picture of Felicity is vibrantly painted by Traherne in the long and elaborate irregular stanzas of "My Spirit," which constitutes a major climax in the Dobell poems. "My Spirit" is invaluable as an expansive poetic catalog of the full range of qualities of this "Wondrous Self" (103). They may be highlighted as follows:

- *Unbounded.* As in the above passages from *Select Meditations*, he informs his reader that, in his Adamic childhood, "My Soul [was] a Spirit infinit" (71), devoid of any external or internal boundaries, including time ("At once Surrounding all Eternitie"[93]). It was completely open and awake to itself as a transcendental phenomenon. Similarly in the poem "Silence" he sublimely states that "A vast and Infinit Capacitie, / Did make my Bosom like the Deitie" (75–76).

- *Pure consciousness.* He stresses early in the poem that there was a oneness, a total identification of his self with lively, non-relative being: "That was the Substance of My Mind. / The Sence it self was I" (4–5). He amplifies in the next line: "I felt no Dross nor Matter in my Soul" (6). His awareness was just that, pure awareness, freed of any overshadowing sensory influences or material contingencies. The experience he is anatomizing was so markedly clear that he can forthrightly state "It was Indivisible, and so Pure [. . .],"

---

[22] *Christian Ethicks:* ed. Marks and Guffey, 201–4

[23] Gladys I. Wade, *Thomas Traherne* (London: Oxford University Press, 1944; repr. Princeton: Princeton University Press, 1969), 26, 94.

or as his revision of this line reads (not preferred by Margoliouth though it keeps the meter): "It was so Quick and Pure" (56). Later he writes in a similar vein that it was an "Indivisible Centre" (92) like an atom or the finest grain of matter.

• *Silent and dynamic.* His silent "Essence" was a shining "Act" (2), a pure "Capacitie / That felt all Things" (8). Or as he repeats some lines later, "Its Essence is Transformed into a true / And perfect Act" (25–26). The point is that he was not lost in some mystical cloud, or afflicted by passive spirits. He fully felt his own inner potential, which is a "Power infinit" (105). The estate of Glory is thus a synthesis of deep silence or pure potentiality and lively dynamism.

• *Full mental enlivenment.* Traherne elaborates in the penultimate stanza that "Twas somwhat evry where. / And tho it had a Power to see / Far more, yet still it shind / And was a Mind / Exerted for it saw Infinitie" (96–100). These lines suggest that he understood by this phenomenon that his brain was more fully "Exerted" or enlivened than before, without any inner or outer hindrances.

• *Source of thought.* He ascertains that this radical category of experience was the result of direct contact with the source of thought within his mind. As he explains: "The Thought that Springs / Therfrom's it self" (9–10). This state is the substratum of the entire thinking process, and the basis of creativity. In "Thoughts. I," in a similar manner, he celebrates felicitous thoughts ("Ye Engines of Felicitie" [6]) as "The Offsprings and Effects of Bliss / By whose Return my Glory is / Renewd" (21–23).

• *Self-referral.* Traherne affirms that "It doth not by another Engine work, / But by it self" (23–24). It is a completely self-contained and self-sufficient mode of reality. It needs nothing to maintain itself or to give it meaning. It is self-referral,[24] operating independently by continually curving back, as it were, upon itself.

• *Simplest state of awareness.* This theme is highlighted in the opening lines,

My Naked Simple Life was I.
That Act so Strongly Shined
Upon the Earth, the Sea, the Skie [. . .]. (1–3)

---

[24] "Pure consciousness is held to be the essential nature of the 'Self' — a 'self-referral' field in which consciousness is fully awake to itself" (Alexander and Langer, *Higher Stages of Human Development*, 22).

Philip Traherne, who inherited his brother's manuscripts and prepared an edition of the poems which he never actually published, changed "Naked Simple Life" to lower case, suggesting a lack of appreciation for simplicity as a controlling idea in the poem. The simple, spirited act of being typifies the Adamic existence which Traherne celebrates here and in other poems, such as "Innocence," where he states that "A Joyfull Sence and Puritie / Is all I can remember" (9–10). He likens this state, towards the end of the first stanza of "My Spirit," to being "Simple like the Deitie" (15), emphasizing the similitude of the individual with macrocosmic creative intelligence.

• *Easy and natural.* Traherne refers to "Dame Nature[']s Law" (39) within the poem in the context of how his awakened consciousness found objects vibrating within itself without over-clouding his sense of being. This phenomenon occurred in harmony with natural law, he states, suggesting an integral harmony between his transcendental experiences and those laws. They do not exist or function, that is, at cross-purposes. In "Ease" he highlights the naturalness of the mind's infusion of Felicity: "How easily doth Nature teach the Soul, / How irresistible is her Infusion! / There's Nothing found that can her force controll [. . .]" (1–3). Here too he demystifies Felicity by commenting from personal experience upon its deep affinity with the mind's nature.

• *Fullness.* This was, in a word, a state of fullness in which Nature's "store / Was all at once within me" (39–40). In "Fullnesse," the shortest poem in the Dobell sequence, he also points out that his "Power exerted, or my Perfect Being" is "a Fountain or a Spring, / Refreshing me in evry thing" (9, 15–16). These lines suggest once again that this experience is fully in accord with the nature of the mind and indeed is the basis of inner wholeness.

• *Blissful.* He describes this state as "The only Proper Place or Bower of Bliss" (79), an "Extended Orb of Joy / Proceeding from within" (86–87), and a "Sphere of Joy most fair" (104). He enlarges that Nature's treasures "Were my Immediat and Internal Pleasures, / Substantial Joys, which did inform my Mind" (40–42). True Felicity, "the Highest Bliss" (10), as he calls it in "The Author to the Critical Peruser," is thus envisioned by Traherne to be the natural by-product of diving into the mind's silent, nourishing source. As he states in the opening couplet of "Silence," "A quiet Silent Person may possess / All that is Great or High in Blessedness" (1–2). Moreover, in "The Rapture" he associates "this Sacred Wealth" of bliss with "Life and Health" (17–18).

• *Unified.* Perhaps the most encompassing quality of this experience is the intimate sense of unity with nature it precipitated. "This made me present evermore / With whatso ere I saw" (35–36). He confesses that "I could not tell [. . .] Whether the Things did there / Themselvs appear, [. . .] Or whether my conforming Mind / Were not alone even all that shind" (46–48, 49–50). This unified state is one in which he is ultimately unable to distinguish whether objects exist independently of his own consciousness, as he had generally thought, or whether in reality they have all along existed within his Self. Through this elated question he raises, if he does not resolve, a tantalizing metaphysical issue. Other lines on the Husserlian theme of the "unitarily, and self-confirming experiential consciousness" (*Essential Husserl,* 71), are as follows: " It Acts not from a Centre to / Its Object as remote, / But present is, when it doth view, / Being with the Being it doth note" (18–21); and "all my Mind was wholy Evry where / What ere it saw, twas ever wholy there" (57–68).

The above characteristics correlate with the personal descriptions of the fourth state of consciousness collected by researchers. As one subject recounted,

> I experience a state of complete silence devoid of any motion, a state of unboundedness and total ease in deep relaxation. There are no thoughts, no feelings or any other sensations like weight or temperature. I just know 'I am.' There is no motion of time and space, but my mind is fully awake and perfectly clear. It is a very natural and simple state.[25]

Upon first learning this meditation technique, another subject reported:

> Following the instructions of the teacher without knowing what to expect, I began to drift down into deeper and deeper levels of relaxation, as if I were sinking into my chair. Then for some time, perhaps a minute or a few minutes, I experienced a silent, inner state of no thoughts, just pure awareness and nothing else; then again I became aware of my surroundings. It left me with a deep sense of ease, inner renewal and happiness. (Qtd. in Alexander and Langer, *Higher Stages,* 312)

Another subject describes below how her experience deepened over time with regular practice:

> Then, with increased familiarity . . . the process of transcending became more and more natural. The whole physiology was by now accustomed to just slipping within, and at some point it would literally 'click,' and with that the awareness would become fully expanded, the breath would almost

---

[25] Quoted in Alexander and Langer, *Higher Stages,* 311. Hereafter cited in text.

cease, the spine would become straight, and the lungs would cease to move. There would be no weight anywhere in the body, the whole physiology was at rest. At this point, I began to appreciate that this inner silence was not an emptiness but simply silent consciousness without content or activity, and I began to recognize in it the essence of my own self. Eventually, even the thin boundary that had previously divided individuality from this silent consciousness began to dissolve. The 'I' as a separate entity just started to have no meaning. The boundary that I put on myself became like a mesh, a net, it became porous and then just dissolved, only unbroken pure consciousness or existence remained . . . the physiology after that state is incredible. It is like a power surge of complete purity, and great bliss and joyfulness are stirred from deep within. (Qtd. in Alexander and Langer, *Higher Stages* 312)

These reports are typical of the results enjoyed by practitioners. They convey the uniqueness of the fourth state of consciousness as one of "heightened inner wakefulness accompanied by deep silence and rest, a state in which all activity of feeling, thinking, and perceiving has come to rest, yet awareness remains wide awake with no objective content to experience" (Alexander and Langer, *Higher Stages*, 92). Alexander and Langer observe that the "striking similarity among these current and historical accounts suggests that these are universally available experiences and not simply idiosyncratic to meditators, a function of shared mental set, or 'Eastern' philosophical belief" (308). This comment would appear to be particularly apposite with reference to Traherne, for the subjective accounts of the self-referral state, such as those above, strikingly reproduce the qualities Traherne ascribes to Felicity: deep rest, pure wakefulness, inner wholeness, expanded consciousness, silent fullness, physiological enlivenment, nourishing bliss.[26] Alexander and Langer add that the individuals "clearly view these experiences as discontinuous with ordinary modes of cognition," and "Subjectively they judge [them] to be more developed, satisfying, and personally meaningful" (308), points also consistent with Traherne's passionate sentiments regarding his experiences.

To return now to *Select Meditations* at large, in "Two Types of *Centuries*" Stanley Stewart[27] contrasts Traherne's persona in *Select Meditations* with that of the later *Centuries of Meditations* manuscript. In *Select Meditations* he is a "stiffly Pedantic" (84) Anglican, who sees himself as "moral tutor and model" (98), whereas in the *Centuries* he is a Neoplatonic spiritual guide. Moreover, while in the former text he "is interested in political issues shaped by pressures of history,"

---

[26] Repeated experience of transcendental consciousness, alternated with normal activity, produces a state in which the physiology is able to maintain it throughout the waking, dreaming, and sleeping states. See Alexander et al., "Higher Stages," 314–18.

[27] Stanley N. Stewart, "Two Types of Traherne *Centuries*," *John Donne Journal* 1 (1982): 81–100. Hereafter cited in text.

in the later work he creates a more mythical persona who "is anxious to extri-cate his reader from precisely such pedestrian concerns" (94). Nevertheless, *Select Meditations* holds much material relevant to an examination of the developmental aspects of Felicity.

It contains, for one thing, Traherne's dazzling accounts of Felicity, analyzed earlier, namely the "Naked Soul" (3.27) and the "Endless Comprehension" passages. In the latter of these he definitively writes, for instance, that "this Infinit space is a Thing so intimately known to the soul, that tis Impossible to remove it" (4.3). Such a seemingly hyperbolic statement takes on more rational import when seen in the context of a new model of adult development founded on growth in pure consciousness. Themes closely tied to Felicity also occur throughout its pages, often in terms of his similitude to divine being (see for example 3.90; 4.6). Phrases such as "Reale Selfe" (4.11) or "clarified Soul" (3.32) equate, it appears, with pure consciousness. In *Select Meditations* Traherne also extols Felicity as "a key that opens all things, whose motto is *facillima suprema*. Nothing is a Riddle, nor inexplicable to it" (3.52), indicating that it is a rational, intelligent phenomenon. The fourth state of consciousness is likewise described as a self-interacting field of pure intelligence.[28] Finally, through its instrumentality one becomes "a Living Sphere" (3.45) — a "sphere of Life including all Things" (3.54), again his singular image for the liberated soul. The essential content of *Select Meditations* is thus on a par with the Dobell poems and, as we shall see, the *Centuries*, his most popular work.

At the outset of the *Centuries of Meditations* Traherne tells his reader that his "Design" is to unfold in a "Plain maner," like St. Paul in Ephesians 3:9, the mystery that has been "Kept Secret from the foundation of the World" — that "lies Concealed" regarding the "interior Beauty" (1.3). "There are Invisible Ways of Conveyance," he elaborates, " by which some Great Thing doth touch our Souls, and by which we tend to it" (1.2). His allusion to a secret ground of a profitable inner life points clearly to the fourth state of consciousness. From this perspective, Centuries I and II constitute an introduction to this intrinsically improved quality of experience. It should be noted, incidentally, that the idea of grouping together one hundred "meditations" in a collection of Centuries evolved and was not established at the outset of writing. As Margoliouth notes, the heading for the first Century "did not occur in the manuscript. Traherne did not start with the idea of 'Centuries,'" but once it took hold an organization unfolded with this "Great Thing" at its heart.[29]

In Century I Traherne traces the psychological origins of Felicity in terms of the dynamics of desire. A dominant idea that emerges is the insatiability of

---

[28] Wallace, *The Physiology of Consciousness*, 8, 20.
[29] *Centuries, Poems, and Thanksgivings*, 1: 235.

desire, but as a positive, self-enhancing phenomenon. He deems infinite want-ing, specifically, to be the prerequisite for infinite enjoying (1.43). As he declares, "You must Want like a GOD, that you may be Satisfied like a GOD" (1.44). For this to occur, however, "You must wake every morning in Heaven" (1. 28), which is to say, your awareness must be cultured to be fully awake inside, crystal-clear and alert. It must also be fully "in Frame" or in a naturally restful and orderly state (1.13). Only then will you be ready to value everything properly and "re-store the Pieces to their Proper Places, being Perfectly Pleased with the whole Composure." This fully enlivened state of mind alone "shall giv you a thorow grounded Contentment" (1.23). These declarations take on resonance when the considerable research on the fourth state of consciousness, which is a state of heightened mental orderliness and coherence as demonstrated by EEG tests, is taken into account.[30]

Several defining points concerning the nature of Felicity are made about midway through the first Century, where Traherne attests that his Spirit "can see before and after its Existence into Endless Spaces," transcending all spatial and temporal boundaries. It is, further, a state in which "the Presence of the under-standing [is] endless" (1.55).

Traherne then amplifies in Century II upon the Soul's unqualified potential. It is brought home, he suggests, by the "Reality of Happiness" (2.98) that one naturally experiences in response to the world, which "feeds you with Joys " (2.1). The joy of artless or "Naked Love" (2.60), which unifies and refines our natures (2.42), is of special interest to Traherne in Century II. He repudiates idolizing "one Creature" (2.66), not because this "Curious and fair woman" in which "Som have seen the Beauties of Heaven" (2.68) is inconsequential, but because "there are 10000 Beauties in that Creature which they hav not seen. They loved it too much but upon fals causes" (2.68). His main point is that "In one Soul we may be entertained and taken up with innumerable Beauties. But in the Soul of Man there are innumerable Infinities" (2.70). Towards the end of the second Century he concedes that "Few will believ the Soul to be infinit" (2.81), but he counters that it is "the first Thing which is naturaly Known" for "Infinity we know and feel by our Souls: and feel it so Naturaly, as if it were the very Essence and Be-ing of the Soul" (2.81). Traherne's words may sound like poetic hyperbole, but set beside representative experiences of pure consciousness subjected to scientific analysis, such as those quoted earlier, they take on more tangible significance. When one such subject reports, as cited above, that "I began to recognize in it the essence of my own self" (qtd. in Alexander and Langer, *Higher Stages*, 312), the cultural/historical boundaries between her and Traherne seem to drop away.

---

[30] Orme-Johnson, "Summary of Research," 62–63.

As mentioned earlier, Century III is biography, but of a kind that sacrifices historical detail for larger, more mythic meanings, with Traherne seeking to bring into full view the "Infancy of this sublime and celestial Greatness" (3.1). Century IV consequently complements *experiences* of Felicity preserved in Century III — especially the "Spectacle" quoted above from 3.60, in which a wonderful evenness came over him and all his desires were satisfied — with *understanding*, which together can be thought of as the two poles of complete knowledge. This intellectual knowledge takes the form of sincere, "active" principles of Felicity, "for besides Contemplativ, there is an Activ Happiness; which consisteth in Blessed Operations" (4.1). It is "a Vain Thing," he laments, "to see Glorious Principles lie Buried in Books [. . .]." They need to be raised up "by continual exercise" (4.2). Perhaps not surprisingly, Traherne spins out fairly standard Christian teachings on virtuous life, with an Anglican as opposed to Calvinistic emphasis on coming into the world only to be happy (4.7). "I will first spend a great deal of time in seeking Happiness," he declares, "and then a Great deal more in Enjoying it" (4.11). The importance of charity (4.22), man as free agent (4.42), his innate goodness (4.51), and the glory of universal love (4.69), are woven together with other principles to create a hopeful, non-deterministic paradigm of human action. His sincere catalog of principles conducive to Felicity, above all else, underscores that perfect happiness is within everyone's reach because it is the reality of one's own shining Self, of which he writes: "The Abundance of its Beams, the Reality of its Beams, the freedom of its Beams, the Excellency and valu of its Beams are all Transcendent" (4.82). Traherne's direct knowledge of the "infinite capacity" of the soul emboldens him to challenge the "Hobbism" of his day, with the statement "The Consideration of one Soul is sufficient to convince all the Atheists in the whole World" (4.81).

To complete this overview, although Century V does not fulfill the hundred meditation requirement for each Century, it brings the work to a grand conclusion by enlarging upon ripened Felicity as a unification of the individual and the "Soveraign Object of all Felicitie" (5.1), the infinite and eternal creator. In the next to last meditation, Traherne lauds his omnipresence as, among other things, "an ample Territory or Field of Joys," "a Castle of Repose," and "an infinit Ocean by means of wherof evry Action, Word and Thought, is immediately diffused like a Drop of Wine in a Pail of Water, and evry where present evry where seen and Known, infinitly delighted in, as well as filling infinit Spaces" (5.9). As we have seen, in the self-referral state of consciousness the brain is profoundly rested, naturally blissful, and wonderfully expansive, all qualities that occur in Traherne's powerful catalog. It is, in short, a transcendental phenomenon, "the life and Soul of the Univers, that in evry point of Space from the Centre to the Heavens, [. . .] inspires us with it self" (5.9).

His *Christian Ethicks*, a conduct manual published soon after Traherne's death, moreover offers a consciousness-based ethical program. His aim is to "to

satisfie the Curious and Unbelieving Soul, concerning the reality, force, and efficacy of Vertue [. . .] ." The practical essence of his philosophy of action is that the
experience of a most enriching happiness naturally motivates harmonious behaviors, which is not the case with the righteous intimidation advocated by other au-
thorities, for "All Goodness is spoiled by Compulsion" (31). Early on he modestly
informs the reader that he has "some advantages from the knowledge I gained in
the nature of Felicity (by many years of earnest and diligent study) [. . .]" (3), thus
linking the two, Felicity and ethics, together. He rather surprisingly admits that
he does "not speak much of *Vice*, which is far the more easie Theme, because I am
intirely taken up with the abundance of Worth and Beauty in *Vertue*, and have so
much to say of the positive and intrinsick Goodness of its Nature" (3).

Traherne cites Aristotle's definition of Felicity as "*the Perfect fruition of a Perfect Soul, acting in perfect Life by Perfect Virtue*" (19).[31] Felicity is thus not so much
the effect of an ethical life as it is the cause. Good choices and acts are the fruits
of an already "perfect" or whole personality. The perfect life Traherne alludes to
is not the result of threats or undue pressure, but instead the spontaneous effect
of having gained Felicity in as much as "Our own Actions, springing from an interiour Fountain, deep within the Soul, when voluntarily and freely exerted, are
more acceptable [. . .]" (31). The principle presented here is that to ensure that
actions will be error-free and of benefit to oneself and the world at large one must
cultivate Felicity, which is a nourishing source deep in the psyche. Then actions
will flow voluntarily and always be in accordance with nature. To experience the
blissful seat of harmonious thoughts and actions in the mind is paramount, "For
to *feel* is as necessary as to *see* their *Glory*" (6). Contrastingly, to search for happiness in the pleasure afforded by objects is ill-advised. "It is Madness and folly,"
he admonishes, "to pursue the first object that presents it self, under the Notion
of felicity" (14). Traherne's statements sound more compelling if it is understood
that the "interiour Fountain, deep within the Soul" is pure consciousness. Its direct experience, Traherne teaches, will satisfy far more than the "first object" that
seems to promise happiness. The natural state of harmony it engenders will compose the mind and prevent it from acting rashly. His realization that the pure interior fountain of consciousness is responsible for stress-free, life-supporting actions is validated by research findings on the effect of the experience of the fourth
state of consciousness on behavior, including that of prison inmates.[32]

---

[31] Marks, in her and Guffey's fine edition of *Christian Ethicks* (which unfortunately
has been out of print for some years), explains that "the real source of the present quota-
tion is such Aristotelian epitomes as that by Eustache" as expanded by Traherne (312).
Hereafter cited in text.

[32] Orme-Johnson, "Summary of Research," 64.

Traherne got only as far as the Bs in his encyclopedically devised *The Commentaries of Heaven* manuscript,[33] so it is not possible to assess it with any conclusiveness. He makes abundantly clear on his title page, however, that Felicity is his inspirational nucleus. The *Commentaries* is conceived from the perspective of the state of "heaven" or Felicity regained. His jubilant announcement reads:

> *Commentaries of Heaven* wherein The Mysteries of Felicitie are opened and ALL THINGS Discovered to be Objects of Happiness EVRY BEING Created & Increated being Alphabetically Represented (as it will appear) in the Light of GLORY.

Everything "(as it will appear) in the Light of GLORY": from a consciousness-based viewpoint this means in terms of the growth of the nourishing fourth state of awareness. How far did he deliver on this intention? The listing for "Adam" helps us to understand how this text exemplifies his goal. "He that would clearly see the Nature of Felicitie," he proposes, "must look back to the Beginning & first Estate of Things [. . .]" (fol. 37ʳ). In doing so, Traherne attributes Felicity to the newly created man:

> When Adam first awaked out of the Dust and Saw so Glorious a Brightness on evry Side, His Soul being a pure and clear Mirror representing the Beauties of the Univers in their Divinity, his [first] Divertisement was a Rapture and Extasie inspired by Sence of the Magnificence of the World. (fol. 37ᵛ)

Human beings, as represented by Adam, were designed to delight in the natural spectacle of the world as mirrored in a crystal-clear state of awareness. Adam is the model of Felicity, the spiritual template for what all can become. He prefigures, of course, the "second Adam," Christ, who is "the Grand Pattern of all Happiness" (fol. 39ᵛ) and who came "to instruct us in the Mysteries of Happiness" (fol. 39ᵛ). Traherne distills his teachings on Christ in the poem accompanying the subsequent section, "The Second Adam." He was "an endless Sphere / Of Light and Glory" (4–5) which the poet aspires to be as well (7–8):

> [. . .] GOD was almost the Soul of Him, the light
> By which he saw; the Splendor infinit
> In which He felt all Spaces, and all Things:
> The Spirit that did cherish with its Wings
> From End to End through all Eternitie
> Extended, all the Treasures of the Skies,
> And all the Wealth that at the Centre lies. (13–19)

---

[33] *Commentaries of Heaven*, microfilm (British Library, Add. MS. 63054).

The crux of his commentary on the second Adam is Traherne's conviction that Felicity is a fully developed mental state. His Christ embodies the boundlessness he perennially associates with Felicity. This freedom from all boundaries is rooted in the "lively Essence in my very Mind" (21–22). As we have seen, pure consciousness is just such a "lively Essence" which Traherne, like Husserl, is convinced lies within everyone's mind. It is in these supremely rational, unsentimental terms that Traherne's Christ is his savior.

Husserl dismissed, as noted earlier, the notion that his speculations were solipsistic. His phenomenology actually evolves into a field of "intersubjectivity and ultimately [. . .] into an ontology of the life-world, embracing the social worlds of culture and history."[34] Traherne also affirms the existence and efficacy of the material world. He indeed endeavored to make his reader "Possessor of the Whole World" (*Centuries* 1.3), a world that he celebrates in the most elated terms. He assures his reader, "That all the World is yours, your very Senses and the Inclinations of your Mind declare" (1.16). He reiterates the point later in Century 1.6 stating that "By the very Right of your Sences you Enjoy the World" (1.21). The world renders services "transcendent to all Imagination," for it not only sustains the body and comforts the senses, but "It feeds you with Joys [. . .] and is the Link of your Union and Communion with [God]" (2.1). He gently warns, "if you be not faithfull in esteeming these, who shall put into your Hands the true Treasures. If you be negligent in Prizing these, you will be Negligent in Prizing all" (1.21). He praises, in fact, the physical sciences such as astronomy, "physicks," and arithmetic,[35] but regards them as ancillary to the study of happiness. Concerning his education he recalls that "There was never a Tutor that did professly Teach Felicity: tho that be the Mistress of all other Sciences" (3.37). He stresses instead that "the Mind / Among all those doth not its Object find," for only "in *Bliss* / Its Rest and Satisfaction seated is" (75–78). He concludes that "All other Sciences are Windows here / And let in Light into this Glorious SPHERE" ("[Aristotle's Philosophy]," 91–92). The quintessence of enlightened education, he drives home, is knowledge of the "single Centre, or a Sphere of Bliss" (66), the state of pure consciousness.[36]

The continuing research on consciousness is important to Traherne studies. It has the potential to offer a viable alternative to the view that Traherne was a lightweight idealist. He emerges rather as a precursor of those researchers who

---

[34] Smith and Smith, *The Cambridge Companion to Husserl*, 1.

[35] See the poem "Aristotle's Philosophy."

[36] See Susan Setzer and Terry Fairchild, "Consciousness and Literary Studies," *Modern Science and Vedic Science* 7 (1997): 108–40 for the implications of a consciousness-based program for the study of literature.

are exploring this most basic human phenomenon and its ramifications for areas such as health and education. The paradox of both his and Husserl's achievement is that, as eye-opening as their writing may be, because they lacked a reliable technique for developing the fourth state of consciousness they could only suggest and not actually reproduce its experience. They believed in its accessibility, but they could not provide for its repeated occurrences. Husserl judged that through the reductive intellectual process of "bracketing" one can achieve this state of unitary consciousness. This procedure may have stirred, to some degree, this subtle level of awareness in his own mind — that is, if his consciousness were already highly refined. That he had advanced experience of transcendental consciousness is supported by his Paris Lectures, in which he reveals that "I reach the ultimate experiential and cognitive perspective thinkable. In it I become the disinterested spectator of my natural and worldly ego and its life [. . .] . The transcendental spectator places himself above himself, watches himself, and sees himself also as the previously world-immersed ego."[37] Husserl seems to be describing an experience resulting from the growth of the fourth state, whereby it begins to co-exist with waking, dreaming, and sleeping.[38] Still, the research makes clear that such a rigorous intellectual method as he advocates actually expends energy, and will not generate the profound restful alertness which characterizes pure consciousness. In like manner, embedded in Traherne's works are what appear to be simple formulations aimed at instilling the "secret Power" underlying the thinking process ("Thoughts. I," 37). He instructs the reader in the *Centuries*, for example, to "let all your Affections extend to the Endless Wideness" (*Centuries* 2.92) and to "Let your Wants be present from Everlasting" (1. 45), and he brings out intriguingly that "Contemplation of Eternity maketh the Soul Immortal" (1. 55). That these grand thoughts will automatically induce a state of expanded awareness is of course dubious. But this fact does not diminish Traherne's accomplishment. His quite fully developed commentary on the transcendental state — a phenomenon given importance in the critical tradition by Husserl — is of serious note. A consciousness-based approach to Traherne makes it possible, in the end, to interpret his poems and prose not simply as exaggerated metaphor, but as descriptions of sublime experience of finer values of awareness.

---

[37] Edmund Husserl, *The Paris Lectures*, trans. Peter Koestenbaum (The Hague: Martinus Nijhoff, 1964), 15.
[38] See Alexander and Langer, *Higher Stages*, 307–27 for of a summary of higher states of consciousness.